# Continuity and Transformation

# Asian Thought and Culture

Sandra A. Wawrytko
*General Editor*

Vol. 41

PETER LANG
New York • Washington, D.C./Baltimore • Bern
Frankfurt am Main • Berlin • Brussels • Vienna • Oxford

Sang Jin Ahn

# Continuity and Transformation

## Religious Synthesis in East Asia

PETER LANG
New York • Washington, D.C./Baltimore • Bern
Frankfurt am Main • Berlin • Brussels • Vienna • Oxford

BL
2233
.A54
2001

**Library of Congress Cataloging-in-Publication Data**

Ahn, Sang Jin.
Continuity and transformation: religious synthesis in East Asia / Sang Jin Ahn.
p. cm. — (Asian thought and culture; vol. 41)
Includes bibliographical references and index.
1. Korea—Religion. 2. Ch°ndogyo. 3. Minjung theology. I. Title. II. Series.
BL2233. A54   200'.9519—dc21   99-049892
ISBN 0-8204-4894-X
ISSN 0893-6870


**Die Deutsche Bibliothek-CIP-Einheitsaufnahme**

Ahn, Sang Jin:
Continuity and transformation: religious synthesis in East Asia / Sang Jin Ahn.
–New York; Washington, D.C./Baltimore; Bern;
Frankfurt am Main; Berlin; Brussels; Vienna; Oxford: Lang.
(Asian thought and culture; Vol. 41)
ISBN 0-8204-4894-X



The paper in this book meets the guidelines for permanence and durability
of the Committee on Production Guidelines for Book Longevity
of the Council of Library Resources.

© 2001 Peter Lang Publishing, Inc., New York

All rights reserved.
Reprint or reproduction, even partially, in all forms such as microfilm,
xerography, microfiche, microcard, and offset strictly prohibited.

Printed in the United States of America

JESUIT - KRAUSS - McCORMICK - LIBRARY
1100 EAST 55th STREET
CHICAGO, ILLINOIS 60615

Dedicated to My Parents

Yong Ku Ahn (1923–1999)

Dong-U Ahn (1927–)

# Contents

| | | |
|---|---|---|
| Preface | | ix |
| Introduction | The Issues and the Problems | 1 |
| Chapter I | Nineteenth Century Spiritual World | 9 |
| Chapter II | The Past and the Present in Donghak | 49 |
| Chapter III | Minjung Theology | 73 |
| Chapter IV | Minjung Buddhism | 101 |
| Chapter V | Ecumenical Implications | 117 |
| Postscript | Religious Synthesis and Being at the Present | 145 |
| Glossary of Names and Terms | | 149 |
| Bibliography | | 155 |
| Index | | 207 |

# Preface

This book is a brief study of Donghak (東學), a syncretic religion founded by Choe Je-U (崔濟愚, 1824–1864) in the middle of the nineteenth century in Korea, and of Minjung theology, a dissent movement by a group of Christian academicians in the second half of the twentieth century. Two books are attributed to Choe: *Donggyông Daejôn* (東經大全), literally, "Great Scriptures on Eastern Learning," and *Yongdam Yusa* (龍潭遺詞 or 辭), "Writings at Yongdam" (the name of the pond Choe inherited from his father.) The former is written in Chinese characters and is a series of discourses, while the latter is written in Korean, and is a collection of didactic songs and poems.

There are numerous editions of *Donggyông Daejôn* with some variations. Some examples are: Nam Man-sung, ed. *Donggyông Daejôn* (Seoul: Ûlyu Munhwasa, 1973); Lee, Se-kwon, ed., *Donghak Gyôngjôn* 東學經典 (Seoul: Jungminsa, 1986); and Yun Suk-san, ed. with commentary, Donggyông Daejôn (Seoul: Donghaksa, 1996). The references of *Yongdam Yusa* are used from the version compiled by Choi Dong-hee, contained in *Han'gukûi Minsok Jonggyo Sasang*, edited by Lee Byung-do (Seoul: Samsung Chulpansa, 1990), pp. 532-606. *Donggyông Daejôn* is also available in Korean under the title, *Han'gûl [Korean] Donggyông Daejôn*, translated, edited, and commentary by Donghak Yôn'guwon (Daejôn: Donghak Yôn'guwon, 1991).

Although the McCune-Reischauer system is still most commonly found in academic writings, this book does not always follow it. Some notable examples are: d for the soft t (ㄷ) sound, as in *d*rama, eg. *D*onghak—the common romanization has been *T*onghak; j for the soft g (ㅈ) sound, as in *J*esus, eg. *J*e-U; ch without an apostrophe for the "ㅊ" sound, as in *ch*air, eg. chôn. One other variation from the M-R system is the use of the ^ symbol instead of the normal use of ˘—due to the practical reason of the font consistency of my word processor program—for example, chôn (천) and ûi (의).

For Chinese, mainly the Wade-Giles system is used, occasionally accompanied by the Pin-yin with a slash (/). The translations from original Chinese and Korean texts are mostly my own unless otherwise indicated.

This book is written in dialogue with myself, as one of those commonly classified as a "1.5 generation" Korean-Canadian. I was born and raised in Korea, and so Korean culture became the very fabric of my being. However, I came to Canada in my late teens, when I was young enough to adapt quite thoroughly to the new context. Moreover, it is in Canada that I received all my higher education: two years in high school and four degrees in the University of Toronto. I have described myself as being culturally shaped in the East and intellectually shaped in the West.

This book is a revision of my dissertation written in search of myself. Like many other immigrants to this continent, I see myself caught somewhere in-between two worlds. This in-betweenness creates within me a certain conflict, which in turn becomes an irresistable force for the question of identity. On the one hand, there is within me the desire to continue to evolve and to be more and more global in outlook. On the other hand, however, there is within me also an urge to reclaim that which brought me into being. This search for identity begs for constant dialogue with and within myself. This book is one such dialogue within.

I want to mention a word of appreciation to some special members of my community. First of all, my thanks go to my supervisors: Professors Julia Ching and Harold Wells. As a former missionary in Africa, Prof. Wells is open to new voices in theology without compromising his confidence in his own Western, Christian tradition. On the one hand, he has always kept me in check with his critical comments, and, on the other, encouraged me to be truthful to myself. Prof. Ching was a resource-person in Chinese religions, especially Confucianism, for my doctoral program. I have been fortunate to have them as my co-supervisors; indeed, this book is a product of East-West collaboration. I also thank the members of Emmanuel College for supporting me financially through teaching assistantships, without which I would not have survived the program.

There are many who have encouraged and supported me in various ways. Dr. David Chung has always been available to explore East Asian worldviews to clear the cloud of confusion in my thinking. Dr. Sang Chul Lee, former moderator of the United Church of Canada, has been helpful for my spiritual journey. The venerable Samu Sunim at Zen Buddhist Temple, Toronto, has often reminded me to stop for a break.

Dr. Sandra Wawrytko, the editor of the Asian Thought and Culture Series of the Peter Lang Publishers read the entire manuscript and made many valuable suggestions. Ms. Jacqueline pavlovic guided me with the preparation for the final "camera-ready" copy of my manuscript.

The following persons/organizations provided financial support for the publication of this book: Dr. Art Van Seters, former principal of Knox College, Council for the Asian and Asian-Canadian Centre for Theology and Ministry at Knox College, and my parents. My father has been fighting with cancer in and out of hospital as I completed this book. Confined in his bed and at times on the couch, suffering from pain "here and there," he often expressed his "last wish" of witnessing certain fruit of my academic ambition. He is now resting in peace. If there is one person who taught me about the value of learning, it would be my mother. She never received any formal education until she came to Canada, but in her seventies she still fixes her lunch in the morning to go to English as a Second Language class. Indeed there must be an intrinsic value in learning itself. I dedicate this book to my parents.

I have been fortunate also to have some of the greatest friends one can have. Jong Ho-yeong at Blanton-Peale Institute in New York has been like my "other self"; he is one who possesses the quality I desire. He has guided me without being physically present around me. Lee Jang-woo recognized my academic aptitude and encouraged me to develop it. Sophia E. Shin has been my dialogue partner in the past few years. I am thankful for their friendship.

A very special word of thanks is due to the members of my extended family and friends. There have been the unconditional love and prayers of parents, both mine and my wife's. My brothers and my wife's brother also helped me in many ways. Without their support, this book would never have been finished. My wife, Kyoung-Ha, and my two sons, Esaac and Kee-seop, deserve my greatest thanks. This book is more their work than mine.

# Introduction

## The Issues and the Problems

This book is a glimpse at the spiritual landscape of East Asian peoples, in general, and Korean people, in particular. The focus of our attention is paid to the religious developments of Donghak, the name of the new teaching founded by Choe Je-U (1824–1864) in 1860 C.E., and Minjung theology, which was espoused by some Christian theologians during the tumultuous period of the 1970s in Korea. Though the two religious doctrines are about a century apart from each other, they are, nevertheless, closely related. I will use Choe's pseudonym "Suun" 水雲 (which means "water-cloud") instead of Je-U, as the former has been the common usage in Korea. The following are some of the most notable themes discussed here: the synthesis of East Asian religious traditions in the Korean context vis-à-vis cultural transformation, gospel[1] and culture,[2] and minjung[3] theological perspectives. It will be stressed time

---

1   I will use the term "gospel" (with small "g") as that which came from outside by missionary activities and distinguish it from "Gospel" (with capital "G") as that which takes roots in the Korean culture, i.e., "contextualized." This will become clearer as the book progresses.
2   "Culture" is not an easy word to define. Clifford Geertz says that "culture" involves interpretation. There are, for him, a "number of ways to obscure it." For example, one can "reify" it by imagining that "culture is a self-contained 'super-organic' reality with forces and purposes of its own." (1973: 10–11) Or one can "reduce" it by saying that culture "consists in the brute pattern of behavioral events we observe in fact to occur in some identifiable community or other." (p. 11) Noting this difficulty we will follow Geertz' compact definition of this term: culture "denotes an historically transmitted pattern of meanings embodied in symbols, a system of inherited conceptions expressed in symbolic forms by means of which men communicate, perpetuate, and develop their knowledge about and attitudes toward life." (p. 89)
3   "Minjung" is a Korean term which can be translated as "common people." It has, however, been used with some ideological overtones. Han Wan-sang, for instance, according to the interpretation of Hyun Young Hak, defines it as those who are "oppressed politically, exploited economically, alienated sociologically, and kept uneducated in cultural and intellectual matters" [Hyun, "Minjung the Suffering Servant and Hope," an unpublished lecture at James Memorial Chapel (April 13,

and again that religious doctrines are contextual constructs and, hence, theological discussions must take place within proper historical context. I begin with the premise that Minjung theology, with its strong political aspirations, is a Korean cultural theology. The subject of culture, however, has by and large been neglected in Minjung theology. Perhaps the intensity of the political struggle in the past three decades accounts for this.

I suggest that, due to that neglect, there are some Korean cultural contextual issues that have not been effectively addressed by Minjung theology. First, we are dealing with a culture that has been shaped by non-Christian ideals for well over two millennia. Theologizing (Christian) in Korea, then, is an attempt by Korean culture to accommodate this rather recent newcomer, Christianity, which in its equally long history was also shaped by very different cultural environments.

Second, we are dealing with a multi-religious situation, in which Christianity is the most recent newcomer among the major religions. Korea has been hailed by many as a remarkable success-story in the history of Christian mission.[4] This success, however, has also brought some problems to the nation. Since the Christian Church was born in Korea, it has not been friendly to the indigenous culture and other religious traditions already established there. Among the early missionaries in Korea, notes Pyun Sun Hwan, while "there were some like M. C. Fenwick, who realized and confessed the limits of the Korean mission as the transplantation of Western Christianity... most missionaries were propagandists of Western culture."[5]

As Christianity became one of the most powerful forces in Korean society, en route to its growth and expansion there has come, in less than a century, the near eradication of some of the indigenous cultural traditions,[6] many of which were not necessarily in conflict with the

---

1982), Union Theological Seminary, NY]. Quoted here from the Preface by James H. Cone in CTC-CCA, ed. (1983: xvii). It is to be noted that most scholars hesitate to give the term "minjung" a fixed definition because of its dynamic nature. We will deal further with this term later in the book.

4  See, for example, Spencer J. Palmer (1967: 91–94); Charles Allen Clark (1937: 18–19).

5  Pyun (1985). Cf. Fenwick (1911).

6  Ahn Byung-mu gives some of the cultural traditions that were seriously affected by the Christian mission and regarded as "idolatry," such as the centuries-old seasons and feasts, the rites and ceremonies for the dead or the new-born and of weddings, and the activities to remember ancestors, etc. The last of these, the rite for

Christian faith. It is clear that the Christian mission brought with it not only a spiritual vision but also competing cultural claims.

The second problem has to do with the way the Church has treated other religions. There have been many instances in which Christians were involved in feuds with other religions, especially Buddhism. Sadly enough, the aggressors have been mainly from the Christian side. This antagonism toward the other is so widespread that Samu, a Korean-Canadian Buddhist priest, was compelled to write a letter to Pope John Paul II, then visiting Korea, addressing this unhealthy situation.[7] I am not going to make any simplistic assertions concerning the root cause of these social clashes. Identifying the problems will suffice for my purpose here.

The task remains for Christian theologians, then, to discern a right relationship between the gospel and culture in Korea. One important presupposition here is that neither the gospel nor culture is a static notion. The question often overlooked—no doubt a difficult one for some—is whether the gospel is a pure notion: is there any expression of the gospel in language that does not need first to go through the medium of interpretation to be understood? Can we single out even a phrase—let alone a sentence—in the traditional Christian doctrinal formulae and use it universally, hoping it will be fully understood by all cultures? Although this book is not an attempt to address or to find answers to these questions, it is fair to say that such questions must be presupposed in all theological discourse on the theme of culture and the gospel.

The purpose of this book is to illustrate the spiritual ethos Choe Je-U exemplies in founding Donghak, namely that a genuine cultural

---

remembering ancestors, for example, has been wrongly translated in English as "ancestor worship," which reflects the early missionaries' perception of it. This is misleading, for it is not "worship" in the way Christians "worship" God. See Ahn (1989: 307).

7 Samu Kim writes: "But the most unfortunate element... is undue criticism of and unprovoked attacks upon Korean Buddhism by some local Christians... And... there is strong evidence that organized and sustained attempts have been made to humiliate and discredit local Buddhism. They range from newspaper ads and handbills declaring 'Buddhism is a dead religion' or 'One surely goes to hell if one believes in Buddhism' etc... to such blatant desecratory acts as defacing Buddha's statues with cross and red paint or pouring sewage over them or destroying them by axe or fire." (1984: 74) Nor have such sentiments against Buddhism been limited to some local Christians; some Christian politicians have also added their weight. For more recent details of similar events, see "Chronology of Events January 1997–December 1998" at *http://www.buddhapia.com/eng/tedesco/chrono1.html*.

transformation is to be sought through a religious systhesis in a particular way. Among the various aspects of the Korean culture Minjung theology finds itself most akin to Donghak. The latter, then, is a nineteenth century precursor, or a spiritual ancestor, for the former. Conversely, Minjung theology is a twentieth century spiritual heir of Donghak.[8] Although this point has been mentioned by many, both Minjung theologians and others alike, it has not been clear how it is so. As well as drawing a sketch of a part of the East Asian religious landscape, this book will also attempt to illustrate some other points as follows: (1) In order to avoid missionary cultural imperialism, as shown in the "problems" described above, theology (or any religious talk) must begin with the local and move to the general or universal, and not vice versa; (2) Donghak provides an instructive Korean example of indigenous religious synthesis which begins with local "praxis," grounded broadly in the Korean religious world and especially in what I call the "shaman ethos," and this approach is taken up later by Minjung theology; (3) The method implemented by Choe Je-U and utilized by Minjung theology is corroborated by other liberation theologies, i.e., what is primarily normative in theology is what reflects the experience of the oppressed and contributes to their liberation.

This book consists of Introduction, Chapters One to Five, and Conclusion. In order to demonstrate some key points of the present work above, in the first chapter, I shall give some of the religious and historical background of Donghak, namely, Shamanism, Taoism, and Confucianism, and in the second chapter I shall expound some of the key doctrines of Donghak, especially *Hanalnim*, *Chiki* and *Shichônju*. Then, in the third chapter, I shall give the background and some of the major contentions of the Minjung theology, and make some connections with Donghak. The fourth chapter, which can be treated as an independent unit, is a look at the similar attempt from some Korean Buddhists, namely, the Minjung Buddhism. In the fifth chapter, I shall engage in a dialogue with some of the contemporary global theologies. Based on the study leading up to the last part, the Conclusion, I shall make some concluding remarks on the study. My contention here is that concerns for context and praxis in religious formulations have more to do with the

---

8 Other similar attempts can also be found among some Buddhists, which is the subject matter of Chapter IV, and Confucians alike. For the emerging, youthful Confucian movement called, "Minjung Confucians United," see *http://my.netian.com/~bookac/page5.htm*.

Introduction 5

present than with the past, for, again, the present is inclusive of the various religious traditions of the past. This book, thus, is also an attempt to find the relationship between religious synthesis and cultural transformation in the context of East Asia.

## Methodology

*Reciprocal Praxis* is a methodological term used in this book. The first word, "reciprocal" may be substituted by other terms like "mutual" or "dialogical," with the understanding that the latter of the two lacks the meaning of interdependence which, in East Asia, is epitomized by Yin-Yang philosophy, according to which one cannot be without the other. If "one" here is the past (spiritual resources or ethos), "the other" would be the present (conditions of human existence). The past and the present are not mutually exclusive; rather, they are interdependent. How can the past be dependent upon the present, as is the case the other way? Obviously, this is impossible when history is understood as a linear movement, in which one gives way to the other. Both past and present, however, are conceptual constructs conveniently located in our consciousness; understanding one presupposes certain understanding of the other.

To put this differently, if "one" is the temporal, "the other" would be the eternal. Spacially, if "one" is transcendence, "the other" would be immanence. In a Buddhist expression, emptiness (*sunyata*) is suchness (*tathata*), and suchness emptiness; the two are reciprocal concepts. Although it is not the aim of this book to explore each of those mind-boggling philosophical issues, a different framework for understanding time and space might be useful in reading it. In other words, the logical framework of the list of the "one-and-the other" above is the operating principle of this book. What is explicitly demonstrated here is this: in reconstructing a Christian theology as a Korean, "one" would be the cultural traditions of my Korean anscestors, and "the other" the Christian traditions of the West.

The second word, "praxis," carries certain ideological[9] implications. Robert Schreiter observes the emergence of a Christian praxis of faith in many oppressive societies. Praxis, generally, as Schreiter points out, has a theoretical and a practical moment, both of which are considered essential to the theological process. The following quotation from Schreiter sums up the notion of praxis well:

> In the theoretical moment an *analysis of the social structure* is undertaken, revealing the relationships of power, oppression, and freedom. The theoretical moment includes reflection on how God is active in human history,... Such analysis and correlation with the perceived activity of God lead to transformative action on the part of the community of believers. In turn that action is reflected upon to reveal God's activity, leading to yet further action. The *dialectical process of reflection and action* are both essential to the theological process (italics mine). (1985: 91–92)

The "process" involved here is a "dialectical" one oscillating between action and reflection. Whatever one fails to accomplish in one's action will be reflected upon later, and the subject of one's contemplation will find fuller meaning in one's action. This insight is important because poverty is not a metaphysical problem; it is an existential one.

Further to the social analysis above there is yet another aspect in some (liberation) theologies, especially Minjung theology: *the traditional spiritual ethos* of the place of theologizing. The type of praxis in view here, therefore, is one which insists on both continuity of the past and transformation of the present. Since the present contains certain tenets of the past, this involves discerning particular traits of the present that are of the past for the transformation of the present to be possible. Why, then, insist on maintaining the spiritual ethos of the cultural past? One important assumption, which is also an argument, in this book is that a genuine transformation of a society is to be done within the framework

---

9   A clear concept of "ideology" is essential for the clarification of our points here, for the term has been used in many different ways, mainly negatively, such as "a 'false consciousness'," which is a legacy of Karl Marx. Harold Wells, however, attempts to trace a positive meaning of the term, using the arguments of Ricoeur and Segundo. "Ricoeur and Segundo are right," Wells says, "that a purely negative use of the term 'ideology' encourages the illusion that this is a disease suffered only by others, and fosters the mistaken notion that there can be an 'ideology-free' and apolitical theology." (1987: 215) I will follow the brief, value-free definition of the term given as the third meaning of the second category in *Webster's Ninth New Collegiate Dictionary* which says, "the integrated assertions, theories, and aims that constitute a sociopolitical program."

of the cultural spiritual ethos of its people. That is, the transformative spirit of the present must be consistent with that of the cultural past of the people in a society. Hence a *reciprocal praxis*!

Since the central notion of Minjung theology is that the minjung are the subjects of history, theological discussion must be undertaken in the concrete historical and cultural situation of the minjung. This means that a theology cannot be constructed outside of the minjung culture and brought there to change the minjung. For then the minjung would not be subjects of history but merely objects for indoctrination. Some questions, however, still remain unanswered, such as, what constitutes the "minjung culture?"

The method of this book is to use the case of Donghak to discern how the concrete place (*Hyônjang* in Korean) of minjung can be the centre of a theology of gospel and culture. One question regarding discernment is, who or what judges Korean culture? Why do we need Minjung theology in Korea? I have already stated above the "problems" in using the Western theological formulations to discern what is right or wrong about Korean culture. As Schreiter argues such is the task of a local theology. Arguing from his own "contextual models," he makes the crucial point when he says, "The role of the community in developing theology reminds us also for whom theology is, in the first instance, intended: the community itself, to enhance its own self-understanding." (1985: 16) Schreiter observes three models of constructing local theologies: translation models, adaptation models, contextual models. He contends that "contextual models are the most important and enduring in the long run."

In Korea, then, it is the task of Korean Christians themselves. A society and its culture is discerned according to what happens to the life of the minjung in their concrete life place. Thus, our methodology— elicited from the methodology of Choe Je-U—is that of looking at and reinterpreting the past in view of the present from the perspective of the minjung. The "past" here denotes the various religious traditions (including Christianity), especially those teachings which have molded our worldviews, and the "present," the contemporary socio-political life situation of the minjung. Hence, the term "methodological" before the "past" and the "present" is used as an attempt to denote this particular meaning. To use a simile, this book is like an open forum in which the minjung extend an invitation to past religious formulations and present life-situations to a dialogue, in which the minjung are the presiders. My contention is that this is the methodology at work in both Donghak and

Minjung theology, and hence, it becomes my methodology in making connection between the two.

Donghak is viewed as an important spiritual root of Minjung theology.[10] There is no need, perhaps, to elaborate on the reasons for taking a non-Christian religion as the spiritual root of a Christian theology. In my observation, a study of this Korean indigenous religion, which was born at the time when the Christian (Catholic) mission was striving to make inroads there, can provide a useful framework in the considerations of (1) the role of religious formulations vis-à-vis cultural transformation and of (2) the clash of cultures and of religious ideas. The assumption, again, is that there is no "pure" theology; all religious ideas and doctrines are cultural products.[11]

---

10  See, for example, Ahn Jae-Woong (1995), where he says, "the most outstanding example of religious wisdom of the Minjung, which arose out of established religions, is the *Tonghak*" (p. 113). Also see, Noh Jong-Sun (1992: 213), where he says, "the Minjung Theological Movement of modern Korea can trace its inspiration, in part, to the Tonghak leaders' thinking."

11  In Zen Buddhism, for example, which strives to overcome the obstacles of time and space for the "transference of the Buddha-mind," one's cultural context often plays more essential role in one's quest than is usually recognized. I plan to deal with this subject elsewhere, using the cases of Tsung-mi (780–841), the fifth and last patriarch of both the Hua-yen school and the Ho-tse branch of the Southern school of Ch'an, and Jinul (or Chinul: 1158–1210), the first patriarch of the Korean Sôn (Ch'an/ Zen) School.

# Chapter I

# Nineteenth Century Spiritual World

## Religious context: The Methodological Past

Suun founded a new Do 道 (in Chinese, Tao/Dao), which means "way, teaching, philosophy, and/or religion,"[1] in 1860 and called it Donghak, literally "Eastern Learning." Like many other religious adepts in history, he too found his own school of thought after a long and intense quest for meaning and being. He searched for, and found, deep cells of wisdom in the several spiritual traditions that existed within his context. He learned from them, critiqued them, and synthesized them. Hence, in this chapter I shall explore the way in which he learned from them and used them to create a new religious outlook for the minjung of his time. This first section, "religious context," will be followed by some discussions on Suun's life and the historical setting, "social context," which, in turn, will be followed by his thought. Thus, I begin by drawing a general

---

1  The term "religion" was not widely used at the time of Suun. In fact, it does not appear in his writings at all. It has been argued by some in East Asia that the used of the term "religion" to depict that particular trait of a culture or the cultural practices of certain tradition is a Western influence. See, for example, Kawada Kumataro, "Bulta Hwaôm: Hwaômgyôngûi Gochal [Hwaôm (Hua-yen) Buddhism: A Study of Hwaôm (Avatamsaka) Sutra]," in *Hwaôm Sasangron* [*Essays on Hwaôm Thought*], ed. by Sok Won-wook (1988), pp. 70–79, where he argues that the term "jonggyo (宗教 religion)" was originally used to denote Buddhism, and that, since Meiji period, it became a generic term to mean religion generally is a Western influence. In Korea, at the time of Jinul (Chinul, 1158–1210), the factional conflict between Gyo-jong (教宗: the reverse of the term "jonggyo" above; stressed the teaching/philosophy of scriptures) and Sôn-jong (禪宗; stressed the practice of meditation only) was at its height. That is, the term "Gyo-jong" was used to denote the particular sect of Buddhism which emphasized diligent learning of sutras, especially, Hwaôm (Avatamsaka) Sutra.

picture of the religious landscape of Korea (and of China) up to the time of Suun, i. e., nineteenth century. Shamanism is our first scene.

## Shamanism

According to Mircea Eliade, who undertook a comprehensive study of world shamanism, "it is difficult to determine the 'origin' of Korean shamanism."(1964: 462) This may be due to his rather cursory look at the Korean situation (one paragraph!). But this difficulty may also be due to the long history of shamanism's existence in the peninsula. Indeed, shamanism has been considered the most basic expression of religiosity for Koreans by specialists and non-specialists alike, both inside and outside the nation.

In this connection, it is important to look at the religious as well as the philosophical aspects of Korean shamanism, as exhibited in such ideas as *shin sôn, sam shin, pung lyu,* and *Han* philosophy with reference to their relation to Suun's thought.

***Shin* sôn.** *Shin sôn* 神仙, *shen hsien* in Chinese, which in Chinese Taoism is usually rendered in English as "Taoist immortals," should be translated in the Korean context as "mountain gods." In the mountainous Korean peninsula, Taoist immortals have always been associated with mountains. According to the Foundation Myth, Korea began in a mountain. In *Samguk Yusa*,[2] written in the thirteenth century by a monk called Il Yôn (1206–1289), we see the following account of the beginning of the nation:

> In the Old Book it is written, "In ancient times Hwan-in (Heavenly King,...) had a young son whose name was Hwan-ung. The boy wished to descend from heaven and live in the human world. His father, after examining three great mountains, chose T'aebaek-san (the Myohyang Mountains in northern

---

2   *Samguk Yusa* (三國遺事) is one of the two chronicles of Korea's earliest period compiled during the Koryô dynasty (935–1392) It is an unofficial history including myths of the preceding three kingdoms of Korea established from around the beginning of the Common Era. Ha Tae-Hung, who translated it into English, finds the title of the book, *Samguk Yusa*, difficult to translate. *Yusa*, he says, "does not mean precisely legends, although that idea is implied by the word. It also carries the ideas of anecdotes, memorabilia and the like." See his Introduction in the book he co-translated, with Grafton K. Mintz, *Samguk Yusa: Legends and History of the Three Kingdoms of Ancient Korea* (1972: 5–20).

Korea) as a suitable place for his heavenly son to bring happiness to human beings... Hwan-ung heard her (bear-turned-woman) prayers and married her. She conceived and bore a son who was called Tangun Wanggôm, the King of Sandalwood.... In the year of Kyông-in (traditionally dated 2333 B.C.) Tangun came to Pyôngyang, set up his residence there and bestowed the name Chosôn upon his kingdom. (32–33)

Cha Ju-hwan (1984) notes two cultic practices in this myth. The first is the trace of a "mountain cult": there is the descent of the heavenly beings to the mountains. The second is the idea of immortality. Dan'gun is said to have reigned for 1500 years and to have lived for 1908 years before he became a *san shin*,[3] literally, a "mountain-god."

Furthermore, as this myth shows, divinity is ascribed more fully to Korean immortals than to their Chinese Taoist counterparts. It is probable that this myth evolved from shamanism.[4] In such a mountainous nation as Korea it is not difficult to argue that mountain-related traditions such as Dan'gun's are indigenous to Korea. According to Cha, Lee Nung-hwa argues that the idea of *shin sôn* originated in Korea.[5] Although Cha is not yet willing to fully endorse Lee's theory, he concedes that it is not difficult to believe that the idea of *shin sôn* or something similar to it existed in Korea much earlier than the written records indicate. Cha also contends that the development of the idea of *shin sôn* is closely related to a certain mountain cult.

Cha's latter idea is contained to some extent in the two Chinese characters, *shin* and *sôn*, themselves. The second of the two, *sôn*, consists of two root characters, which mean "human" and "mountain," respectively. Since the first character *shin* means "god" or "ghost," a literal translation of *shin sôn* indeed comes closer to the Korean rendering, "mountain gods," than to "Taoist immortals." The fact that *shin sôn* in Korea is closely related to mountains can be seen from that *shin sôn* is used interchangeably with *san shin*, "mountain-god," which Dan'gun is said to have become. Though not always the case, sacred

---

3   This *san shin* (山神), though pronounced the same, should be distinguished from *san shin* (産神), "fertility god," which is the later development of *sam shin* (三神), "three gods." See the subsection on *sam shin* in this chapter.
4   The etymology of the term "dan'gun" suggests a strong shamanistic origin. Scholars generally agree that the Dan'gun Myth originated from shamanism. See, for example, Yu Chai-shin, "Korean Taoism and Shamanism," in Guisso and Yu, eds. (1988: 98).
5   See Cha (1984: 103), or Lee Suk-ho (1991: 229). This theory is first advocated by Lee Nung-hwa (1981, chapter 4).

mountains were also favoured by some Taoist immortals in China. The Queen Mother of the West (*Hsi wang mu*), the symbolic divine figure of immortality (longevity) in China, is said to have lived in the peaks of Kun-lun Mountains. One can thus speculate that the idea of *shin sôn* first originated in shamanistic mountain cults and then later became assimilated in other schools of thought, such as philosophical Taoism and Confucianism.

***Sam shin.*** The idea of *sam shin*, three gods, is one of the best-known examples of a mountain-related cultic philosophy in Korea. The three gods are Hwan-in, Hwan-ung, and Hwan-gôm (Dan'gun) who appear in the Dan'gun myth above. Together they form a trinity in both heaven and earth.[6] The roles the three gods play are creating/ cosmogony, teaching/religion, and governing/harmony, respectively. They thus represent the beginnings of the world, of religion, and of society, respectively. None of the three, however, is said to have left the Taebaek Mountain, which is situated in the northern part of Korea. For the early inhabitants of the Korean peninsula, mountains must have appeared both mysterious and sacred, an ideal place for the union of humanity and divinity. They thus associated power (politics) and meaning (religion) with mountains. If the Taoist *sôn* (*hsien*) cult did not originate in the shamanistic mountain cult in Korea, the two forms of religious expression, at least, found each other compatible and merged smoothly in the Korean version of *shin sôn* philosophy. Suffice it to say here that there is continuity between humanity and divinity in both traditions.

***Pung lyu do.*** Although the idea of *pung lyu* 風流 (in Chinese, *feng liu*), "wind and stream," was first developed in China[7] and later came to

6  There are other versions of *sam shin* in Korean shamanism. For Choe Gil-song, for example, the three gods in *sam shin* (三神) are Heaven, Earth, and Humanity, which, in fact, may be derivative form of the three gods of Hwan-in, Hwan-ung, and Hwan-gôm above. See Choe G. S. (1994: 147). According to Choe Nam-son, *sam shin*, "three gods," becomes *san shin* (産神), "fertility god," in later shamanism. It seems that the idea of child-bearing came to be attached to "three gods" of heaven and earth, as the latter became the object of prayer/petition for blessings for women, especially during the Yi dynasty (1392–1910) when giving birth to a boy was considered a blessing for women. See Choe N. S. (1948: 43).
7  See Fung (Fêng) Yu-lan (1958, chapter 20). Surprisingly enough, some Korean scholars who have been enthusiastic about this tradition for many years seem to be unaware of (or unwilling to recognize) the Chinese origin of it. Ryu Dong-sik, for example, depends entirely on the alleged statement of Choe Chi-won in Kim Bu-

Korea, it has probably exerted more influence in the latter country, especially in the Silla Kingdom (57 B.C.E–918 C.E.)

During the Silla dynasty Taoist influence was clearly visible in the *Pung lyu do*, literally, the "way of wind and stream," which can also be translated as "the way of aesthetic pursuits." According to Kim Bu-sik (1075–1151), the author of *Samguk Sagi*, "History of Three Kingdoms," compiled in 1145, this philosophy, or "way," is first explained by Choe Chi-won (857–?), arguably the greatest scholar of his time in Korea. Choe's pseudonym, Go-un 孤雲, a "solitary (piece of) cloud," or a "recluse," suggests his strong affinity with philosophical Taoism. Choe here is alleged to have stated that *Pung lyu do* is an indigenous Korean idea,[8] yet one that contained the kernel of the three religions, Buddhism, Confucianism, and Taoism. The essence of the three traditions is contained in it, for Choe, however, not because of an eclectic mixing of elements. Rather, he explains, it is the art of *Pung lyu do* itself that manifests the same power and quality as the kernel of each of the other three. That is, the message of *Pung lyu*, on its own merit, exhibits what each of the other three aspires to teach.

According to Han Jong-man, what Choe emphasizes is the art of *byung haeng* 竝行, "parallel movement," of the three traditions. All three return to one and the same reality in the end. The art of such a movement, says Han, is what Choe calls *Pung lyu do*, and this can be seen as the way the three traditions manifest themselves at their best. (1991: 33)

However, this does not mean that these three traditions are not mixed in *Pung lyu do*. In fact Choe himself alludes to the syncretic nature of the philosophy of *Pung lyu do* by relating its essential ideas to those of the three traditions: Confucian filial piety, *Lao Tzu*'s *muwi* 無爲 (*wu wei* in Chinese; "inaction," or "non-action"), and the Buddhist

---

sik's *Samguk Sagi* 三國史記 mentioned here (next page), namely that *Pung lyu do* was an "indigenous Korean idea." While, according to Fung, the tradition of *feng liu* (*pung lyu*) was a popular current among literati since the 3rd and the 4th centuries in China, Ryu theorizes that it was originated in Korea in the 6th century. See Ryu (1982 and 1992). Due to the respect Ryu commands in the Korean theological circle, younger scholars tend to follow his theory in good faith; some dissertations have already been written on the basis of Ryu's theology. See, for example, Andrew Sung Park, *Minjung and Pungryu Theologies in Contemporary Korea: A Critical and Comparative Examination*, a dissertation (Graduate Theological Union, Berkeley, 1985).

8  Kim, *Samguk Sagi [History of Three Kingdoms]*, Silla, Chapter 4, Period of King Chinhûng (三國史記, 新羅本紀, 第四, 眞興王條).

emphasis on good deeds.[9] Scholars now generally see *Pung lyu do* as a mixture of the three religions, with shamanism as its unifying principle. The shamanistic *Han* philosophy, in which "oneness" is emphasized, is operative in this synthesis. *Pung lyu do*, for this reason, is considered a distinctly Korean philosophy, which development perhaps contributed to the disputable claim of its origination in the Korean soil.

That *Pung lyu do* is the way the three religions manifest themselves by means of a "parallel movement" also does not mean that there was no school established on the basis of this philosophy. Its most well-known representative is *Hwa-rang do* 花郎徒, "the way of the flower youth." *Hwa-rang* was a group of youths mainly composed of the sons of aristocrats in the Silla society. Some of the major activities of these youths included writing/reading poetry, riding horses, performing certain religious rituals, and so on. Originally, they seemed to have aspired mainly to religious and aesthetic pursuits, such as reading poetry in and around the beautiful mountains and their streams. However, as the war among the three Kingdoms[10] intensified, they shifted toward a more military purpose. The commander-in-chief of Silla at the time of unification, Kim Yu-shin, is also from this group. Such was the shamanism of Silla society.

Lee Nung-hwa summarily states that the philosophical substance of Silla coincides with the *muwi* of Lao-Chuang. Silla, says Lee, was (nature loving) Taoist before learning about Taoism. (1981: 68–70)

***Han*[11] Philosophy.** Unlike philosophical Taoism, in which there are representative classics, namely, *Lao Tzu*, *Chuang Tzu*, and *Lieh Tzu*, there is no established classic which can represent philosophical Shamanism. Although the word *Han* has been used by Koreans since antiquity, "*Han* philosophy" is rather a recent term. It evolved as a result of modern scholars' effort to identify the kernel of Korean thought. Situated on the borders of China, Korea has always produced a religious and philosophical correspondence with Chinese ideas. Throughout history various religions and philosophies have found their way to this peninsula, and yet scholars have observed that there is something unique about the way Koreans received those traditions. For example, not too

9  Lee, Nung-hwa (1981: 318–319).
10  Koguryo (37 B.C.E.–668 C.E.), Baekje (?–660 C.E.) and Silla (57 B.C.E–918 C.E.).
11  Note that this term is different from "Han 漢," the Chinese dynasty (206 B.C.E–220 C.E.).

long after Buddhism came to their land, Korea tailored it to suit Korean needs.[12] Whether this was intentional or not, what is important here is that there is a consistent pattern in the way Koreans have handled foreign doctrines. What is the nature of this pattern? What is the philosophical axis of the Korean mind? Many scholars now identify it with the notion of *Han*.

*Han* has many meanings, such as "great," "one," "totality," "the ultimate," etc.[13] Etymological research shows that "han" is from the cardinal number "hana," meaning "one." According to Lee Ul-ho, the Dan'gun myth is the source of *Han* philosophy.(1990: 14) As shown above, however, there appear in the story of Dan'gun not one but three deities, Hwan-ung, Hwan-in, and Dan'gun. How can three be the origin of one? "Han," says Lee, is more than the cardinal number "one." It is a philosophical number in which all numbers converge. Hence, "han" is also "great," or "the ultimate." As a number it is both "one" and "two." As a philosophy it is both monotheism and polytheism. Metaphysically, *Han* is both monism and dualism, both pantheism and anthropomorphism. Whereas the *Lao Tzu* ascribes the ultimate meaning of the Tao to nature, *tzu jan* 自然 (*jayôn* in Korean), and accepts things as they are, *Han* ascribes *shin* 神, "god," or "spirit," to myriad things. This partly explains why Korean shamanism became thoroughly animistic. It also partly explains why in Korea there has been such a consistent effort to find a unity in all the different religious philosophies that came there. The "three religions in one" of *Pung lyu do* is but one of many such attempts.[14] This tendency, say some scholars, like Lee, is characteristic of Korean thought.

We can summarize our observations as follows: like Taoism, in which a general distinction is made between the religious and the philosophical (this will be discussed below), Korean Shamanism can also

12  Since Wonhyo (617–686), the greatest scholar monk of his time in the Silla Kingdom, attempted to unify diverse Buddhist sects that came in Korea mainly from China, a search for unity became a recurrent pattern in Korean Buddhism. Korean Sôn (禪: *Ch'an/Zen*), for example, is the syncretized combination of the meditative Sôn and the doctrinal Gyo-sects since the time of Jinul (or Chinul) in the beginning of the 13th century. We will come back to this subject in Chapter IV.
13  It is neither possible nor necessary to deal with a full philosophical exposition of this notion here. For a more detailed account see Lee Eul-ho, et. al., *Han Sasangkwa Minjok Jonggyo* [*Han Philosophy and Korean Religion*] (1990).
14  Modern attempts, which became established religions, are Donghak, Jûng San Gyo, Dae Jong Gyo, and Won Bul Gyo, each of which seeks to find a unity among diverse religions.

be divided into the religious and the philosophical. We can also say with some confidence that the ideas of *shin sôn* and *sam shin* belong to the religious strand and the *Han* philosophy to the philosophical one. *Pung lyu do*, however, is both religious and philosophical; it includes the *sôn* 仙 (*hsien/xian* in Chinese) practices and formulates doctrines along the lines of *Han* philosophy. In Korean shamanism such a combination is possible because, unlike philosophical Taoism (see below)—the *Chuang Tzu*, in particular, which "unequivocally condemns" some of the central pursuits of religious Taoism—*Han* philosophy prescribes no such condemnation against religious Shamanism. This leads us to the subject of Taoism.

## Taoism

In this section I will attempt to give a brief introduction to Taoism, especially in connection with Suun's thought, which, for example, can be found in his idea of immortality. He frequently mentions his joy in the "miraculous" signs in his physical condition, such as *sôn pung do gol*, "stature of immortals," *bul lo bul sa*, literally, "no aging and no death," and *yông se mu gung*, "immortality."[15] This suggests that Suun clearly aspired to a long healthy life.

In connection with Taoism, however, there are two things one must consider. Firstly, Taoism as a religion needs to be separately treated from Taoism as a philosophy. Secondly, Suun's idea of immortality is to be understood not only in connection with Chinese (religious) Taoism but with Korean Shamanism. I shall, therefore, first deal with Taoism in its philosophical and religious aspects separately and then move on to its relationship with Shamanism in Korea up to the time of Suun.

There are some notable differences between philosophical and religious Taoism. Their respective attitudes toward *tzu jan*, for example, which can be translated as "naturalness," or "things as they are," show some of these differences. While philosophical Taoism lays its stress on the importance of embracing things as they manifest themselves in nature, religious Taoism seeks "things as they are meant to be" or "things as they ought to be." Of course, like any generalization this is not always unambiguously the case. In the *Chuang Tzu*, for example, one is admonished to endeavor to perfect oneself in pursuit of sagehood. One

---

15   仙風道骨, 不老不死, 永世武窮, respectively; "Anshimga," *Yongdam Yusa*.

also sees in the *Lao Tzu* the notion of "cultivating the Tao" which is done through discarding knowledge. The basic thrust of such pursuit here, however, may be understood to mean a "mystical union with the Tao."

Due to the preoccupation of religious Taoism with "things as they ought to be" it tends always to find a way to improve the status quo, be it through personal longevity or through the collective expectation of a "messiah."[16] At times the aspirations of the two kinds of Taoism are contradictory to each other. For example, whereas philosophical Taoism stresses spontaneity devoid of artificiality, religious Taoism actually prescribes specific behaviors for the betterment of life. Furthermore, as will be mentioned below in regard to immortality, while philosophical Taoism accepts death as a natural part of life, religious Taoism searches for ways to avoid, or at least temporarily delay, death. For this reason some scholars like Herrlee G. Creel and Holmes Welch contend that the two aspects of Taoism originated in entirely different sources. (1970: 11f.) I shall deal with some of these differences between the two in relation to the theme of immortality, followed by some discussions on how Taoism can be compared to shamanism, especially in Korea.

Welch observes that there are four distinct schools or cults in Taoism: philosophy, P'eng-lai (one of the Isles of the Blest), alchemy, and hygiene. These four, he contends, were *separate* when they flowed into history in the middle of the fourth century B.C.E. (1965: 95) Much in the same manner as Creel, Welch also argues that the four "streams" of the separate schools came to merge "in the river of Taoism" in the middle of the fourth century B.C.E. (1965: 89) Whether those four listed by Welch were originally separate is not our concern here. However, we still need to account for the fact that the central ideas contained in the *Lao Tzu*, *Chuang Tzu*, and *Lieh Tzu* are often critical toward the aspirations of the latter three schools. The *Chuang Tzu*, in particular, "unequivocally condemns" those who indulge in cultic practices in pursuit of immortality. "In this respect," says Welch, "at least, the (true) Sage is not a *hsien* (an immortal)." (parentheses mine; 1965: 93)

Since it is beyond the scope of this study to trace the roots of all the four schools mentioned above, we will simply make a broad distinction between philosophical Taoism and religious Taoism, with particular attention to the development of the *hsien* cult in religious Taoism. As

---

16  For the study of Taoist messianism, see Anna Seidel, "Taoist Messianism," in *Numen*, 31, 2 (1984); also Seidel, "The Image of the Perfect Ruler in Early Taoist Messianism: Lao-Tzu and Li Hung," in *History of Religions*, 9 (1969).

shown above the point of contact between Chinese Taoism and Korean Shamanism may be made through the disputable claim of some Korean scholars that the origin of *sôn* (*hsien*) may be found in the Dan'gun Legend, the founding myth of Korea.

**Taoism as a Philosophy.** If it were possible to summarily state the central message of the Taoist philosophy, what would this be? From the perspective of the Tao all things are relative. No matter what we say, it would still be incomplete. At times I have said to the perplexed students in the introductory course in Chinese Religion that "when our intellect does not help us, stop thinking and start feeling." I was alluding, in particular, to the way of Chuang Tzu. When the reality before us is one of overwhelming nature, our intellectual analysis does not lead us very far. In that case, one would only hope to absorb that reality with one's entire body-and-soul.

Is the "mystical union with the Tao," then, a central message of philosophical Taoism? How mystical is the *Chuang Tzu*, for example? How different is the latter from other classics/philosophers? "Most of the philosophies of ancient China are addressed to the political or intellectual elite;" says Burton Watson, "Chuang Tzu's is addressed to the spiritual elite."(1964: 5) For Fung Yu-lan, Taoist philosophy in fact aspires to a mystical union with the universe. One is, Fung says, "to forget the self, and by this means to enter the sphere of undifferentiated oneness with all creation."(1962: 79-80) The spontaneity of Lao Tzu and the satiric craftsmanship of Chuang Tzu weave their insights with ordinary words to lead us to the realm where our studious words cannot reach. If Fung's description above is too complicated, one can consider the following words of Chuang Tzu:

> You forget your feet when the shoes are comfortable. You forget your waist when the belt is comfortable. Understanding forgets right and wrong when the mind is comfortable. (chapter 19)

Is there any word here that is too profound to understand? In the world of Chuang Tzu the most profound is not profound enough when it cannot make an impression on the least complicated. Such is the way of Tao for Chuang Tzu.

**Tao.** Tao is both Cosmic Substance and its Principle, for Tao, the "Way," is also the "Ultimate." Fung explains the two meanings of the term Tao: "One denotes that by which all things come into being," and "the other denotes the knowledge of that by which all things come into being."(1962: 72) The first is the Ultimate, which is unthinkable, inexpressible, and unnamable. And the second is the Way which leads us to such "knowledge which is not knowledge." Should we use the term "knowledge" for Tao, then, it is "the highest kind of knowledge."(1962: 73)

As the Cosmic Substance and its Principle, Tao is not only the cause of all things but also their effect. In Giancarlo Finazzo's words it is "the vital force that pervades and ordains the nature of all things."(1968: 34) Being, in the case of Lao Tzu, is a child of non-being; the former comes from the latter. "Non-being," then, is a higher philosophical category than "being." For Tao is "the nameless uncarved block" (*Lao Tzu*, chapter 37). It is cosmic and hence "non-personal and amoral."(Lau) Tao is non-personal because it existed before personal attributes, or any attributes for that matter, became useful. It is also amoral because it lies beyond good and evil; that is, it transcends such value-distinctions.

Transcending value distinctions, however, does not lead us to an other-worldly realm in the case of Tao, for it is also thoroughly immanent in nature. Tung-Kuo Tzu asked Chuang Tzu, "This thing called the Way—where does it exist?" Chuang Tzu said, "There is no place it doesn't exist." "Come," said Tung-Kuo, "you must be more specific!"

"It is in the ant."
"As low a thing as that?"
"It is in the panic grass."
"But that's lower still!"
"It is in the tiles and shards."
"How can it be so low?"
"It is in the piss and dung," said Chuang Tzu. Tung-Kuo gave no response. (chapter 22)

The Tao of Chuang Tzu forces us to go beyond conventional values to the realm where such distinctions as life and death, good and bad, high and low matter no more. For conventions are artificial arrangements of human intellect, which can never fully grasp the truth of Tao. Perhaps the best description about the Tao is *via negativa*, as the opening words of *Lao Tzu's Tao Te Ching* attest it, "The Tao that can be spoken of is not an eternal (constant, or real) Tao."

***Te.*** Most commentators translate the term *Te* 德 (in Korean, dôk) as "virtue." Fung Yu-lan, however, argues that, in many cases, *Te* "would be better translated as the 'efficacy' or 'power' inherent in a thing," for the term denotes the principle underlying each individual thing. Drawing on such passages as the Lao Tzu's "Tao gave them birth[.] *Te* reared them" (ch. 51), Fung explains that "*Te* is what individual objects obtain from Tao and thereby become what they are."(1952-3, vol. 1: 179-180) If Tao can be described as Being Itself, then, *Te* would be the Power of Being.

For Authur Waley as well, "virtue" is rather a Confucian reading of the term *Te*. Hence, in his translation of the Lao Tzu, he too opts for "power." It is "a power over the outside world undreamed of by those who pit themselves against matter while still in its thralls." (1934: 46) It is also "the only power that can 'benefit without harming,' that can dissolve the myriad contradictions and discordance of phenomenal existence." (1934: 88)

When translated as "power," however, does it provide the right connotation for the term *Te*, which is so rich in meaning? This is the question Wing-tsit Chan raises. "Power," for him, "does not connote moral excellence which the word *te* involves."(1963: 790) He thus prefers to translate it as "virtue" or "character."

What becomes clear from all this is that in translating such key terms as "*Tao*" or "*Te*" one must take pains to reconstruct the cultural values taken for granted by the authors in the ancient Chinese civilization. When E. R. Hughes translated Fung's book, *The Spirit of Chinese Philosophy* (1962), such pains are duly acknowledged by the latter, who said, "the translator and I sadly agreed that there seemed no way of rendering the full sense of the original." The pains here can easily be multiplied when crossing over not only cultural barriers but also temporal ones, which in the case of Lao-Chuang is more than two millennia. Noting this difficulty, *Te* can be broadly understood as the (moral/ spiritual) power of Tao inherent in things.

***Wu Wei.*** *Wu wei* (*muwi* in Korean) is another key term for an understanding of Tao as the uncarved block, the nameless, water and, in the case of Chuang Tzu, freedom. Literally, *wu wei* is "non-action." But it is not the denial of any action. Rather it is taking no (artificial) action that is contrary to nature. Put it another way, it is taking action in a such a way that it involves neither purposeful motives for a certain end nor attachments to anything. In short, *wu wei*, negatively, is "no unreal (unnatural) action" and, positively, a natural, spontaneous, and, therefore, "real action."

In the *Lao Tzu*, this term *wu wei* as the way of Tao is expressed as the principle and efficacy of Tao. "The way [Tao]," it says, "never acts yet nothing is left undone."(chapter 37) This may sound strange to the average Westerner. How does the Tao do all things by never acting? The myriad creatures, the same chapter in the *Lao Tzu* continues, "will be transformed of their own accord." Can we, then, still regard these as the work of the Tao? How immanent is the Tao?

There is more immanence in the notion of the Tao than, for example, in Aristotle's Unmoved Mover. For the latter the Absolute is the First Cause of all causes of change. But for the former, Tao is more than the first cause; it is also the last of all the causes in nature. As mentioned above, when asked about this immanence of the Tao, Chuang Chou[17] explained that "there is no place that the Tao does not exist" high and low, from the heavenly constellations to "piss and dung" (chapter 22). All things in nature come from the Tao. For "from the viewpoint of the Tao," says Fung, "things which are different 'interpenetrate and become one'."(1962: 68) Thus is the way of *wu wei*, which, viewed this way, becomes an active principle and not a passive one.

**Taoism as a Religion.** "Taoism," says Henri Maspero, "is a salvation religion with aims to lead the faithful to Life Eternal."(1981: 266) For the search of the ancient Chinese for immortality was not simply a physical matter; it was a spiritual quest as well. Unlike the ancient Greeks, Maspero points out, who were used to separating the spirit from the body, insisting on making the former oppose the latter, the Chinese did not do so. Instead, for the Chinese, who have "never made any distinction between Spirit and Matter, but for whom the world is a continuum which passes without interruption from void to material things,"(1981: 266) "nourishing the body" was closely related to "nourishing the spirit." Hence the Taoist would combine a proper diet with meditation to achieve immortality, which is the most important theme in religious Taoism.

---

17  According to the account in *Shih Chi* 史記, "Records of Historian," given by the historian Ssu-ma Ch'ien (司馬遷), Chuang Chou is the alleged author of the book *Chuang Tzu*. Scholars, however, are certain about neither this account nor other details of Chaung Chou. Hence, the use of the name "Chuang Chou" here is no more than a matter of convenience, that is, to distinguish the author, or the group of authors, from the book.

*Yang-sheng* 養生 (*Yang-saeng* in Korean) is a key term in understanding the major difference between philosophical and religious Taoism. It is a key term in the sense that it can make the whole picture blurred. The term *yang sheng*, which literally means "preserving life," occurs frequently in the *Chuang Tzu*. In the light of the philosophy of the book as a whole, the appearance of *yang sheng* becomes problematic because the general tendency of the book is to maintain that death is but a part of the natural process of life. This means that in the *Chuang Tzu* there are ambiguities regarding this theme of immortality. How, then, should we interpret the term *yang sheng* in the *Chuang Tzu*? Should we associate the *Chuang Tzu* with the immortality cult? On this scholars are divided.

Noritada Cubo, for example, while admitting that *yang sheng* in the *Chuang Tzu* is "probably" meant to indicate the spiritual (or the metaphysical) sense of longevity rather than the physical, claims that there is a close relationship between the *Chuang Tzu* and the theory of *shen hsien*.(1990: 74) There appear in the book, for example, such legendary symbols of longevity as the Queen Mother of the West and P'eng-tsu.[18] This for Cubo clearly suggests that the link between the *Chuang Tzu* and the immortality cult cannot be denied. The idea of immortality, he contends, is an important part of the *Chuang Tzu*.

However, Creel argues that the notion of *yang sheng* in the *Chuang Tzu* should not be interpreted as "prolonging life." Using the position of the *Lieh Tzu*, which severely criticizes such an idea propagated by the immortality cult, the term *yang sheng* in the *Chuang Tzu*, Creel contends, should be understood to mean the way the term is interpreted by the *Lieh Tzu*, i. e., "to give free rein to one's desires, regardless of whether this shortens one's life or not."(1970: 22) Creel partly bases his argument on the fact that some adherents of religious Taoism, such as Ko Hung (circa 300 C.E.), later criticized the *Chuang Tzu* for regarding life and death as the same.[19]

The question whether the *Chuang Tzu* alludes to the immortality cult in support of its doctrines, such as *shen hsien*, must be considered in the light of the philosophy as a whole. As Fung Yu-lan contends, the central conception of the *Chuang Tzu* vis-a-vis immortality is a mystical

---

18   Section 6. "P'eng-tsu's life span as given here extends, by traditional dating, from the 26th to the 7th centuries B.C." (Watson's trans., 1964: 78, note 12.)

19   Ko Hung says, in *Pao P'u Tzu* 抱樸子, *Nei* 8, 3b, that "this doctrine [that life and death are the same] is separated by millions of miles from that of *shen hsien* (spirits and immortals)."

union with the universe. "Therefore," says Fung, "if we can unite ourselves with the universe to form one ... then, since the universe has no beginning or end, so too shall we be without beginning and end." (1952-3, vol. 1: 238) Chapter VI of the *Chuang Tzu* is an important source for Fung's conclusion. Chapter VI says:

> So I began explaining and kept at him for three days... After he had put life outside himself, he was able to achieve the brightness of dawn [Bodde (Fung's translator) translates this as "enlightenment"], and when he had achieved the brightness of dawn, he could see his own aloneness. After he had managed to see his own aloneness, he could do away with past and present, and after he had done away with past and present, he was able to enter where there is no life and no death. (Watson's trans.)

In short, the attainment of *yang sheng*, for Chuang Tzu, is to reach the state of life where death becomes an ingredient of life.

Since scholarly opinion today tends to date the immortality cult to a much earlier age, it need not be doubted that the author of the seven "inner chapters" of the *Chuang Tzu* had a certain relationship with the cult. There is ample evidence in the book to support this assertion. However, this author did not in fact subscribe to the idea of physical immortality; instead, he radically reinterpreted it in a mystical way. This shows that he was not an ardent adherent of the cult; for such a radical reinterpretation would have been anathema to the cult. Also, considering the thrust of his philosophy as a whole, which seems to consider such preoccupation for physical immortality an "unenlightened idea," he himself would not have supported it. It would be truer to say, however, that this does not mean that the *Chuang Tzu* is against the life-prolonging practice of the cult; what is in fact the case is that for this philosopher those who were seeking to avoid death in order to live longer simply missed the point. Rather than being an attempt to avoid death, the same practice would be undertaken by this mystic to be one with the universe in the sense of going beyond that which separates death from life.

Thus, Creel argues that the two aspects of Taoism, the philosophical and the religious, the "Hsien Taoism," "not only were never identical; their associations, even, have been minimal."(1970: 11) But if this is the case, then, how did both come to be called by the same name? "During the Han dynasty," Creel says, "those seeking immortality gradually took over the name of Taoism" without taking over its philosophy. (1970: 11) Creel further contends that they went on to take over Buddhist practices to develop a popular Taoist religion in later Han times. Who were these seekers?

According to Creel, they were a group of shamans who, from Shang oracle bones, are known to have existed already in the second millennium B.C.; they took over the name of Taoism without taking over its philosophy, and, in the same way, they took over Buddhist practices without taking the name of Buddhism. *Wu* 巫, shamans, explains Creel, are important in the background of Hsien Taoism. (1970: 11-12)

## Religious Taoism and Shamanism: Distant Relatives

This section is a comparative study of Chinese religious Taoism and Korean Shamanism. I cannot, of course, explore the whole of these two great traditions, but shall consider their relation as this is relevant to Suun's synthesis. There has been relatively little attention paid to this subject, considering the close relationship between the two. Religious Taoism has always been a source of Korean philosophy/religion since the former made inroads in Korea during the Three Kingdoms Period (57 B.C.E–918 C.E.), even when Koreans did not know it by name. Paradoxical though it may seem, this is the reason why religious Taoism as such never became a substantial spiritual force in Korea, as Buddhism and Confucianism have been.

Thus, it is difficult to trace religious Taoism in Korea because of its rather diffused influence. While during the Koryo dynasty (918–1392) Taoism received some official sanction, it did not become an established religion. Instead it was used mainly for the purpose of blessing and protecting royalty. By and large, Taoist religions (sects), which had thrived in China, were absorbed into local shamanistic practices in Korea, becoming more "this worldly" in the process.

Suun, hence, taught his followers that they should aspire to be *ji sang shin sôn* 地上神仙, "earthly divine immortals." The idea of staying on earth instead of going to heaven can be found in both Chinese Taoism and Korean shamanism. *Shin sôn*, "divine immortals," which had been a Taoist ideal in China, was made more this-worldly by Suun in Korea.[20] In the case of Chinese Taoism, Creel explains that "a *hsien* who goes to heaven must take a lower place; since he has no seniority; this is why some prefer to stay on earth." (1970: 8–9)

---

20   For more discussions on this subject, see Yun Suk-san (1989: 327–343).

If we follow Creel, then, while some religious Taoists in China had preferred to stay on earth for strategic reasons, in Korea the idea of going to heaven was abandoned altogether. This, I believe, is an example of the characteristic way in which Chinese religious Taoism became absorbed into Korean shamanism.

However, Korean shamanism is not simply this-worldly; it has always sought a way out of the present human situation through shamans' usual activities, such as healing, exorcism, exhortation, and predictions about the future. In short, Korean shamanism aspires to a "this-worldly transcendence." Thus, like Chinese religious Taoism, Korean shamanism also seeks "things as they ought to be." This particular aspect of Suun's cultural heritage becomes important for him, for in his writings he clearly exhibits his disgust with the contemporary socio-political situation, hence aspiring to the improvement of the status quo.

We have thus far seen the close affinity between Taoism, especially the religious, and Korean Shamanism. Although the influence of Taoism in Korea is generally diffused, its influence on Suun, some argue, is the most decisive among the different traditions.[21] The reason for this decisive nature is because of the way the religious Taoism was immersed in local shamanistic practices, hence, being connected to the minjung's religious culture.

One more observation we have made is that the synthetic practices of different traditions into one, as Suun does, is not atypical in Korea, as *Han* philosophy epitomizes. The obvious difference between Suun and his intellectual predecessors is the importance of the social context in his intellectual activity. We will deal with his social context later, but now we need to discuss his Confucian background.

## Neo-Confucianism

Of course, I cannot offer here a full study of the vast Confucian tradition. Thus, the scope of this section is limited to the philosophical debate of some Neo-Confucian scholars in China during the Sung dynasty (960–1279) and in Korea during the Yi dynasty (1392–1910). My purpose here is to trace the Confucian roots of Suun. With respect to Confucianism, Suun identified his teachings with the former in its *li* 理

---

21  See, for example, Shin In-chul (1987: 532).

(principle) and slightly differentiated in its *do* (*Tao*).[22] *Li* here can be interpreted as the basic principle of the Confucian quest for sagehood and *do*, the path or manner of such a quest. That is, for him, the goals of the two (Confucianism and Suun's Teachings) are the same but the ways to attain them are different. Suun calls his newly-found "way" *Mugûk Daedo* 無極大道, "the Great Way of the Non-Ultimate." Where did the term *Mugûk* (*Wu Chi*, in Chinese), "Non-Ultimate," or "Ultimate of Non-Being," originate? The frequent appearance of the name of Chou Tun-i[23] (1017–73) in Suun's writings show the latter's indebtedness to the former. For Chou, the term *Mugûk* is closely related to *Taegûk* 太極 "Great Ultimate"; *T'ai Chi* in Chinese). In this section, therefore, I will focus on the development of this term, *Taegûk*, and that of the *li-ki* debate in Sung China and Korea during the Neo-Confucian Yi dynasty. Among the authors considered particular attention will be paid to Chou Tun-i and Chu Hsi (1130–1200) in China and Yi Toegye (1501–1570) and Yi Yulgok (1536–1584) in Korea.

The unique aspect of Confucianism from its early development is its social dimension. In comparison, the other two competing traditions, Taoism and Buddhism, are generally considered more individualistic than Confucianism. There are, for example, some important non-Confucian Chinese notions such as *wu wei*, "non-action" or "inaction," discussed above. *Wu wei*, however, as William T. de Bary points out, "provided no ground on which to stand against human injustice or exploitation."(1989: 5) At least that was the way it was understood by Confucianists, whose preoccupation had been, "What is one's appropriate role in family and in society?"

In answering this age-old question, neo-Confucianists set themselves apart from their sage mentors of the past by employing some key metaphysical concepts which had mostly been favored by Buddhists and Taoists. Classical Confucian authors had taught on the basis of some key notions like *jen/ren* 仁 (human-heartedness) and *i/yi* 義 (righteousness). For Confucius human-heartedness was a fundamental moral quality; one who was not human-hearted was one who lacked a genuine nature. *Jen/ren* has an altruistic character for others: "*jen* is the denial of self and response to the right and proper (*li*, 禮 'propriety, 'rites' or 'ritual')." (Analects, XII, 1)

---

22  "Sudokmun (On Disciplining Virtue)," *Donggyông Daejon*.
23  Chou is the first of the major thinkers, commonly known as the Sung School, of Neo-Confucianism in China.

Along with this term *jen*, *i* was made a central concept for Mencius. "He who outrages human-heartedness (*jen*)," says Mencius, "is called a robber; he who outrages righteousness (*i*) is called a ruffian." (Mencius, Ib, 8) No doubt the importance of these ideas in the Confucian societies of East Asia cannot be exaggerated. One's meaning and being is viewed in the light of those terms. With this brief note on ancient Confucianism, now we need to begin our exploration of the world of metaphysical Neo-Confucianism with the ideas of *Taegûk* and *li-ki*.

**The Ideas of *Taegûk* (T'ai Chi) and *Li-Ki* (Ch'i).** Although the "notion of Tao," as Michael C. Kalton points out, "or *li* (underlying Principle of all things, noumena) as Tao, explicates appropriateness and the norm for what is appropriate," it does not explain deviance.(1994: xxiv) That Ch'eng I (1033–1107) and later Neo-Confucians paired this term, *li*,[24] with another constituent of all things in reality, *ki* 氣 (ch'i/qi in Chinese; breath, ether, ethereal force [25]), was a natural move to explain deviance and evil.

In the face of the rising dominance of such competitive philosophies as Buddhism and Taoism, Neo-Confucians were compelled to respond from the Confucian side. Hence such key terms as *T'ai Chi* (Great Ultimate), *li* (Principle), and *ch'i* are newly introduced into the writings of Neo-Confucianism. For example, in *Lun-yü* (Discourses or *Analects* of Confucius), which is considered the most reliable source of Confucius' teachings, *T'ai Chi* and *li* do not appear at all. Even when used, they do not have the same meaning as they do when Neo-Confucians use them later. As Wing-tsit Chan notes, the term *ch'i* "appears several times [in the *Analects*], but is not used in the sense of material force."[26] (1963: 14) In this sense, Neo-Confucianism is more than a new interpretation; it is also a new creation. It added metaphysics to the old humanism. In the words of Joseph Percy Bruce, "the great achievement of the Sung School was to rescue the ethical teaching of the Classics from its threatened oblivion by bringing that teaching into close relationship with a reasoned theory of the universe, which in comparison with that of Buddhism or Taoism may at least be called a sane philosophy." (1973: 25)

---

24   For Ch'eng I's discussion on *li*, see A.C. Graham (1958: 8–21).
25   For the discussion of the concept of this term, see Lee Rainey (1992: 263–284).
26   In Mencius' notion of *huo jan chih ch'i* (浩然之氣), "active force," or "moving force," we see the development of this term *ch'i* as material force (energy), which, if properly nurtured, "fills up all between Heaven and Earth." (*Mencius*, IIa)

Bruce further attributes this achievement to the doctrine of the Supreme Ultimate (*T'ai Chi*) of Chou Tun-i, who is commonly considered the founder [27] of the Sung School.[28] We will now consider this notion of *T'ai Chi*, first in the Book of Changes (*I Ching*) and then in the work of Chou.

***T'ai Chi* in *I Ching*.** The term *T'ai Chi* first appears in the Book of Changes (*I Ching*/ *Yijing*). James Legge contends that "it [*T'ai Chi*] found its way into this [Third] Appendix [in the *I Ching*] in the fifth (? or fourth) century B.C. from a Taoist source."(1885: 373) Perhaps this strong Taoist flavour gives Ch'u Chai (and Winberg Chai) confidence to claim that the "Supreme Ultimate (*T'ai Chi*) given here is different from the *T'ai Chi Tu* (Diagram of the Supreme Ultimate), in which the Sung scholar Chou Tun-i elucidated the origins of 'Heavenly Principle' and probed into the beginning and end of all things."[29] Chai's rationale in this claim is centred on the notion of *I*, which means both "change" and "easy." "Change," it is said, is simple and easy. There are in the concept of *I* the meanings of "tranquility in movement" and "simplicity in complexity." Chai quotes the following passage from *Hsi Tz'u* (Appendix III in the *I Ching*) for which, he says in the corresponding note, a "similar passage is found in Ch. 42 of the *Lao Tzu*":

> Therefore, in (the system of) the *I*, there is the Supreme Ultimate (*T'ai Chi*), which produced the Two Modes (*Yi*). The Two Modes produced the Four *Hsing* (Symbols), which in turn produced the Eight Trigrams (*Kua*). (Sec. I, Ch. II)

The pertinent question in the *I Ching* is, "What lies behind, or enables, the ever-changing phenomena?" This classic, then, is an attempt to formulate a theory of the evolutionary process of the universe in an easy and simple formula centered on the notion of *I* 易, yôk in Korean. What is the ultimate cause of change?

Similar questions were also asked by the early Greek philosophers. The outcome of those, however, was quite different from that of the *I*

27  Chan contends that calling Chou "the founder" of Neo-Confucianism is "going too far." Instead, he describes Chou as the pioneer of Neo-Confucianism who "really opened its vista and determined its direction." (1963: 460–1)
28  The Sung School is generally associated with the following philosophers: Chou, the brothers Ch'eng Hao and Ch'eng I, their uncle Chang Tsai, and Chu Hsi.
29  "Introduction" in *I Ching: Book of Changes*, trans. by James Legge, edited with Introduction and Study Guide Ch'u Chai with Winberg Chai (1964: xliii).

*Ching*. For Aristotle, for example, the necessity for the First Cause called for the theory of the existence of the Unmoved Mover, which caused things to come to be in the manner of a chain reaction. Hence, between this First Cause and the myriad things in reality no direct contact is necessary.

In the case of the *I Ching*, however, the Great Ultimate subsists not only in its immediate modes, *yin* and *yang*, but also in every aspect of phenomena. As Legge contends, it was neither creation nor cosmogony but the Yi [I]—the ever-changing phenomena of nature and experience that was before the mind of the author of *I Ching*. The two cosmic forces, *yin* and *yang*, interact with each other in alternation. Out of this interaction all patterns of both things and ideas are evolved. Certainly, Chan is not alone when he says, "philosophically speaking, it [*I Ching*] has exerted more influence than any other Confucian Classic" (1963: 263), and it was Chou Tun-i who shaped the course of Neo-Confucianism, whose works were decisive in shaping Neo-Confucianism in both China and Korea.

**Chou Tun-i (Chou Lien-hsi, 1017–1073) and *T'ai Chi T'u*.** Chou's philosophy may be said to be an attempt to explain the unity of the double modes, *yin* and *yang*, using the notion of *T'ai Chi* as the source of both modes. Chou first drew *The Diagram of the Supreme Ultimate* (*T'ai Chi T'u*), then he expounded it in the *Explanation of the Diagram of the Supreme Ultimate* (*T'ai Chi T'u Shuo*). According to the *Explanation*, the *Great Ultimate* generates *yang* through movement (activity) and *yin* through tranquility. These two modes, *yin* and *yang*, together produce the Five Elements, Fire, Water, Wood, Metal, Earth, which, in turn, cause the cycle of the four Seasons through harmonious distribution. At the peak of the winter, for example, when the tranquility is at its height, activity ensues. In like manner, at the peak of the summer, when activity is at its height, tranquility begins its course. Such is the way of *yin* and *yang*. At this stage, however, a difficult part of Chou's thought emerges, namely, the introduction of *Wu Chi*, literally, "non-ultimate," in his system.

The term *Wu Chi*, which can be translated as "Ultimate of Non-being," was first used by Lao Tzu (chapter 28). Because Chou used it side by side with *T'ai Chi* at the beginning of the *Explanation*, he had to risk a logical difficulty as to how two such different terms can be associated with the necessity for the one Final Cause. Do the two terms, *Wu Chi* and *T'ai Chi*, denote one and the same reality, or do they mean different things? If they mean the same, why are there two terms? If, on the other hand, they mean different things, how can both be the Final Cause? This was the chief criticism made by Lu Hsing-shan (Lu Chiu-yuan, 1139–1193). If "the Great Ultimate is fundamentally the Non-ultimate," as Chou himself says,[30] how can the Ultimate derive from non-being?, asks Lu. Hence he charged Chou as a faithful follower of Lao Tzu. Lu says,

> Lao Tzu regarded non-being as the beginning of Heaven and Earth and being as the mother of all things, and tried to see the subtlety of things through eternal non-being and to see the outcome of things through eternal being. To add "non-being" to "ultimate" is precisely to follow the teaching of Lao Tzu.[31]

In the beginning, for Lu, was the Principle (*li*) and not non-being. Chu Hsi, however, defended Chou by arguing "that Chou never meant" the two, *Wu Chi* and *T'ai Chi*, to be separate entities. According to Chu Hsi, *Wu Chi* is meant by Chou to denote "the state of reality before the appearance of forms," while *T'ai Chi* is "the state after the appearance of forms," and, therefore, "the two form a unity."[32]

What of the difference which Chai indicates between the *I Ching* and Chou in their notions of *T'ai Chi*? Obviously, there is a formal difference between the two. In the *I Ching*, *T'ai Chi* produces the Two, *yin* and *yang*, which, out of their interaction, in turn produce the Four *hsing* 象 (symbols, emblems), major and minor *yin* and *yang*. These Four then give rise to the Eight *kua* 卦 (Trigrams). For Chou, on the other hand, *T'ai Chi* generates the Two, which in turn produce the Five Elements (neither *hsing* nor *kua*), Fire, Water, etc.

Nevertheless, it is truer to say that this difference stems from the difference in the symbols or metaphors which they employ in explaining the nature of reality. The Four *hsing* and the Eight *kua*, for example, are more metaphorical than actual. This is indicated by the meaning of the word *hsing*, which connotes symbols, patterns, and ideas. It is further illustrated by the fact that when the Eight trigrams become sixty-four hexagrams through combinations, they are taken to represent all possible

30 *Chou Tzu ch'uan-shu* (*Wan-yu wen-k'u* edition), chapter 1; Chan (1963: 463).
31 In *Hsing-shan ch'uan-chi* (Complete Works of Lu Hsing-shan), a collection by Lyman Van Law Cady, entitled "The Philosophy of Lu Hsing-shan, A Neo-Confucian Monistic Idealist," typescript, 2 vols. (1939); Chan (1963: 578).
32 *Chu Tzu wen-chi* (Collection of Literary Works of Chu Hsi), CTTC, 36: 8a–12a; Chan (1963: 464–5).

forms of change, situations, and possibilities. In the case of Chou, on the other hand, the Five Elements form the spiritual-material basis of the world and human nature. The difference between the *I Ching* and Chou, then, is more in the figures of speech than their philosophical viewpoints. If there is a new element in Chou's philosophy, which was not obvious in the *I Ching*, it is the emphasis on human nature.

Furthermore, this apparent difference does not warrant the view that Chou did not base his theory of *T'ai Chi* primarily on the *I Ching*. The argument seems to be somewhat ideologically motivated. An underlying question is, "how Taoistic is Chou?," which is also the point of debate between Lu and Chu above. We have already noted above the strong possibility of a Taoist influence in Appendix III of the *I Ching*. In dealing with the notions of "tranquility" and "movement (or activity)," for example, Taoists and Neo-Confucianists are diametrically opposed. For the former, tranquility is the way of Tao, while the latter claims that only through activity can the mind of Heaven and Earth be seen. It is to be noted that Chou's objective is undeniably Confucian; the causality of the Great Ultimate in *yin-yang* and the myriad things is fundamentally ethical in nature. As Li Kuang-ti (1642–1718) argues, in Chou's mind tranquility is never divorced from activity.[33] That is, for Chou, the implication of the Great Ultimate is more ethical than mystical. That Chou employed the Five Elements instead of the *hsing* and *kua*, as discussed above, is a clear indication that he wanted to deal with the subject of human nature in his cosmology. Carsun Chang likens the idea of the Five Elements to the Monads of Leibnitz, "which are neither mind nor matter separately, but are immaterial and material at the same time." (vol. I: 145) One wonders, however, whether this similarity is outweighed by the difference between the Monads and the Five Elements; the former are self-contained "windowless" aggregates, whereas the latter are much more mutually interdependent in their constant interaction. Be that as it may, Chang is right in saying that these Five Elements, "stand for matter and also for moral values."

Herein lies Chou's achievement: using the expression of Chan, "in spite of [Chou's Taoist influence], he steered Neo-Confucianism away from it." (1963: 465)

---

33 *Jung-ts'un T'ung-shu p'ien* (Essay on *Penetrating the Book of Changes*) appended to the *Chou Tzu T'ung-shu* (Penetrating the *Book of Changes* by Master Chou); Chan (1963: 465).

**Chu Hsi (1130–1200).** Chang describes Chu Hsi as neither a monist nor a dualist. Drawing from the Western philosophical tradition, Chang calls Chu both a Platonist and an Aristotelian.(vol. I: 254–257) In the realm of the physical world, Chang argues, Chu is an Aristotelian. Like Aristotle, he contends, Chu rejects the idea that the Form, or the Universal Principle (*li*), exists apart from the concrete objects (*ch'i*).

In the realm of moral values, Chang continues, Chu is a Platonic Idealist. Like Plato, Chu held the view that the perfect unchanging Principle exists. Why, then, does this Perfect principle not become realized in the world? It is, for Chu, due to the way of *ch'i*. *Li*, he explains, is one, but its manifestations through *ch'i* are many. As the same Supreme Ultimate subsists in *yin* and *yang* and the Five Elements in diverse ways, the One resides in the Many. Strictly speaking, then, for Chu to be consistent, it would be incorrect to speak of the manifestation of *li*. For *li* cannot manifest itself; it can only reside in *ch'i*'s manifestations. Hence, *li*, the metaphysical, is the same everywhere, while *ch'i*, the physical, is manifested in diverse ways.

There is here in Chu's system a logical vacuum. While, on the one hand, "*li* cannot exist without *ch'i*,"[34] the two are, on the other hand, clearly separate in essence; *li* is the pure good devoid of evil, while *ch'i* is not immune to evil influences. Whence, then, comes the evil? For Chu does not identify *ch'i* with evil, in the same way as he identifies *li* with good. In order to examine Chu's explanation of evil in the world, a comparison may be made with one exemplary figure in the Western philosophical/theological tradition: Augustine.

The problem of evil has also been an important philosophical issue in the West. Augustine was among those who attempted to solve the problem. He developed his theory in the light of his Christian doctrines of Creation and Redemption. Since, argued Augustine, God said, "it is good," after creating the Heaven and the Earth, the original creation must have been good. How, then, could God's creation have been spoiled? Augustine contended that evil is the privation of good. With God's creation, which was originally good, in mind, he said that whatever is is good, and whatever is not, not good. Hence Augustine laid an important foundation for Western philosophy, namely, that being is good, and non-being is bad.[35]

---

34  Wang Mou-hung, Book 1, Section on Ri and Ch'i; Chang, vol. I, p. 257.
35  Masao Abe traces this subject to early Greek philosophies of Parmenides and Plato. See his book, *Zen and Western Thought*, ed. by William R. LaFleur (1985: 122–

In East Asian worldviews, however, being and non-being are not separately attributed to good and evil, respectively, in the way Augustine made them. In the *Lao Tzu*, as well as in the *I Ching*, for example, both being and non-being are closely related to each other, and, together, they constitute reality. For the former, *Lao Tzu*, in particular, non-being is the source of being, and hence it is of a higher and nobler category, which is the opposite of what Augustine argued. Also in the *I Ching* what is ideal is not the dominance of being over non-being but a harmony between the opposites. Even the "opposites" here are not opposites in the sense of being good, for one, and bad, for the other; they are rather essential components for any thing to be. Perhaps, this cultural ethos of East Asians, whose way of thinking is "both-and" rather than "either-or,"[36] was a contributing factor to the difficulty for them in explaining the existence of evil in the world.

For Chu Hsi, following the idea of Mencius, original human nature is good. What Mencius did not do, Chu points out, is explain how the originally good nature can become bad. This, Chu felt, was due to the fact that Mencius "takes account of the Nature but not of the Ether, and thus in some respects his statement is incomplete."(1973: 80). What had been incomplete in Mencius, says Chu, was completed by the Ch'eng brothers. The following words show Chu's indebtedness to the Ch'engs: "The Ch'eng School, however, has supplemented this doctrine with the doctrine of the physical element, and so we get a complete and all-round view of the problem." (1973: 80)

Within the moral framework of Mencius, that is, the doctrine of the original goodness of human nature, Chu attempted to show how the evil of the world can be explained. The metaphysical term *ch'i*, therefore, is employed to explain what was not explained in Mencius. In Chu's philosophy, as in that of most Neo-Confucianists, the metaphysical is at the service of the ethical. How, then, does the introduction of this term, *ch'i*, solve the problem of the existence of evil in the world? Chu identifies what is originally good with *li*, and associates the reason for the existence of evil with the way of *ch'i*. The relationship between *li* and *ch'i*, for him, is like that of a rider and a horse, respectively. An ideal situation is when the horse obeys the rider's command. The question constantly asked is, how does one become able to put *li* in control of *ch'i*

---

123).
36  Lee Jung-Young argues that the perspective of the *I Ching* is "both-and." See his book *Cosmic Religion* (1973) or *The I: A Christian Concept of Man* (1971).

in oneself ? Hence, the concern for proper education becomes important. For that reason, some argue, the question of good and evil, for the Chinese, is in essence the question of pedagogy rather than that of ontology or theology. (Ching, 1977: 116).

Now the problem in Chu's system is that although his preoccupation is the ethical in nature,[37] as in other Neo-Confucianists, in all this speculative reasoning the major difficulty in his system is his metaphysics. Augustine, again, held the view that evil is the privation of good, that is, that there is nothing which contributes to the evil state of affairs except the fact that there is less of being than desired. For Chu Hsi, on the other hand, it is the lack of *li*'s control in the being of *ch'i* which produces evil. Although it is true to say that Augustine, whose thought is greatly indebted to Plato's, is generally more dualistic than Chu Hsi, the latter exhibits more dualism on this particular point.

Herein lies the practical difficulty in Chu's ideas of *li* and *ch'i* as they may be summed up in the following two ways: (1) *li* is always good, and the evil in the world is due to the way of *ch'i*; (2) *li* is logically prior to *ch'i*; and (3) there is no instance, however, where *li* can exist apart from *ch'i*. It appears that the problem is in Chu's insistence on the essential priority of *li* over *ch'i*. That is, on the essential level, *li* is prior to *ch'i*, whereas on the existential level, the two are not separated. He emphasizes *li*'s priority to the point of somewhat contradicting his own point about the inseparability of *li* and *ch'i* when he says, "Before the creation of the world, *ri [li]* exits."[38] By attributing an ontological meaning to the term *li* and prioritizing it over the physical notion of *ch'i*, Chu puts himself in a logical difficulty.

In Korea this difficulty is inherited by many Neo-Confucians, perhaps, most notably Toegye. We will deal with Korean philosophers later, but now we need to discuss some Buddhist elements in Chu Hsi.

**Some Buddhist Influence on Chu Hsi and *Li-Ch'i* Philosophy.** Chu associates *li* (Principle) with *hsin* 心 (mind-and-heart). Since he also identifies *li* with the Supreme Ultimate (*T'ai Chi*) and Heaven, this means that there is an undisturbed continuation among *T'ai Chi, T'ien* (Heaven), *li*, and *hsin*. On one occasion he says, "It is correct to say that

37 Wing-tsit Chan argues that "the concept of *Jen* ["humanity," the central notion of the *Analects*] was clearly far more important than those of the Great Ultimate and other philosophical categories" to Chu Hsi. See his book, *Chu Hsi: New Studies* (1989: 152).
38 *Chu-tzu yu-lui*, Book 1, the first question and answer; Chang (vol. I: 258).

mind is what rules." He then continues, "What rules is principle/reason [*li*]." Is this ruler an anthropomorphic Being? "It is incorrect," Chu explains, "to say that a person sits in heaven who judges the sins of men." Nor is it correct, Chu adds, "to say that there is no ruler at all."[39] Since *hsin* (mind-and-heart) is also a central notion of Buddhism, Chu's metaphysical use of this term can be seen as his response as well as indebtedness to Buddhism. As Ching explains,

> Ironically, since the rise of Neo-Confucianism signaled the decline of Buddhism, Buddhist influences on Chinese thought are best discerned afterwards in the structure of Neo-Confucian thinking. (1993: 156).

There are, for Chu Hsi, two natures, or minds, in a person: *tao-hsin* and *jen-hsin*. The first, *tao-hsin*, is literally "the mind of *Tao*." This is the moral nature endowed by Heaven. It is hence inherently good and pure. The second nature, *jen-hsin*, which means the "human mind," on the other hand, is imperfect and prone to mistakes and evil influences. It is "that aspect of the mind-and-heart expressive of man's psycho-physical nature, that is, for appetites and desires... become selfish if not guided or directed by the *tao-hsin*."(de Bary, 1989: 10). From what has been said thus far, it is natural to say that this dual aspect of human nature is the way of *li* and *ch'i* in a person. One question arises here: aside from the aforementioned "response"-characteristic of Chu in treating *hsin*, how serious is he about this predominantly Buddhistic term?

The dichotomy in Ch'eng (I)–Chu (Hsi)'s "school of principle" (*li-hsueh*) and Lu (Hsiang shan)–Wang (Yang-ming)'s school of the mind (*hsin hsueh*), argues William Theodore de Bary, is misleading. Fung Yu-lan, for example, argues that the two are rival schools. De Bary, however, agrees with Ch'ien Mu, who contends that Chu-Hsi's thought encompasses both *li* and *hsin*. The dichotomy, for Ch'ien Mu and de Bary, lies not in their emphasis on either *li*, for Ch'eng-Chu, or *hsin*, for Lu-Wang. Rather the difference between the two, says Ch'ien Mu, lies "squarely in [their different views of] the learning of the mind." (de Bary, 1989: 10) For Ch'ien Mu and de Bary, then, *hsin* is a central notion of Chu Hsi.

One wonders, however, whether Chu Hsi is not in fact using the Buddhist concept to explain his thought more effectively rather than making it his central idea. There is a difference between using a certain idea within one's philosophical category and making it one's central

---

39 *Chu-tzu nien-p'u*; Chang (vol. I: 259).

frame of thinking. Chu Hsi's use of *hsin* belongs to the former; although he uses it with a more metaphysical connotation than does Mencius, the former still works within the moral philosophical tradition of Confucius-Mencius. Moreover, dividing the mind into two, Buddha-mind and human-mind, is not common among Buddhists. That humans possess the Buddha-mind, as Buddhism claims, is not usually interpreted in the way Chu Hsi distinguishes between *tao-hsin* (mind of the Tao) and *jen-hsin* (human mind). For Chu the two minds can be in conflict with each other in a person. The *jen-hsin*, therefore, must obey the *tao-hsin*'s lead. This falls under the same principle as that of *li* and *ch'i*; the former is the rider and the latter, the horse. Now, then, what of these two terms of his that concern us mostly here: *li* and *ch'i*?

The two notions of *li* and *ch'i* show the influence of Buddhism, especially the Hua-yen (Kor. Hwaôm; Jap. Kegon) School, on Neo-Confucianism. Hua-yen, which is based on the Avatamsaka sutra (Flower Garland Scripture), explained reality under the two aspects of *li* 理, the noumenal, and *shih/shi* 事, the phenomenal, and their combination, which together make reality fourfold in the concept of the Universal Causation of the Realm of Dharmas: the Realm of Facts (*shih*), the Realm of Principle (*li*), the Realm of Principle and Facts, the Realm of All Facts interwoven and mutually identified. These noumenal and phenomenal aspects, *li* and *shih*, form a "Perfect Harmony" through constant interaction and interpenetration.[40] The One is interdependent with the All: when one dharma rises, all dharmas rise with it, or the entire universe rises at the same time. One (*li*) is all (*shih*) and all is one. Each of the phenomena interpenetrates all others.[41] Some of the well-known illustrations used by Fa-tsang (or Hsien-shou, 643–712),[42] such as "the Buddha statue and the Mirrors" and "the Ocean and the Waves," have been favored by both Buddhists and non-Buddhists alike, including Chu Hsi.[43]

---

40   理事無碍
41   事事無碍
42   Buddhist monk commonly considered the founder of Hua-yen (Hwaôm in Korean; Kegon in Japanese) school of Buddhism in China.
43   Chu Hsi modified this and gave the following analogy: "Fundamentally there is only one Great Ultimate, yet each of the myriad things has been endowed with it and each in itself possesses the Great Ultimate in its entirety. This is similar to the fact that there is only one moon in the sky but when its light is scattered upon rivers and lakes, it can be seen everywhere. It cannot be said that the moon has been split." Chan (1963: 638).

However, as Chan points out, there is a fundamental difference between the Hua-yen and the Ch'eng-Chu schools with respect to the relationship between *li* and *shih*. While for the former, "all phenomena are manifestations of the mind," it is in accordance with *li* that the universe produces and reproduces constantly for the latter. Moreover, the idea of *li* in opposition to *shih* can be traced back to the third century C.E., i.e., before the development of Hua-yen Buddhism in China.[44]

## *Li-Ki* Debates in Korea

**Chong Do-Jon (1342–1398).** Chong was one of the most important predecessors of the *li-ki* (*ch'i*) debate in Korea. He used the philosophy of Chu Hsi as a theoretical tool to criticize the then dominant Buddhism. Because of his preoccupation with anti-Buddhist activities, he has been considered more a political figure than a scholar. As Chung Dae-hwan argues, however, it is important to treat him seriously because he clearly set the ideological tone for later scholars to follow. (1992: 1–43).

For Chong *shim* 心 (Ch. *hsin*), mind-and-heart, as the central notion of Buddhism, is inferior to *sông* 性 (Ch. *hsing*), the (human) nature, of Chu Hsi's Neo-Confucianism. Chong argues that "[w]hen *li* is of metaphysical and *ki* physical, how ridiculous it is that Buddhists consider themselves the most exalted while preoccupied with the physical phenomena."[45] In his *Bulssi Japbyôn* 佛氏雜辨, "Various Confusions of Buddhism," Chong argues that whereas in Confucianism there is the monistic union of the opposites between Void 虛 and Existence 有 (虛而有) and between Quiescence 寂 and Transformation 感 (寂而感), in Buddhism Void leads to eventual Nothingness 無 (虛而無), and Quiescence to Perishing 滅 (寂而滅). Hence, for Chong, Confucianism maintains the dialectical continuity between the positive and the negative, but Buddhism falls into dualism by insisting only on the negative.[46]

---

44 A.C. Graham (1958), referring to the findings of Demieville in the *Annuaire du Collège de France* (1947), says, "Neo-Confucianism returned to the old sense of 'un principe d'ordre naturel', but without fully freeing itself from the Buddhist conception of *li* as an Absolute immanent in the self and in all things." (21, note 1)
45 Source from Chung (1992: 26).
46 "Yu sôk dong i ji byôn (儒釋同異之辨) [Confucianism and Buddhism: a Comparison]," *Bulssi Japbyôn*; source Kum Jang-tae (1994: 20)

Ironically, however, Chong himself relates *shim* to *ki* and *sông* to *li* in a clearly dualistic way. This shows some variance from Chu Hsi. *Ki* as the substance of natural phenomena is considered inferior to *li*, which, as the original nature, enables the former. Chong identified *ki* as the representative notion of Taoism and *li* as that of Neo-Confucianism, and hence he treats Taoism in much the same way as Buddhism. Chong hence used Sung Neo-Confucianism eclectically for his ideological purposes.

**Kwon Kun (1352–1409).** Kwon was a contemporary of Chong Do-jon, and while the latter was preoccupied with introducing Neo-Confucianism as a philosophical tool to oppose Buddhism, the former was more interested in developing the same tradition as an academic discipline. This is an important shift that Kwon established from the ideological course of Chong, whose polemics were mainly directed against Buddhism.

According to Yun Sa-soon, the central purpose of Kwon in treating such notions as *chôn* (Ch. *t'ien*, Heaven), *in* (*jen*, human-heartedness), *shim* (*hsin*, mind-and-heart) and *sông* (*hsing*, nature) through various diagrams is to illustrate the possibility of *chôn-in-hap-il* 天人合一, "heaven and human are one",[47] which is an important notion for Suun later. Whereas Chong related *shim (hsin)* to *ki*, treating it as separate from and inferior to *li*, Kwon taught that *shim* comes to be in a mysterious union between *li* and *ki*, and is that which humans received from the Heaven, and hence, it supervises physical activities.

Another peculiar aspect of Kwon's thought is also found in his contention about the path to sagehood. For him knowledge (ji; 知) and action/practice (*haeng*; 行) are like two wheels of a wagon; both are legitimate ways of learning and discipline. Hence, on this particular point, Kwon departs from Chu Hsi, who held the view that an erudite search is the way of enlightenment.

**Suh Kyong-Dok (Hwadam, 1489–1546).** Suh was a Taoist Confucian scholar in the early part of the Neo-Confucian Yi dynasty. His thought echoes the monistic philosophy of Chou Tun-i's *Diagram* and that of Chang Tsai (Chang Heng-ch'u, 1020–1077). For Suh, there is neither beginning nor end in *ki*, which is the original substance of the universe

---

47 Yun Sa-soon, *Josôn Chogi Sônglihakûi Jôn'gae [Development of the Study of Human Nature in Early Josôn (Yi) Dynasty]*, p. 140; Chung (1992: 55–56).

and the ground of being. *Ki* divides itself into two, *yin* and *yang*. *Yin* condenses itself and become Earth, and *Yang* moves to turn into Heaven.

Although Suh was greatly indebted to Lao Tzu,[48] he departed from the latter in his theory of the origin of existence. For according to Lao Tzu, existence/ being 有 comes from non-existence/ non-being 無 and therefore *ki* (*ch'i*) is from the Void. Suh "adamantly" rejected this theory and believed that "the condensation or dispersion of *ki* is carried out under the power of its own force and is not influenced by outside elements."[49] This last point was originally argued by Chang Tsai.

Chang insisted that *ch'i* (*ki*) produced and reproduced through its own condensation and dispersion. By identifying *ch'i* with the Great Ultimate (*T'ai Chi*), Chang held the view that the universe is one but its manifestations are many. Both "one" and "many" here are *ch'i*. In connection with *ch'i*, Chang—and also Suh—uses another term, "Great Void (*T'ai hsü* 太虛)," which is the ultimate reservoir for *ch'i*; the latter condenses from and disperses into the former. When *ch'i* condenses there is form and shape, and when it disperses into the Great Void it becomes formless existence. Thus Void here does not imply the absence of or opposite from existence. On the contrary it indicates existence in fullness like that of great water, hence without concrete form and shape.[50]

This is the reason why Chang cannot accept the proposition of Lao Tzu who claimed that being is born of non-being (有生於無). Much the same way as Suh later, Chang criticized Lao Tzu for failing to understand the eternal principle of the undifferentiated unity of being and non-being by arguing that the former comes from the latter. The ethical implication of this monistic view was that under Heaven and Earth, our "universal parents," we were to be one with the universe through our love for all beings. Such, for Chang, was the way of Tao.

The common feature among these thinkers, as Kalton explains, is that "Tao is simply the pattern inherent in *ki*, and *ki* is the concrete

---

48  Since the historicity of the author of *Tao Te Ching* is uncertain, we will simply use Lao Tzu as both the author and the book.
49  Pak C. H. (1983: 66).
50  It is noteworthy that in his commentary to *Awakening of Faith in Mahayana* (大乘起信論疏. 別記), Wonhyo (617–686), about 4 centuries before Chang, also used the term "Great Void" in the context of explaining the meaning of Mahayana 大乘, using the notions of existence 有 and non-existence 無. For Wonhyo, too, the Great Void is not mere emptiness but is in a state of formlessness like a vast and wide ocean. There will be more discussion on Wonhyo in Chapter IV.

vehicle in which the Tao is realized; [there are two] terms, but they are complementary to the point of being virtually monistic."[51] This monistic view, however, is not followed by Toegye, one of the major figures in Korean Neo-Confucianism.

**Yi Hwang (Toegye, 1501–1570).** Toegye is commonly known as an exponent of *Juriron* 主理論, a theory of the priority of *li*. For him *sông* 性 (*hsing*), human nature, is conceived as a dual-nature: the nature of *li* and that of *ki*. *Li* is the "original, Heaven-bestowed nature," which was related to *tao-hsin* 道心, the mind of Tao, for Chu Hsi, and manifests itself in the *Sadan*,[52] Four Beginnings (sympathy, shame, concession and reason).

The Four Beginnings were first suggested by Mencius as the basis for the four virtues: humanity 仁, righteousness 義, propriety 禮 and wisdom 智. Hence, the Four provided Mencius a philosophical rationale to proclaim his doctrine of the goodness of human nature as follows:

> If you let people follow their feelings (original nature), they will be able to do good. This is what is meant by saying that human nature is good. If man does evil, it is not the fault of his natural endowment. The feeling of commiseration is found in all men; the feeling of shame and dislike is found in all men... The feeling of commiseration is what we call humanity; the feeling of shame and dislike is what we call righteousness... Humanity, righteousness, propriety, and wisdom are not drilled into us from outside. We originally have them with us. (2A, 6)

Bae Jong-ho takes the view that Toegye's notion of *li*, Principle, is similar to that of the Hua-yen school and hence signifies the *gongli* 空理, "void *li*," which is the pure spiritual entity. (1989: 600) As discussed above, however, Hua-yen's influence on Neo-Confucianism is already clear among the Sung Philosophers, most notably Chu Hsi. It is more likely, therefore, that the influence of Hua-yen on Toegye is indirect, i.e., through Chu Hsi.

The influence of Chu Hsi on Toegye is unmistakable. For Chu Hsi *li* is the final cause, the Supreme Ultimate. Toegye's dilemma is how both to be faithful to Chu Hsi's orthodoxy and sensitive to the question of the "whence" in regard to the presence of evil in life, which is supposed to be governed by *li*. Any deviance, therefore, must be dealt with in the realm of human emotions.

51   Kalton (1994, "Introduction")
52   四端: 惻隱, 羞惡, 辭讓, 是非

As opposed to *li*, which is the pure good, *ki* (*ch'i*) is a sensual nature originating in human passion, and manifests itself in the Seven Emotions (pleasure, anger, sadness, fear, love, hate, and desire.[53]) These Seven, which are first mentioned in the *Book of Rites*, are the comprehensive depiction of the human emotions. In the *Doctrine of the Mean*, which is named by Chu Hsi as one of the four most authoritative books, namely, Four Books,[54] there are four emotions instead: pleasure, anger, sadness, and enjoyment.[55] There is no difference in meaning between the Seven Emotions of the *Book of Rites* and the four emotions of the *Doctrine of the Mean*, except in number. Unlike the Four Beginnings, which are inherently good, the Seven, or the four (emotions), can become either good or bad. As Chu Hsi identified *jen-hsin* 人心 as that part of human mind which is fragile in the face of evil influence, Toegye relates the Seven to *ki*.

Ki Dae-sung (Kobong), one of Toegye's disciples (or junior colleagues), raises the issue of the possibility of evil in the Four Beginnings by arguing that some people become confused as to when it is proper to practice *Su-O*, "shame," or *Sa-Yang*, "Concession." In this case it becomes possible that the Four can be used for both good and bad alike. Kobong hence challenges Toegye's dualistic treatment of *li* and *ki*. For Kobong, Toegye makes this interpretation possible by separating *li* and *ki* as he does. Kobong points out the phenomenal aspect of the Four, which is often bad, while Toegye explains the original nature of the Four, which is only good.

Kobong's contention is that the functions of *li* and *ki* cannot be as distinct as Toegye makes them. The Four, for Kobong, are but the good aspect of the Seven; both *li* and *ki* are related to both the Four and the Seven.

After seven years of debate between Toegye and Kobong, the former came to soften his assertion by amending it so that the Four Beginnings are in manifestation of *li* followed by *ki* while the Seven Emotions are the revelation of *ki* participated in by *li*.

Kim Ki-hyon describes Toegye as an idealist and Kobong as a realist.(1992: 53) The difference between Toegye and Kobong, then, stems from their different starting points; while Toegye begins with the

---

53   喜怒哀懼愛惡慾
54   *Lun Yu* (論語 ) or *Analects (of Confucius)*, the *Mencius* (孟子), the *Ta Hsueh* (大學) or *Great Learning*, and the *Chung Yung* (中庸 ) or *Doctrine of the Mean*.
55   喜怒哀樂

way human nature should be, as espoused by Mencius, Kobong starts from the way human nature actually appears among human beings. Each of the two thinkers has his own preoccupation: Toegye with the metaphysical and Kobong with the phenomenal. Hence, it can be said that the former is prescriptive and the latter descriptive.

**Yi I (Yulgok, 1536–1584).** In contrast to Toegye, whose philosophy is considered a *juriron*, the thought of Yulgok is generally called a *jukiron* 主氣論, which is a theory of the priority of *ki*. For Yulgok *li* does not manifest itself; it always follows, or accompanies, *ki* when *ki* manifests itself. What, then, is *li*? *Li* is the *reason* for *ki*'s manifestation and the *manner* of *ki*'s being. There is no instance in which *li*, the principle, can manifest itself without *ki*, the substance, also having revealed itself; *li* is the principle, the way, or the mode of *ki*'s manifestation. Therefore, what reveals itself is *ki*, and *li* merely participates in this revelation.

Song Sok-ku argues that Yulgok's philosophy of *li-ki* is a combination of those of Hwadam and Toegye. Yulgok, he says, attempts to unify the diametrically opposed views of Hwadam's *ki*-monism and Toegye's *li-ki* dualism.(1985: 252) Neither *ki*-only-existence nor *li-ki*-alternate emanations is accepted by Yulgok. Instead, he advocates *ki-bal-li-sûng* 氣發理乘, "*ki* emanates and *li* rides on it," rejecting Toegye's *li-bal-ki-bal* 理發氣發, "both *li* and *ki* emanate [alternately]." Yulgok's *ki-bal-li-sûng* is in fact a partial acceptance of Toegye's *hobal* 互發, "alternating manifestation." Toegye argued that *ki* follows when *li* emanates in the case of the Four, and *ki* emanates and *li* rides on it in the case of the Seven, hence separating not only *li* from *ki* but the Four from the Seven.

However, unlike Toegye who contended that there is an essential separation and a temporal precedence of one over the other, for Yulgok, there is neither separation nor sequential precedence between *li* and *ki*. For him, like Kobong before him, the Four are the good side of the Seven. One wonders, then, why Yulgok insists on retaining the notion of *li* at all. Could he not free himself from the linguistic paradigm of Chu Hsi?

It becomes clear here that Yulgok's philosophy is more dualistic than is suggested by the conventional category of "*ki*-monism" which some scholars use without qualification. If Yulgok espoused *ki*-centred philosophy, this is so because for him physical human experience is bound by the phenomenal entity which is *ki*. *Ki*, which has form and shape, is what informs us of the moral nature of reality. *Li*, on the other hand, is formless and shapeless, and therefore it cannot be discerned empirically. Nevertheless its existence cannot be denied, because without it *ki* cannot exist. Yulgok in this sense is epistemologically a dualist, and existentially a monist. The two, *li* and *ki,* are distinct in essence but not separate in existence.

Some liken Yulgok's contention of the presence of *li* in all sensual things to Chuang-tzu's treatment of Tao. "In a chapter of *Chibukyopyôn* (chap. 22)," says An Pyong-ju, Chuang-tzu said that Tao can be found in an insect,"... in piss and dung, "thus advocating the omnipresence of Tao." In a letter to Song U-gye in which Yulgok asserted the theory of *li* pervading and *ki* accommodating, Yulgok maintained the omnipresence of *li*, showing a striking similarity to Chuang-tzu's theory of the omnipresence of Tao. (An, 1983: 109).

The difference between Toegye and Yulgok is similar to that between Plato and Aristotle in the Western philosophical tradition. If Toegye's notions of *li* and *ki* may be compared to those of Plato's Form and the visible world, respectively, Yulgok's *li* and *ki* will correspond to Aristotle's form and matter.

Chung Yak-yong (1762–1836) explained that the apparent difference between the two thinkers, Toegye and Yulgok, is due to their different philosophical orientations. While Toegye explained *Hobal*, "alternate emanation," in the light of his understanding of human nature, Yulgok espoused *Ildo* 一途, "one way" or "one manner," in accordance with his cosmology. Following Chung a comparison may be drawn between these two figures and two exemplary Chinese thinkers, Chu Hsi and Chou Tun-i; Toegye is closer to the former and Yulgok, to the latter.[56]

Toegye and Yulgok made such a lasting impact on Korean Neo-Confucianism that scholars who followed Toegye's line of thought started a circle called the Yôngnam School (Yôngnam is Kyôngsang Province which is Toegye's hometown), while the followers of the latter formed the Kiho School from Kyônggi, Yulgok's hometown, and Hosô (Chungchông Provinces). In the beginning, notes Pak Chong-hong (1983), while Toegye's followers in the Yôngnam School were generally older and conservative, those of Yulgok from the Kiho School were

---

[56] The obvious difference between Chou Tun-i and Yulgok is the latter's use of *li*, which is absent in the former. This shows that although Yulgok differs from Chu Hsi at times, the former struggles to remain within the orthodoxy of the latter.

progressives in the field of politics. We shall return to this subject of Confucianism later to discuss how Suun made use of it in his system.

## Social Context: The Methodological Present

**The Setting.** Korea in the nineteenth century experienced crises as a result of both the internal corruption of the ruling group and external threats from foreign nations. At this time the Yi dynasty (1392–1910) was tightening its grip on people in order to maintain the nation's centuries-old feudalism. The way the rulers did so made the minjung feel helpless in the present and hopeless about their future. They were unable to cope with ever increasing economic, social and political oppression. The words of Chung Yak-yong, a positivist Confucian scholar who attempted to reform Chinese Neo-Confucianism to suit the needs of the Korea at the time, portrays the social scene vividly:

> The people made farming land out of the earth, and the government functionaries made farming land out of the people. In this way the government functionaries stripped the skin of the people and thwacked their bones as the farmers cultivated and tamed the land. They counted the number of the people and conscripted them just like the farmers gathered their harvest.[57]

Corruption was so widespread, from the central governing body centred on the monarchy to the smallest local authorities, that the people had nowhere to turn but to themselves.

At the centre of this situation the dynasty saw the rise to and fall from power of different factions, one after another, for over three centuries. The most well-known family in power in the nineteenth century was the "An Dong" Kims. An Dong was the name of the place from which these Kims traced their ancestry. The Kims, like most other powerful figures in the history of the dynasty, were related to the kings by marriage and maintained their power for over 60 years. During this period (1802–1863) there were 1,238 reported cases of illegal activities by local aristocrats reported by the "Amhaeng Ôsa," i.e., the royal secret inspectors traveling incognito.

---

57   This quotation is taken from the inscription of the inside cover of Kim Chi-ha's book (1978), *The Gold-Crowned Jesus and Other Writings*, edited by Kim, Chong Sun and Shelly Killen.

Instead of trying to tackle the root cause of the problem, i.e., corruption, the aristocrats consistently turned their backs against the demands of the people, producing countless street-beggars who became thieves and robbers to feed themselves and their families. These bandits gradually organized themselves to attack the houses of the rich and powerful as well as corrupt local aristocrats. They were no longer simple robbers out of basic economic necessity; they were now political rebels beginning to send clear messages to the central government. These revolts, however, were met with stronger suppression by the central authorities. The leaders of the revolts were without exception executed and the participants faced severe punishments.

Among the uprisings, there were large-scale rebellions, such as the Pyung-An Province Farmers Revolt (1811) and the Im-Sul Farmers Revolt (1862) which drew tens of thousands of participants. The demands these uprisings put forward showed that the people were beginning to question the feudalistic social structure itself. Although none of these revolts achieved their objectives, they nevertheless paved the way for the most well-known popular uprising in the nineteenth century, namely, the Donghak Farmers Revolt (1894), which forced the nation to put an end to feudalism.

**Confucianism and Suun's Fate.** Any discussion of the Confucian influence on the Korean society should not fail to mention *Samgang Oryun* 三綱五倫, the Three Bonds and the Five Moral Rules in human relations. *Samgang* depicts the three fundamental principles between a king and his servants, father and his children (sons), and husband and wife. The former in each of the three groups has the (heavenly) authority over the latter. Thus, the relationship between the two in each group is marked by obedience and subjection.

*Oryun* means following five cardinal articles of morality: (1) the affection between father and son, (2) the faithfulness between master and servant, (3) the separation (or distinction) between husband and wife, (4) the right order between the old and the young, and (5) the confidence among friends. All of these, except the last, again, presuppose inequality.

The place of these social teachings in the Confucian Yi dynasty was that of the divine commandments of any religious culture. These doctrines were taught in a more rigid manner in Korea than in China, so that the former became more Confucian in outlook than the latter as a result. One example of the rigidity is shown in the regulations prohibiting widows to remarry. Whereas in China widows were allowed to remarry but not recommended, the same teaching was more strictly legislated in Korea. Suun was one of the victims of such socio-religious rigidity.

**Suun the Founder of Donghak.** Suun was a fallen aristocrat. His ill-fate was decided at his birth: he was born to an aristocrat and a widow. As mentioned above, according to the custom of the time, a widow was not allowed to remarry. Hence, the marriage between his parents had no legitimacy. Being an "illegitimate child," Suun could not enjoy the same social status and prestige his father had as an aristocrat. In such a highly moralistic Confucian society he was, instead, destined to be an outcast. No matter how much he studied, the opportunity to climb the social ladder was not available to him. He was expected to study like other aristocrats but could not hope for a bright future. Perhaps this predicament gave him his sensitivity toward his fellow minjung and also enabled him to work out his revolutionary ideas. He began to make an emotional connection between himself and the society he had belonged to since he was young. Suun himself wrote[58] how much he had lamented the sickness and turmoil in society at the age of ten. He was deeply concerned that in this "dark age," no one was able to function his/her appropriate duty in society, neither king as king, nor father as father, nor anyone else for that matter.

Suun had a sense of calling to change the contemporary social situation from its root cause. The religious (or spiritual) consciousness, he realized, constituted the most fundamental structure of human beings, individually as well as collectively. The current turmoil of his nation, then, reflected both an inner spiritual depletion and the social corruption at large. He felt that the influx of enormous Western imperial power in the East was due not only to the military superiority of the West but to their mental-spiritual might. This conviction made him delve into such traditions as Confucianism, Taoism, Buddhism, and Christianity. He knew that Confucianism, which had been used as a state ideology by the Yi Dynasty to control the masses for over five hundred years, was unable to correct the ills of the society. Indeed, this ancient Chinese moral philosophy, especially in the way it was taught in Korea, had been a strong supporter of the political and social status quo. And the other two traditions in Korea, Taoism and Buddhism, had been established in the nation for many generations, but were unable to provide a concrete way

---

58 "Mongjung Noso Mundapga 夢中老少問答歌 [Song of Dialogue Between an Elder and a Youth in a Dream]," *Yongdam Yusa.*

of liberation for the people in despair. Suun felt that a new "way" (*do*, *Tao/Dao* in Chinese), with more relevance to the present situation, must be sought to save the nation. Where, or what, was this "way"? How about Christianity? Could it be, for him, the new "way"?

The Catholic mission in Korea had begun in the late eighteenth century. By the time of Suun's search, therefore, there were many followers of the Christian religion. Since the early nineteenth century, however, the influence of Christianity was joined by Western colonial expansionist activities and other international political developments that began to add strong external pressures to those internal troubles in Korean society. Naturally, the missionary activities were suspected of concealing imperialistic motives. The Opium War (1840–42) and the humiliation of China by the Western powers intensified this feeling. Hence, Suun looked upon Christianity as a selfish, individualistic and dangerous foreign doctrine. For him, it was unthinkable that the Western religion would advance as a force distinct from Western political imperialism. In fact, some of the historical events taking place at the time showed their close connections.[59] Moreover, the missionaries were highly antagonistic toward many of the cultural traditions in Korea. Hence, the Christian mission itself, for Suun, was a serious threat to the integrity of his nation and the spiritual well-being of the people. The very naming of his new found "way" as "Donghak," which means "Eastern Learning," demonstrates his sense of threat from the influx of Western influence, especially that of Christianity, which was commonly called "Sôhak" 西學, i.e., "Western Learning."

It is noteworthy that saving people from their socio-political predicament as well as from spiritual poverty was the major motivation of Suun, as shown in much of the Donghak literature, such as the following:

---

59  There is no need for elaborate documentation to prove this much discussed point. Some military assaults had been made in Asia by the Western nations after their missionaries had been killed there. France, for example invaded Peking, the capital of China, for killing their missionary and forced China to sign the 'unequal treaty' and open its market to France (1856–60). It was soon followed by the construction of the huge cathedral in Peking with full scale mission work. Suun heard about this while he was still searching for the "way." See Shin Yong-ha (1987: 141).

## Chapter One

> Our teacher, Choe of Yongdam, receiving a direct order from God, tried to spread widely the virtue of Donghak as the Way in which Heaven and human are one, in order to save the people from suffering.[60]

How should a religious philosophy be thought out so as to have some socially emancipatory implications for the suffering people? This leads us to some of the important philosophical notions of Suun.

---

60 In an attempt to redress the wrongful execution of Suun, the founder of Donghak, as well as to stop the ongoing persecution of the followers of the religion, this petition, written by Haewol, the second leader, was sent to Lee Kyoung-jik, the governor of Jônla Province. This letter is recorded in Lee Don-hwa (1933, 1969: 46–7). The translation here is taken from Benjamin B. Weems (1964: 23), except for the following two words: *Donghak* instead of *Tonghak* and *human*, *Man*. The date of this petition was November 1, 1892 (it seems that Weems' dating of it as December is a misreading of the original text). For the background of the failed petition, see also Oh Ji-young (1974: 90–103).

# Chapter II

# The Past and the Present in Donghak

In this chapter we shall consider some of the key doctrines of Suun, which reflect not only his indebtedness to his intellectual mentors of *the past* but also the socio-political situation of his time, *the present*. There are different cultural currents flowing into the stream of *the past*, which are in turn filtered through his socially conditioned perspective. We shall examine this point through the following ideas of Suun: *Hanalnim, Chiki*, and *Shichônju*.

## Basic Doctrines of Suun

***Hanalnim* (God, or Supreme Reality).** Suun's philosophy of human subjectivity, as Hong Jang-hwa argues (1990: 52), is different from the Western humanism of the nineteenth century. For Suun's thought is profoundly pneumatological. The immanence of the Spirit[1] is *sine qua non* for understanding his teachings. But there is no absoluteness with regard to the doctrine of the priority of spirit over matter. Neither is reality simply a materialistic evolutionary process of nature. Suun's philosophy may be viewed as a combination of a seemingly incompatible Platonic Idealism and scientific materialism. Although the existence of God is presupposed, this God is not the creator of all things *ex nihilo*.

---

1  Suun's terms for "Spirit" are *ki* (*ch'i*), *lyông* (靈), and *shin* (神). As shall be mentioned again below, *ki*, which means "material ether," "breath," or "etherial force" is more impersonal and *lyông*, which can also be translated as "ghost," and *shin*, "god" with small g, are more personal. For Suun these terms are not that which are used in contrast to "matter"—which is, generally, the case in the West.
   Joel Kovel finds it "remarkable" that in the West, too, the "original and primary meaning" of the term "spirit" is "a vital and material force pervading the entire universe" (1991: 22).

The relationship between God and humans is not one of "I and Thou"; the divine and the human are not as clearly separable as I/Thou. There is a radical oneness between God and humans. The noumena and phenomena, using Kantian terms, coincide without the precedence of one over the other. The evolution of the physical world is the process of noumena themselves. Is Suun's theism, then, pantheism? Not quite. Or rather, I should say, not in the sense that the term is understood in the West. For the relationship between an individual and the universe here is not identical with that of a part and the whole. His philosophy, again, is deeply pneumatological. Panentheism, then, rather than pantheism, would be a better description of the theism of Suun.[2]

It is important to note here though that pantheism in East Asia, generally, has not been devoid of certain pneumatological characteristics. The distinction between matter and spirit in East Asian philosophies has not been as clear as it has been in those of the West since the time of early Greek philosophers. In this sense, then, calling Suun's theism pantheism would not be altogether a mistaken view.

In fact, taking this one step further, one wonders whether the term "panentheism," is really necessary in Asia. The usage of the term "panentheism" may be viewed as an attempt to "fill the gap," so to speak, between traditional theism and pantheism in the West. The most commonly felt problem of this traditional distinction is that one becomes either "too dualistic" by opting for the former or "too materialistic," or even atheistic, by choosing the latter. Should there not be an understanding of God, which is less dualistic than the former and yet not quite as materialistic as the latter? Panentheism was conceived out of this want of a remedy in line with modern sensibilities.

However, in East Asia, where theism is not caught between dualism and materialism, where one is not in need of making an existential decision between theism and atheism, philosophical preoccupations and struggles have been entirely different from those of the West. One would not use the same remedy when problems are different. Take, for example, the case of the generally pantheistic framework of Buddhism. This pantheism is also profoundly religious. Let's take the philosophy of Chou Tun-i above as another example. His notion of *Tai Chi*, the Great Ultimate, is both monistic and pantheistic. But his pantheism is not reduced to materialism, as shown in his notion of *ch'i*, "breath," "ether," or "ethereal force," which is both immaterial and material at the same

---

[2] For other similar observation see Kim Kyung-jae (1988: 101–117).

time. I am of the opinion that in East Asia pantheism already includes what is attempted by "panentheism" in the West. Thus, the use of the term "panentheim" may be superfluous; using it without qualification can easily confuse the issue in this cultural context.

Due, perhaps, to the danger of using such categories beyond cultural boundaries, Hong is cautious about any attempt to describe Suun's theism in such terms. In fact, Suun himself was reluctant in defining the Ultimate Reality. That is, there is an apophatic character in Suun's treatment of the term *Hanalnim*, "Heavenly Sovereign," the term which had been used to designate the Supreme Reality by the Koreans throughout their history; Suun never attempted to explain *Hanalnim*. Among the Magical Words, consisting of twenty-one Chinese characters, which all the adherents of Chôndogyo (later name of Donghak) are to recite regularly, the term *chôn* (Heaven; *t'ien/tian* in Chinese) is the only character Suun did not explain. Considering the importance of the term, there is no doubt that it was an intentional omission. Suun did not feel that words are adequate to describe the Ultimate Reality, by which one can only be absorbed in one's entire being.

Let us briefly consider here some etymological elements of this term *Hanalnim*, which is one of the oldest in the Korean language. Put briefly, it designates the One Supreme Being, outweighing any other ontological notions of its sort. *Hanalnim*, which later became *Hananim*, or *Hanûnim*,[3] with its strong Shamanistic roots, has been for Koreans "that than which nothing greater can be conceived," to use the expression of St. Anselm. This Being is the One who sends rain and thunder as well as punishment and reward to people in accordance with their behaviors. "*Han*," the first part of *Hanalnim*, meant both "one" and "great."[4] Choe Dong-hee argues that *Hanalnim* has been a proper name for Koreans much as Yahweh has been for Jewish people, or *Allah* for Muslims, rather than one of the generic names, such as *Chôn* 天, "Heaven," *Sangje* 上帝, literally, "Lord-of-Above" ("Supreme Being" in Taoism/Confucianism), and *Deus* (1993: 39).

Surprisingly enough, Suun used this term, *Hanalnim*, identifying it with *Chônju* 天主, "Lord-of-Heaven," or "Heavenly Lord," which the Catholics used for "God." There is no doubt that Suun was well aware of

---

3  "Hananim," with its emphasis on monotheism ("hana" means "one"), is the Protestant choice, while "Hanûnim," which connotes the "Heavenly Sovereign," is favored by the Catholics.
4  For the discussion on the etymology of this term, see Yun Sung-bum (1964: 46–60).

the profoundly anthropomorphic nature of the God of the Catholics. Hence, although Suun did not define *Chôn* and *Hanalnim*, which are his terms for God, anywhere in his writings, it is not difficult to suggest that his notion of God is not completely devoid of anthropomorphic characteristics.

There are some, such as David Chung, who suggest that this aspect of Suun shows his indebtedness to Christianity.(1986: 140–1) At the end of the nineteenth and the beginning of the twentieth centuries, Protestant missionaries made use of this indigenous term *"Hananim"* to their advantage, borrowing it as the translation of "God."[5] *Hanalnim*, for Suun, however, cannot be equated with "God" of the Western religious culture. Hence, Hong asserts that Suun's theism cannot be explained in terms of Western philosophical categories, viz., monotheism, pantheism, or even panentheism.

Suun operates on the basis of the two ontological currents of his time in Korea: one from outside, the other indigenous. The former comes from the Chinese philosophies of Neo-Confucianism and philosophical Taoism, and somewhat from Buddhism, which are generally regarded as being pantheistic. This current is most evident in the notion of *Chiki* 至氣 in *Donggyông Daejôn*, which is written in Chinese. The latter, indigenous ontology, is the monotheistic tradition of *Hanalnim* which has shaped the Korean mind for many centuries. This latter current is clear in Suun's use of the term *Hanalnim* in *Yongdam Yusa*, which is written in Korean with occasional Chinese characters. The sources of Suun's theism, then, are philosophical pantheism and cultural monotheism. Whence, then, in the mind of the Korean is the trace of monotheism?

Shamanism immediately comes to mind. This religious strain in Korea is as old as the story of Dangun, the founding myth of the nation, attests. The influence of Shamanism on Suun is seen in the anthropomorphic side of his theism.

Among the most important terms in Suun's thought are *Chiki*, the Ultimate Reality, and *Shichônju* 侍天主, "Nurturing, Bearing, or Serving God." I will now explain these terms in connection with Suun's other points.

---

5  For the discussion on this subject, see, for example, Spencer J. Palmer, who says, "Hananim was a point of contact with Korean culture..., considerably facilitating their work" (1967: 18); Charles Allen Clark (1981: 195–197); and Homer B. Hulbert (1906: 104–5).

**Chiki.** *Chiki*, which can be translated as "ultimate (*chi*) energy (*ki*; *ch'i*/*qi* in Chinese)," is the monistic energy-stuff of the universe. It is that through and in which all things came into existence. This is the point at which it becomes clear that the nature of the human relationship with God is not that of "I and Thou," for *Chiki* is the totality of existence. It is both Alpha and Omega. Through [*Chiki*'s] self-manifestation, it constantly evolved and interacted within. Humanity is the highest stage of evolution it has reached thus far, for it is where we find the divine nature most fully. For a human being, not just symbolically but essentially, is the fullest exhibition of the evolutionary process of *Chiki*. In a sense, there is a similarity between Donghak and scientific evolutionism in that "all living beings evolved from lower forms to higher forms of life resulting in millions of different life forms in the universe."[6] Unlike Darwinism, however, Donghak holds that behind the evolution of nature lies the movement of the Spirit. The world, according to its *Chiki* doctrine, is the self-evolutionary manifestation of *Chiki*, which is the Ground of being. Enlightenment, for Suun, then, is seeing the unity of oneself with one's own depths. In his mystical experience, for example, Suun hears the voice of this Ultimate saying, *o shim jûk yô shim ya*,[7] "My (God's) mind is your (Suun's) mind."

One is reminded of Meister Eckhart, the German mystic, who insisted on the "soul's union with God," taking possession of God without any mediation. That the true nature of the Ultimate is beyond definition is shown in Eckhart's use of the term "Godhead," provided that God is conceived as Creator. The difference between Eckhart and Suun is that whereas the former prescribes detachment as the way to such realization, the latter prescribes no such detachment; he simply begins with the acceptance of external things as they are because God is already immanent in nature and most fully in oneself. What happened afterwards is the logical outcome of their difference: Eckhart founded the mystical school called "Rhineland Mystics," and Suun founded a religion which later spread among the less sophisticated mass.

**Shichônju.** At this point Suun relates *Chiki* to another important doctrine of his, namely, *Shichônju*, "nurturing (bearing) God," or "serving God." Kim Chi-ha interprets the first of the three Chinese characters, *Shi* 侍, "serving," or "bearing/nurturing," as signifying the organic nature of the

---

6  Lee Don-hwa (1963: 15f.). Or see Paek Se-myong (1956: 42).
7  吾心卽汝心也; "Nonhakmun [Discourses]," *Donggyông Daejôn*.

spirit, containing three unions: the ecological union between humans and the cosmos, the social union among humans, and the revolutionary union between individuals and society (1994: 16). As such *Shi* points to a holistic vision of Reality.

There is in *Shichônju* a radical union between God and humans. However, the relationship between an individual and the universe here is not identical with that of a materialistic part and the whole. For its philosophy, again, is deeply pneumatological. This can be argued from what was thought to be the revelatory experience of Suun. At the moment of the mystical experience, Suun was shaken by a sudden touch of the spirit and a realization. Then he heard the voice saying, "My mind is your mind... People do not know *guishin* 鬼神, spirit/ghost, but *guishin* is also I."[8] This became for Suun the moment of enlightenment, which he repeatedly recalls later.

What is the nature or source of this experience of enlightenment of Suun? Obviously, there is someone, identified as God, with whom Suun converses. In that sudden experience, which happened after his long meditation for forty-nine days, there is both an external source and an internal realization. Firstly, there is the "touch" of the spirit from without.[9] Secondly, there is the realization/understanding from within.[10] The source of the "touch" of the spirit is identified as *ki* (*ch'i/qi* in Chinese). That there is an external source suggests that enlightenment, for Suun, is not simply a psychological state of affairs. Moreover, when the existence of spirit and matter is understood in a monistic sense, as was for Suun, the spirit within resides not only *in* a human body but *as* his/her body as well. Rather than saying, anthropomorphically, that God has personal characteristics, divine attributes inform human beings for the doctrine of *Shichônju*. Humanity is the presence of the Spirit in the universe. The universe as a whole is the appearance of the Ultimate Energy (or the Spirit, *Chiki*) itself, and the Ultimate Energy is the power of the universe. There is no matter/spirit dualism here. Haewol, Suun's

8  吾心卽汝心也　人何知之　知天地而無知鬼神　鬼神者吾也: "Nonhakmun" [Discourses]. The term "guishin" used by Suun here is understood more as the way of natural (cosmic) phenomena than as a being apart from the world. The first of the two Chinese character, gui 鬼, is the yin side and the second, shin 神, is the yang side of nature. This is a good example of Suun's non-anthropomorphic theism. A similar experience is also recorded in "Podôkmun" [Preaching Virtues]. Both incidents are said to have happened in the year 1860.
9  外有接靈之氣
10 內有降話之敎

successor and the second leader of Donghak, took this doctrine one step further and said,

> there is nothing in nature that does not *shi chônju* [*shi* as a verb, i.e., "bear or nurture" the Ultimate/God], and hence *i chôn sik chôn* [以天食天: literally, "heaven/god eating heaven/god"] is a cosmic principle. However, if you harm a being or destroy a creature unnecessarily, it is none other than God destroying God.[11] [parentheses mine]

Since *Shichônju* is the universal principle of nature, eating to nurture body is understood by Haewol as not only a necessary activity but a harmonious part of nature's process. Any other harmful activity, however, constitutes a violation of cosmic principle, and hence Haewol admonishes his followers to take a good care of their cohabitants around them. For nature as a whole is a sacred living organism. In the face of the present ecological crisis, this is where some contemporary critics of Donghak find its doctrines resourceful.

**Suun and Western Philosophy**. In the Western philosophical tradition, one may compare Suun's thought with the philosophies of G.W.F. Hegel, A.N. Whitehead, and, perhaps, P. Tillich. It would be true to say that between Suun and Hegel the difference is far greater than the similarity. Hegel's idealism, for example, would not be accepted by Suun. For the former history or historical process is the self-actualizing activity of the Spirit (*Geist*)—and, hence, there is always something higher in reality than the actualized world. However, for the latter, there is nothing behind or beyond the world we see.

Such difference nothwithstanding, it would still be interesting to compare the notions of Suun's *Chiki* and Hegel's *Geist*. Alan M. Olson (1992) describes Hegel's philosophy as a speculative pneumatology. Following Olson's interpretation of Hegel, both Hegel and Suun are speculative. The difference is that Hegel's speculation is propositional/rationalistic—claiming that the state of self-alienation is only fully overcome in philosophy, that is, in unlimited thinking-through—while that of Suun is intuitive/experiential, which, perhaps, is the difference between the West and the East, generally. Another difference is that while Hegel is centered on historical events and their major players, Suun focuses on human nature as such.

---

11  From a sermon delivered in 1885; Choe (1993: 54).

Some comparison has been made between Suun and Whitehead.[12] One difference, among others, is that while the former regards *Chiki*, i.e., Ultimate Energy (or God), as the supreme reality, the latter holds that process, and hence creativity, itself is the reality. In short, the role of God for Suun is greater than that for Whitehead in change and process. The striking similarity between the two, though, is that for both God is not an exception to the principle of process and change—"God keeps the rule," using Whitehead's expression, except that for the former, process is the self-evolutionary activity of God, while for the latter, the process includes God and others. In other words, God is what changes in process for Suun, while God is an active agent for Whitehead—hence the distinction between the Primordial and the Consequent Natures of God. To put it in a somewhat abbreviated form, Suun is more monistic and Whitehead more dualistic.

One comparison may be made between Suun's enlightenment experience and Tillich's notion of revelation. Enlightenment for Suun is the realization of oneself being one with the Ultimate Authority, while revelation for Tillich is achieving the unity of what are in conflict under the conditions of existence, "autonomy against heteronomy," "relativism against absolutism" and "formalism against emotionalism."[13] For both Suun and Tillich, there is a sense of fallenness in the human predicament. Suun sees human nature being ignored and robbed by the oppressive socio-political structure. And Tillich connects his devastating war-time experience as a chaplain during World War I to the traditional Christian doctrine of original sin, which he terms the state of "existential estrangement." The remedy for this condition shows the difference between the two: while Suun asserts the basic goodness of human nature, Tillich reaffirms the Lutheran formula of *sola gratia*, in his words, "accepting the unacceptable."

As mentioned above, for Hong, Donghak's theism cannot be explained in terms of Western philosophical categories, viz., monotheism, pantheism, etc. Hong also argues that Donghak's theism unifies the opposites and contradictions between monotheism and pantheism in a dialectical way. There is, he contends, a harmony of the transcendent and the immanent, the absolute and the relative, the changing and the constant, the eternal and the temporal, matter and spirit,

---

12   See, for example, Kim Kyung-jae's article in the book he coedited with Kim Sang-il (1988).
13   *Systematic Theology*, I. I. 5.

and the universal and the particular (1990: 11–18). But this God is also in process as noted above. It seems that what Hong alludes to is a combination of dialectical theism and process theism.

Suun, again, operates on the basis of the two cultural currents of his time in Korea: one from the intellectual circle, the other from popular religiosity. The one from the intellectual circle is composed of the Chinese philosophies of Neo-Confucianism and Taoism, especially those centred on the ideas of Taegûk (*T'ai Chi*) and Mugûk (*Wu Chi*), which are regarded as being pantheistic. The latter, popular religiosity, is the indigenous monotheistic tradition of *Hanalnim*, which is related to the philosophy of Han and which has shaped the Korean mind for many centuries. Hence, the sources of Suun's theism can be described as philosophical pantheism and shamanistic monotheism.

## Basic Principles

**The Eclectic Principle of Suun and Confucianism.** In the light of the survey of the Neo-Confucian thinkers above, some observations about the Confucian influence on Suun can be listed in an attempt to discern his eclectic principle in using the religious resources of the past. First, there is a clear line of philosophical development within Neo-Confucianism prior to the time of Suun: Chou Tun-i–Kwon Kun–Hwadam–Yulgok. This line, however, should not be understood in the light of do-tong 道通 (*tao-t'ung* in Chinese), as a sort of apostolic succession. Yulgok, for example, preferred to follow in the footsteps of Toegye, who repeated somewhat dogmatically Chu Hsi's dualistic tendency, to accept the creative but "mistaken" view of Hwadam. The lineage, then, should no more than demonstrate the eclectic activity of Suun for his philosophical/religious purpose from the Neo-Confucian tradition in both China and Korea.

The line of thought drawn above is centered on human nature as it is shaped by the environment. In the debate between "nature and nurture," for example, this line would emphasize the importance of nurture and the influence of the context, without, of course, neglecting the role of nature. Such a view focuses on the struggle to improve the socio-political situation as a precondition for the wholeness of one's being.

Secondly, there is here a consistent effort to view reality as one undivided whole. When viewed against the ideological background of Neo-Confucian orthodoxy, as it is systematized by Chu Hsi, Yulgok's somewhat dualistic tendency is also not an exception to this. Suun, however, went further; he deleted *li*, Principle, altogether in his discussions on *ki* (*ch'i*), material-immaterial energy. In that sense, there is something unique in his doctrine of *Chiki*, the Ultimate Reality, in that it maintains the monistic framework without discarding the anthropomorphic understanding of the Reality, by combining the materialistic notion of *ki* (*ch'i*) with the monotheistic concept of Hanalnim.

How, then, one wonders, could Suun overcome the dualism that Yulgok struggled against without much success, even after the latter criticized Chu Hsi for being dualistic? This shows that the religious and ideological freedom of Suun was different from that of Yulgok. For Suun orthodoxy was to be continuously reinterpreted and reformulated in the light of the needs of the present situation. The teachings of the sages of the past are relevant today in so far as they possess the spiritual efficacy for the present. In short, the present is what informs us of the way of the past, and not vice versa. He used some of the key Neo-Confucian terms, such as Taegûk (*T'ai Chi*), Mugûk (*Wu Chi*), and *ki* (*ch'i*), in this principle. Suun shared the Confucian quest for sainthood, but he departed from his intellectual predecessors in the substance of the quest; for him it was the spiritual/ontological, not the ethical, which was the proper path to sainthood—the former includes and informs the latter. That the centre of his philosophical system is spiritual/ontological is evident from his notion of *Chiki*, the Ultimate Reality, which is generally considered Suun's key concept. Suun sought the organic union of self, others, and Reality.

**Pneumatology as the New out of the Old.** Suun did not create new terms. Instead, he used familiar terms in new ways. This means that Suun sought something new out of the old; for him, there is nothing new under heaven. A reform is to be made from within. Even in founding a new religion, which Suun clearly did, the new concepts discussed by him were but a revitalization or reinterpretation of the "old tradition," as he called Confucianism. For Suun the traditional religions in Korea, Buddhism, Confucianism and Taoism, were "dead" since they had lost the spiritual power to defend Korean people from the "assault of the Western nations." In particular, Suun had in mind the dominance of

"Western Learning," i. e., Christianity (Catholicism), in Korea.[14] Behind the rapid success of this foreign teaching Suun saw the desperate condition of the Korean people. Suun felt that Christianity, at least in the way it came to the East, was not contextually suited to the latter. Suun's Donghak, therefore, was not conceived so much to negate Western Learning as to complement it and to fulfill what he considered was lacking in it. This is evident in Suun's contention that Western Learning, which for him was the force of *Yin*, must be "suppressed" by the power of the *Yang* of his Eastern Learning. In light of the traditional doctrine of *Yin-Yang*, however, the two forces of *Yin* and *Yang* must be kept in balance. Thus, by saying that *Yin* is to be suppressed by *Yang*, Suun wanted to complement or balance the dominance of *Yin*. The overwhelming malaise of the present socio-political situation in Korea was interpreted by Suun as the domination of *Yin* over *Yang*. It was believed that whenever the balance of the two modes of *Yin* and *Yang* is destroyed, confusion and chaos ensue in a person and in society.

As a remedy for this imbalance, Suun shifts emphasis from the outward expression of *in-ûi-ye-ji* 仁義禮智, the four basic virtues emphasized by Mencius, meaning "compassion-righteousness-propriety-wisdom," to the inward solidity of *su-shim-jông-ki* 修心正氣,[15] literally, "cultivating mind and possessing right *ki* (*ch'i*)," which, for him, was more fundamental than the Four Beginnings of Mencius. Choe Haewol, Suun's successor and the second leader of Donghak, explains:

> *su shim jông ki* is that which provides the life-spirit of Heaven and Earth whenever in need, and, hence, without *su shim jông ki*, it is difficult to practice *in ûi ye ji*.[16]

That is, spirituality constituted a more holistic centre of one's being than ethics. Pneumatological reinterpretation of the ethical is Suun 's way of revitalizing the ancient teachings. That humans are the most elevated beings is not simply due to their intellectual capability. Rather the ability for the highest consciousness of humans is the result of the holistic make-up of the human spirit.

14  The Protestant mission was not actively present in Korea until late nineteenth century.
15  "'*In ûi ye ji*' is what ancient saint had taught, but '*su shim jông ki*' is what I introduce/propose" (仁義禮智先聖之所敎 修心正氣惟我之更定): "Sudôkmun [On Disciplining/Cultivating Virtue]," *Donggyông Daejôn*.
16  *Han'gûl Donggyông Daejôn*, ed. and trans. by Donghak Yôn'guwon (1991: 145).

There are two questions that need to be asked in regard to the peculiarity of Suun: what did Suun want? and how did he pursue it? In response to these I select two points respectively: the minjung-consciousness and the pneumatological synthesis. The former is the substance, and the latter the form of his thought. He wanted the liberation/salvation of all, and pneumatological synthesis was his way of connecting past resources to the present oppressive situation.

The first aspect of Suun's peculiarity is shown in his starting point, the present human situation, not the classics of the past. This was indeed a revolt against the intellectual current of his time; the first and foremost requirement of a Confucian scholar was to be well-versed in the classics. For him, however, digging through piles of ancient literature was not as important as possessing the heart able to suffer the plight of one's fellow people. This I call a "minjung-consciousness."

The second aspect of Suun's peculiarity is the pneumatological thread which runs through his system. To the ethical teaching of *in ûi ye ji*, again, for example, he gave a spiritual flavour in his doctrine of *su shim jông ki*. For the people who had been shaped by shamanistic/animistic culture, this device was effective in enlivening the "dead" religions and provide empowerment.

As mentioned earlier, it is my contention that Suun was a liberation theologian of his time. What made him so effective was his never-ending engagement in the life of the minjung, which shaped his thought. With genuine passion for transcendence of the present socio-spiritual situation of the nation, he was in constant dialogue with his religious and social contexts.

Suun was deeply in touch with this religiosity of his compatriots. The pluralistic nature of Korean culture was well depicted by early missionaries. Since, for Suun, the religious realm constitutes the most basic structure of human beings, he attempted to achieve liberation through religions; the theology of liberation and that of religion must coincide for the realization of the most thoroughgoing transformation. In my opinion, the most peculiar aspect of Suun is the pneumatological connection between the past (various religious ideas) and the present (an oppressive social situation). The past and the present are united in his pneumatological thought. Thus, I identify Suun's theological methodology as the following: *pneumatological synthesis of the past in view of the needs of the present*. This is also the methodology with which I attempt to make a connection with Minjung theology, which is the subject matter of Chapter III.

**Syncretism Suun's Way.** As mentioned earlier, at the time of Suun there were various religious/philosophical traditions such as Confucianism, Taoism, Buddhism, and Christianity, the most recent newcomer to Korean soil. Although the Chôndogyo officials have not fully agreed, there is a general consensus among secular scholars that Suun was influenced by all of those traditions, including the last one, Christianity. *Chôndogyo Changgônsa* records the following conversation between a Buddhist priest, called Songwôldang, and Suun:

> Priest: Do you study Buddhism?
> Suun: I like Buddhism.
> Priest: Why did you not become a monk?
> Suun: Understanding the Buddhist principles without having to become a monk would be better.
> Priest: Then, are you Confucian?
> Suun: I like Confucianism, but I am not Confucian.
> Priest: Well, then, are you Taoist?
> Suun: I like Taoism, but I am not Taoist.

At this point, the priest is puzzled, becoming more anxious to get into the mind of Suun:

> Priest: What do you mean exactly? What do you like best among those?
> Suun: You have two hands. Do you have to like one more than the other?
> Priest: Now, I understand. You mean you like the whole body, don't you?
> Suun: I am neither Buddhist nor Confucian, nor Taoist still. I love the whole principles. For there is no place where *Chôndo* (Heavenly Way) does not reach.

When the priest asks which of the three exhibits the highest principle, Suun answers:

> There is no such thing as high or low among those. Using a simile, there is no need for a comparison among the dead. Which is more terrifying: a dead lion or a dead dog? When they are both alive, the lion would be strong and the dog, weak. But once they are dead, there would be no difference. Truth is like this: once any truth is no longer able to enliven and give soul to that time and its people it becomes a morality of the dead.

Then Suun gives what may be considered his rationale for the foundation of Donghak:

> This is a time when such old traditions as Buddhism or Confucianism cannot lead people on. What we need to do now is grasp the limitless energy that

could induce a living soul out of the dead bodies and open the new heaven, new earth, and new human (or being).[17]

From this conversation we can see a few important aspects of Suun's thought. First, he makes a distinction between the form and the substance of a religion/tradition. Hence, although Suun draws from each of the three traditions named above, he does not tie himself to any of them. For him, eliciting the substance is possible without subjecting oneself to the rules of the tradition of that faith. Here we have an example of his "pneumatological" emphasis. Eliciting the substance of a tradition is being in touch with the living spirit behind the tradition. This enables Suun to freely reject whatever seems irrelevant for his time. Second, he has a keen sense of time vis-à-vis reality. It is analogous to Paul Tillich's notion of *kairos*.[18] What is the criterion, for Suun, for rejecting and accepting any given tradition? It is, third, whether a certain tradition is able to "enliven and give soul" to the time and its people. If any tradition is no longer able to do so, no matter how great it once may have been, it is likened to a dead body. That means the (present needs of) people have priority over (the past religious) traditions. For Suun, religions are there to serve people, and not the other way around. In other words, philosophically speaking, the term "people" belongs to a higher category than does "religion."

**Dialectics East and West.** Lee Hang-nyong compares the dialectics of East and West. (1982: 16) For example, he points out, Hegelian dialectic in the West reaches its synthesis through anti-thesis. In the process there is always the stage of negation. However, Lee argues, synthesis is not reached through negation in the dialectics of the East. Instead, he says, it is thesis-thesis-return (to the origin). The doctrines of *Bul-I* 不二, "non-duality," of Buddhism and *Yin-Yang* of Confucianism as well as the

17 *Chôndogyo Changgônsa [History of Chôndogyo Foundation]*, ed. by Lee Don-hwa (1933, 1969: 33–4).
18 See, among others, Tillich (1956), *The Religious Situation*, trans. by H. R. Niebuhr. For Tillich, "Kairos is fulfilled time, the moment of time which is invaded by eternity" (pp. 138–9). He calls for a "belief-ful realism in contrast to unbelieving realism and to belief-ful or Utopian idealism." It is important, for Tillich, to "wait and act" because there is the higher category of "eternity" coming into the not yet realized present. While for Tillich, therefore, "eternity" is not to be objectified and must be waited upon to break into the present, it is, for Suun, almost entirely up to the enlightened to "grasp" the "limitless energy" to change the present.

philosophy of *Han*, "One, or Great," in Korea are examples of Eastern dialectics.

For any thesis (A) there is normally an alternative thesis (B). The word "alternative" here, however, can be misleading, for the latter (B) does not necessarily negate the former (A). Nevertheless, the presence of such different theses creates a certain struggle, which in turn produces a synthesis. Unlike the Hegelian dialectics, in which such struggle creates a competitive mood, calling for a synthesis of A and B, the synthesis here (Eastern dialectics) is the outcome of the process which negated neither A nor B; the spirit of this synthesis is "both/and" rather than "either/or." The Neo-Confucian doctrine of *Yin/Yang* is a prime example of this. Each of the two modes, *Yin* and *Yang*, opposes as well as requires the existence of the other.

Moreover, in the dialectics of the East, the synthesis is not so much the result of the struggle between A and B as it is that of an appeal to the past. In other words, it is more a reinterpretation of the past than a progressive synthesis for a new creation. According to this dialectical framework, progress normally means continuous dialogue with the past. The culture in which such dialectics prevail would be somewhat backward looking, as East Asian cultures generally have been.

For Lee this is the type of dialectics at work in Suun's thought. For Suun the relationship between God, or the Ultimate, and I is one of non-duality. This, however, does not mean that God and I are identified without any distinction. Rather, the relationship between God and I, for Suun, is to be understood as undifferentiated duality or non-dualistic duality. As illustrated above this can be seen through Suun's key doctrines of *Chiki* and *Shichônju*.

There is in Suun's thought, however, a more progressive forward looking tendency than Lee's thesis entails. Suun, for example, repeatedly mentions the beginning of the "New Heaven and New Earth" (*hu chôn gae byôk*).[19] As mentioned above, Suun's thought contains certain elements of evolutionary process. Within the framework of the Eastern dialectics which Lee demonstrates, what is the difference between Suun and his intellectual predecessors? The most distinctive characteristic of this religious thinker, again, lies in his use of pneumatology. In making

---

19   *Hu chôn gae byôk* (後天開闢), literally, "opening of new era, or beginning of latter/next heaven," is Suun's idea of millenarianism. According to this doctrine, by founding Donghak, Suun declared the beginning of the New Eon, which will last for fifty thousand years, ending the old eon of fifty thousand years.

use of Confucian teachings, for example, Suun spiritualized their predominantly ethical doctrines. According to Suun's own explanation of the term *Chiki*, for example, there is a pneumatological union between God and humanity. *Ki* (*Ch'i*), again, is a monistic notion denoting both material ether-stuff and immaterial energy (or etherial force). As explained above, this philosophical term is combined with *chi*, "supreme," or "ultimate," to denote that reality which is more deified than *ki* alone. *Chiki* has personal attributes like will and consciousness. It is at the same time non-personal in the sense of being the totality of existence. *Chiki*, then, is that which is beyond the personal/non-personal distinctions. Suun made the predominantly non-personal notion *ki* into the reality which can even be worshipped as a deity. Suun explains *Chiki* in connection with his other doctrine, *Shichônju*, as "the spirit within"[20] and "the *ki*-ization without".[21] Each of the two characters of the "spirit 神靈 (*shin-lyông*)"—which appears in both Chinese religious Taoism and Korean shamanism—is the term used by Christians for the second of the two characters in "Holy Spirit" (聖神 *Sông Shin* or 聖靈 *Sông Lyông*).[22] The keen interest in spirit perhaps may be due to the generally shamanistic/animistic tendency of the Korean people. However, although one can distinguish between *shin-lyông*, "spirit-ghost," or "ghost-god," and *ki* (*ch'i/qi*) in Suun's writings—the former contains more personal attributes, and the latter more impersonal ones—the nature of his enlightenment is such that the two are inexorably connected as the unity of self/time and the ultimate/space, of being/realism and meaning/idealism, and of one/individual and many/society.

20  內有神靈
21  外有氣和
22  The term "holy" before "spirit" obviously presupposes a certain dualistic worldview, from which the overall East Asian cultural outlook is excluded. Indeed, the terms "Sông Shin 聖神" and "Sông Lyông 聖靈" as the translation of the Christian "Holy Spirit" are somewhat culturally alienating. A better translation would have been "Shin Lyông (神靈, literally, 'Ghost-Spirit,' or 'Spirit-God')," which appears in Suun, or "Saeng Ki (生氣, literally, 'Live, or active, Breath/ Ether/ Energy')." The underlying assumption, of course, is that the world is a living organism.

## Donghak the Yeast of the Gob-O Revolt

Donghak is often considered in connection with the Gab-O Revolt of 1894 (also known as the Donghak Farmers Revolt), which helped Korea modernize. Although scholars disagree as to how much connection can be made between the religion Dongahk and this revolt, there is no doubt that the former was a significant factor in the latter. This is the subject matter in this section.

**A Struggle for Relevant Ontology.** Having been born out of such an intense social and political climate, Suun made a clear attempt to formulate a realistic solution drawing on the old traditions, such as ethical Confucianism and metaphysical Taoism. "The humanism of Chôndogyo[23] (the later name of Donghak)," says Hong Jang-hwa, "is that all humans become deified regardless of status or class." It is an "interiorization of God" within us (1990: 52). The *gunja* 君子, "an exemplary gentleman" or a "sage," had been a Confucian ideal. Although a realistic image, it was limited to the noble class. And the *shin sôn* 神仙, literally, a "divine person," or an "immortal," had been a Taoist ideal. But this figure was a mystical dream that existed only in myths and, therefore, was far from the ordinary human reality. Suun proposed, instead, *ji sang shin sôn* 地上神仙, "earthly divine person (or immortal)." Since all humans are in essence divine, they are expected to live up to this characteristic. In this doctrine, ontology and ethics also coincide. Egalitarianism is a logical social teaching based on this philosophical position. Considering the highly authoritarian feudalistic nature of the society, it is not too difficult to imagine what Suun's teachings meant to people and the authorities. In 1864, four years after he began to teach his thought, he was executed for "agitating the public with impure thought."

**Coincidence of Ontology and Ideology.** For Suun and his successors all the ontological religious doctrines that did not consider the human situation seriously were subject to revision. Ontology was to be thought out in terms of human political and economic situations, and it must be able to address the social infrastructure in an unambiguous manner. The ontological, for Suun, must be revolutionary, and vice versa. The social

---

23  天道敎, "Teachings/Religion of the Heavenly Way," is the new name of Donghak changed by Sohn Byung-hee, the third leader in 1906.

situation of the oppressed people, the minjung, was the source of his ontology, and his ontology, in turn, provided the ideological impetus for social change. There was a close relationship, therefore, between his ontology and his political thought, both of which have been the result of his analysis of the religio-cultural data (past) and the socio-political climate (present). In this sense, therefore, we can interpret his religious synthesis as a form of "reciprocal praxis," for his doctrines clearly contained some political implications.

Suun's political thought was the outcome of his critical analysis of both the internal and the external situations of his time. Throughout his writings, he constantly criticized the corruption of the aristocratic ruling group in the face of the rapidly rising scale of Western influence in the East. Many people became organized bandits to rebel against the rich and the powerful, while some sought to find refuge in the newly instituted Catholic mission, and others could only wait for a messiah-like hero to come to save them. The people were without a clear vision because the rulers were neither willing nor able to provide them with one. Suun thought that the time was ripe for a new political philosophy. This philosophy was to be concrete enough to be an ideology and ontological enough to be religious. To be concrete meant, for Suun, to meet the most urgent needs of the people. He viewed the inequality among the people and all the different social ranks as the first cause of the widespread corruption, for had there not been an imbalance of power, there would be no one to misuse it. What was the ruling ideology that legitimated the social caste system? Although Suun himself was by and large shaped by the Confucianism of his time, this was the point at which he departed from it. Confucianism had been used by the rulers of the Yi dynasty to effectively divide the people into different social statuses.

Suun's way of tackling the oppressive social and political ideology was a radical reinterpretation of human nature, one that could offset the givenness of the socio-political structure. His notion of *Shichônju*, "serving God" (within oneself and others) suggested the identification of the highest ontological notion, *Hanalnim*, or God, with human nature. According to this doctrine, no human was subject to any socio-political conditioning, for *Hanalnim* (universality) resided in human nature (particularity). The political implication of this was that community and (individual) identity were no longer separable from each other. Without community, identity was futile, and without identity, community was empty. Totalitarianism and individualism were both evil products of a false ideological framework. Hence Suun viewed the Western capitalist expansion in the East as a serious threat, not only to his nation and the people but to human nature itself. His critiques of the centuries-old feudalism and Western capitalism were clear: the former exemplified (particular) class-centred morality, and the latter, individual-centred morality.[24] One finds an interesting work-ethic in his notion of *chôn jik chôn lok* 天職天祿, "*Hanalnim*, or God, always wants jobs and fortunes for all humans," or "a job for each human is the will of Heaven". For Suun, there were some things that were fundamental human rights, such as work and basic subsistence.

Suun's call for human rights is summarily expressed by Shin Bok-ryong under the following five headings: (1) the dignity of human nature; (2) minjung-oriented thought; (3) an anti-feudalistic social caste system; (4) the improvement of the status of women (unlike now, at the end of the twentieth century, when feminism is only beginning to make inroads in Korea, such a call was unheard of then); and (5) the value of children in society (1985: 239–246). Suun's objective was to dismantle inequality in all aspects of human life. One can only wonder at how far Suun was ahead of his time.[25] That he was sincere was seen in the way he set his slaves free: he made two of his maids members of his family, one his daughter-in-law and the other, his adopted daughter.

**The Eventful Year of 1894.** It was the beginning of 1894 when the peasants organized themselves to engage in a massive war against the corrupt local aristocrats. After Suun, the founder of Donghak, was executed in 1864 for "agitating the public with impure thought," the entire Donghak organization went underground. Choe Shi-hyung, whose

---

24  See Hong (1990: 98–99), especially his interpretation of *Donggwi Ilche* 同歸一體, "solidarity of humanity" (Hong), or, "oneness of truth (Choe D. H.)," and *Sain Yôchôn*,事人如天, "treat humans as heaven/God." Although the latter term is not Suun's but Haewol's, Suun's successor, Hong sees it as a natural development from the former's thought.

25  The influence on Suun of Hung Hsiu-ch'uan (1814–64), the mystic leader of the Taiping rebellion of China, is an interesting subject for further study. According to Jean Chesneaux, "This [i.e., the Taiping] most spectacular and exceptional of the great peasant movements of the mid-nineteenth century was more profoundly 'pre-conditioned' than peasant risings in general throughout the history of China. It occurred at the point when the traditional social crisis coincided with the penetration of China by the Western powers." See Chesneaux, *Peasant Revolts in China 1840–1949*, translated by C. A. Curwen (1973: 24). One notable difference between Hung and Suun in their general sentiments and doctrinal outlook, Christian influence is much more visible in Hung than in Suun.

pseudonym was Haewol, and who had succeeded Suun and become the second leader of Donghak, wandered about for 30 years without a fixed residence, secretly teaching people the new "way" found by his teacher and predecessor, thus solidifying the organization. Under the leadership of Haewol, Donghak spread quickly in the lower class of the society. The new religion was also appealing to the fallen aristocrats who had been discontent with the current corrupt state of affairs throughout the nation. The place where the flames of the peasants were ignited was Gobu, a county in Jônla Province.

The date was February 15, 1894. With its fertile land, Gobu was known as the leader in rice production. Since the unequal treaty with Japan in 1876,[26] Gobu had been hit hard by the enormous exploitation of the rulers, who found every possible way to squeeze the farmers to export rice to Japan. The peasants, who were at the height of their discontent, gathered around Jun Bong-joon, a fallen aristocrat whose father had been beaten to death by the magistrate of the county Jo Byung-gap, to lead them to attack this corrupt official. Jun agreed and led the people to victory. This news quickly swept across the Jônla Province and beyond. Although the extent of Jun's connection with the Donghak is not clear,[27] the role of the religion in the revolt is not in question; Donghak by then was solidly organized with a good network of communication that proved to be effective. Now the entire nation was buzzing with the wishful rumors that the corrupt nation was finally coming to its end. There are great discrepancies among the records of this war, which lasted a year, as to the number of peasant participants, discrepancies ranging from tens of thousands to over two-hundred thousand.[28] Whatever the exact figure had been, the central government of Korea felt greatly threatened and asked China to send its military to

---

26 In 1876, Japan forced Korea to open its market to Japanese exporters. This unequal treaty forced Korea to sell rice, which Japan needed most at the time, cheaply, and to buy the Western goods which Japan was forced to buy from the Western nations. See details in Han'guk Minjungsa Yôn'guhoe, ed. (1986, vol. II: 61–64); and Dolbegae Pyunjipbu, ed. (1980: 73–79).

27 There have been disagreements on how much Jun Bong-joon, the rebel leader, was religiously committed in leading the revolt. According to the Hang'uk Minjungsa Yôn'guhoe (1986, vol. II: 80) he is described simply as a people's leader who used the religion for the war, while Oh Ji-young, who took part in the revolt, says that Jun was a follower of Haewol, then leader of Donghak (1974: 161).

28 For low end, see Dolbegae Pyônjipbu (1980: 320–327), which puts the number at twenty thousand. And for the other end, see Oh Ji-young puts it "over two-hundred thousand" (1974: 160–164).

The Past and the Present in Donghak 69

put down the revolt. As China became involved, Japan, fearing a Chinese monopoly in the Korean peninsula, also sent its army. This caused the war between China and Japan in Korea, which Japan, armed with advanced Western military equipment, won. In this civil war-turned-international-war, the civilian casualties caused by the united force of the Japanese and the Korean government armies, are said to have numbered around three- to four-hundred thousand.[29]

**Donghak and the Gab-O Revolt.** The way this event has been described varies greatly among scholars. Some examples are: war, revolution, revolt, uprising, movement, insurrection, and rebellion. Shin Bok-ryong divides the perspectives of the scholars into two different categories, each with two opposing groups: the first category is "colonial historical consciousness" versus "national historical consciousness," and the second, nationalism versus Marxism (1977: 31). As Korea is becoming more democratized in the 1990s, i.e., as scholars find room to express their views more freely, there is an increasing degree of awareness among the Korean people on how to interpret their past. The first category, colonialism vs. nationalism, may be redirected chronologically as pre- and post-1945, the year Korea was liberated from Japan.

A brief historical sketch would, perhaps, help us understand the rationale behind the first category above. After Korea was annexed by Japan, the ruling Japanese authorities found it necessary to re-culture, or re-educate, Koreans in a way that would make them easier to control. During this period, 1910–1945, much of Korean history was re-interpreted to make the people believe that Korea needed Japan's "help" (which scholars have called "colonial historical consciousness.") This re-culturing was done with force—some examples are: the Korean language was banned, the people were forced to participate in worship of the Japanese Emperor, and they had to use Japanese family names. After Korea was liberated in 1945, much went back to normal, except that this time the dictatorship which lasted over four decades needed to continue the "colonial historical consciousness" to make the people believe that "Koreans needed 'strong' leadership."[30]

---

29  Han'guk Minjungsa Yôn'guhoe (1986, vol. II: 86).
30  There have been many publications of historical books recently to redress this century-old problem, among which Han'guk Minjungsa Yôn'guhoe, ed., *Han'guk Minjungsa*, 2 volumes, is a good example.

The first category, colonialism vs. nationalism, therefore, is based on whether one takes the perspective of the Japanese-inspired historical consciousness of Korea or the Korean nationalistic perspective. The former condemns the Revolt of 1894 as an "armed bandits' war." This is not surprising when we consider the fact that the Revolt protested against the increasingly obvious influence of Japan in Korea. The latter, i.e., "nationalistic perspective," however, generally views the event as a "revolution." Although I take the latter perspective, I will, nevertheless, use such value-free terms as "revolt" or "uprising."

The second category, nationalism vs. Marxism, is more obvious than the first. The perspective of nationalism focuses on the call for national sovereignty, free from any domination by the foreign nations. This would be the position of many Western influenced South Korean scholars.

The second group, Marxism, stresses the economic struggle of the oppressed people in the revolt. They view it as a fight against the feudalistic structure of the society. North Korean scholarship would belong to this group. The strength of this perspective, which is shared by some South Koreans, is that it also considers the first aspect, i.e., nationalism, to be important. For this group, the revolt of 1894 was a "revolution."

**Political Significance of the Gab-o Revolt.** The historians who call the revolt of 1894 a revolution do so on the basis of the significant change it brought to the nation, viz., the termination of some of the most oppressive feudalistic customs. Among the most significant changes in the nation, called the Gab-o Reform, occurred later in the same year, 1894, were the following: (1) elimination of the centuries-old social caste system, which had divided the society into the upper and the lower classes, (2) abolition of the slave law, which had legitimated the slave system, (3) abolition of the law that kept widows from remarrying, and so on. Those are similar to what the peasants demanded at the treaty with the central government, namely the Jônju Treaty (June 10, 1894), except "equal and fair distribution of land."

Now we must consider the following questions: what connected the Donghak to the spirit of minjung?; what distinguished this religious philosophy, or philosophical religion, from other traditions which had thrived in Korea for many centuries? In answering these questions, we can now go on to discuss the contemporary developments of the Minjung theological perspective.

I will begin with the shamanistic religiosity of the Korean culture and the related issues of syncretism and inter-religious dialogue. Our objective in the second part of the book is to relate Minjung Theology to Donghak as its theological paradigm. As I stated in the Introduction, I do not want to endorse the term "inculturation" on the basis of my insistence on a genuine inter-subjectivity between the gospel and culture. My question is, what, or who, should be the final discerning authority in theological discussions in Korea?

# Chapter III

# Minjung Theology

## Religious Context: Methodological Past

Although Donghak has not been the only religious source in the cultural context of Minjung theology, I shall limit the scope of this book to this particular religion in connection with the rise of Minjung theology. Donghak, again, was a syncretic religion, with doctrines borrowed from such others as Confucianism, Taoism, Buddhism, and Christianity. One thing must be mentioned here regarding which religious element was mostly at work in making the people rebel in the revolt of 1894. Although, Confucianism has been at the centre of social reform both in China and Korea, at the same time, it taught respect for rulers, teachers, and elders as its important ethical doctrine, and, hence, it would not be a suitable candidate[1]; reforms have been carried out mainly by ruling literati within the confines of the Confucian orthodoxy. Taoism, as a philosophical system with certain religious features, discusses such metaphysical themes as Tao, *muwi* (*wu wei*), "non-action," as a cosmic principle, and balance and harmony. Unlike Confucianism, religious Taoism had been attractive to the lower class in society both in China and Korea and had much contact with local shamanistic practices. But because of its philosophical notions, which had by and large been removed from the life of common people, pointing beyond the immediate daily struggle, it had not been an influential factor for political change in Korea. Buddhism, although some of its monasteries have regarded national defense as a principle, has been by and large apolitical. It has not taught people to unite to defend themselves in times of crisis. What, then, was the most important source or religious/cultural

[1] Whether the way Confucianism was taught in Korea was a perversion of its original intent is not the point here. Of course, Confucius and Mencius sought a harmonious society through teaching righteousness and compassion. My focus here is on how the Neo-Confucianism was generally used in the Korean society during the latter half of the Yi Dynasty (1392–1910).

phenomenon that has played the role in getting people together in such a large scale revolt? Before one attempts to answer that question, one needs to keep in mind that the event that happened in 1894 was only a continuation of similar events that had occurred for over a century, except that it was larger in scale. The point here is that as far as the spirit of the uprising is concerned, there was something more than the three major traditions involved in Donghak. As indicated above, these three systems that were blended in this new teaching gave it a highly philosophical and conceptual character that did not in itself account for its real impact. It was something indigenous beyond these three traditions that gave it such impetus. What was it?

The spirit, I argue, which gave rise to the revolt came mostly from that part of the cultural tradition which had been shaping the mind of the Koreans since the beginning of their history: shamanism. As already noted, the importance of this religious phenomenon cannot be exaggerated. Suh David Kwang-sun, for example, also contending that shamanism is the most pervasive popular form of religiosity in Korea, calls shamanism "the religion of the Korean minjung," for it is "the most basic mind-set of the Korean people high and low." (1991: 94)

The succession of revolts, large and small, including that of 1894, followed is what I call "shaman ethos" of the Korean minjung. As it will be discussed again below, it was this "shaman ethos" that provided the spiritual impetus for the people in the face of threats from both inside and outside their nation. The "spiritual-prophetic" aspect of shamanistic cultural practices prevailed in this critical event. This should not be difficult to accept when we consider the well-known and widely accepted proposition that in the deepest part of Korean religiosity lies indigenous shamanism. It is this that has provided Koreans with the zest for making decisions on the most basic level of their life. This phenomenon is aptly described in the words of Homer B. Hulbert: "As a general thing, we may say that the all-round Korean will be a Confucianist when in society, a Buddhist when he philosophizes and a spirit-worshipper when he is in trouble."(1906: 403–4) This suggests that a certain degree of cultural accommodation of shamanism is unavoidable if any religion is to produce spiritual fruits in Korea. Hence, I shall begin this chapter on Minjung theology with shamanism as the cultural/religious context which, along with the tradition of Donghak, becomes the "methodological past" to be considered in conjunction with the "methodological present," namely the contemporary socio-political situation of the minjung in Korea.

**Shamanism: the Melting Pot in the Korean Mind.** There is a general consensus among scholars, both inside and outside of Korea, that shamanism best represents the religiosity of Koreans. As Hulbert rightly observed, the average Korean, young or old, educated or illiterate, becomes shamanist in times of crisis. This phenomenon is so deeply imbedded in Korean culture that the success of religions coming into Korea is largely dependent upon how well those religions are planted in the shamanistic soil of the culture. Students of the phenomenology of religions in Korea, for that reason, cannot ignore this aspect. There are many Western authors who observed the pervasive phenomena of shamanism in Korea. The following statement of W. M. Clark, made in 1925, is a good example: "Today it may be safely said that this Shamanism is the strongest power, from a religious point of view, in Korea."[2]

Suun also utilizes all the traditional sources available to him in this melting pot of the shamanistic Korean mind. In so far as shamanism is concerned, we need to deal with the religious ritual called *gut*[3] in connection with *han*[4] at least briefly. This is our next subject.

**The Gut Ritual in Korean Shamanism.** Among other things, exorcism has been at the centre of the *gut* ritual of Korean shamans. In a sense, a shaman is the caregiver, or guardian, of one's soul from the intervention of exterior forces like spirits. There are various signs of the spirits' intervention in human affairs. A member of one's family, for example, suddenly acquires an unexplainable illness. When physicians can not

---

2   Clark, *Korea Mission Field Magazine* (1925: 79); Quoted here from his brother Charles Allen Clark (1981).
3   *Gut*, or *kut*, is the traditional Korean shaman ritual, performed by mudangs, mainly female shamans. For more elaborate study of Korean shamanistic practices available in English, see Suh David Kwang-sun (1991: 89–117); Lee Jung Young (1981); Guisso and Yu, eds. (1988); Kendall, Laurel (1988).
4   Although *han* (恨) is a Chinese character which is also used in other Asian languages, it has a peculiar Korean meaning which is difficult to translate. It is a deep aggravated feeling of resentment caused by the accumulation of unresolved unfair treatment and oppression from powerful forces over a long period of time. Suh David K.S. defines *han* as "a sense of unresolved resentment against injustice suffered, a sense of helplessness because of overwhelming odds against, a feeling of acute pain or sorrow." (1991: 195, note 3.1). Note that this word, *han*, should be distinguished from *Han*, "one, great, totality," discussed in Chapter I above. The former, again, can be written in Chinese and used by some other Asian peoples, while the latter is a purely Korean notion.

cure, or explain, the nature of the illness, a shaman is consulted as the last resort. The shaman, usually female, would then perform a routine ritual, called *gut*, to find out which of the spirits is at work in the sick person. It may be one of the deceased ancestors, upset at his unruly descendents, bringing a clear message to correct their path. It may also be other spirits who could not go to the other world because of injustice they had suffered in their earthly lives. They need the recognition of the living about the injustice they experienced, and then would be free to go to their world with some soothing words from the shaman. For the culture where such rituals are commonly practiced, even the dead can speak to the living. That is, there is no perfect crime. Perhaps one can give a very simple illustration of a theological meaning of *gut* as the following diagram.

**A Theological Look at *Gut***

| *Gut* as *ritual* | *Gut* as *hanpuri* (literally, "resolving *han*") |
|---|---|
| Formal and religious aspect of the shaman tradition | Spiritual and prophetic aspect of the "shaman ethos" |

"The Shamanist *gut*," says an EATWOT[5] statement, "is a ritual where in the spirits of all those who suffered unjustly are rendered present so as to impel the participants to protest against all kinds of oppression and injustice."[6] The theological notions of Karl Barth and Paul Tillich illustrate the distinction between the two aspects of the *gut* ritual: *gut* as ritual vs. that as *hanpuri*. In the case of Barth, the formal and religious aspect would correspond to his notion of religion (defined as "unbelief"), and the spiritual and prophetic to his "faith" (defined as a positive human response to God's self-revelation). Religion, so defined, can be an obstacle to faith. One question here is whether reification of the term "faith" can be justified, for it seems that faith is always the faith of some persons or of a certain group of peoples rather than an independent entity.

Notwithstanding the answer to that question, I feel that in the Korean shaman ritual tradition of *gut* the analogy would be closer to

---

5 Ecumenical Association of the Third World Theologians
6 "Religion and Liberation. Statement of the EATWOT Consultation, New Delhi, December 1–5, 1987," in *Dialogue*, 15 (1988), n.1–3, 11–27.

Tillich's notions of religious symbol and the Protestant Principle. A symbol must always point beyond itself to what is ultimate to maintain its role as a symbol. Otherwise, it is static and becomes demonic. The Protestant Principle is a constant challenge to what becomes static by pointing only to itself. The shaman ritual, for this reason, must always point beyond itself to its spiritual-prophetic aspect of *hanpuri*, through which all han-ridden experiences get redressed. The cultural-religious activity called *gut*, for that reason, becomes demonic when it loses its purpose, which is *hanpuri*. The power does not come from the shaman or, in Korean, *mudang*, nor from the religious ritual itself. Rather it is manifested through the medium of the sacramental activity of *gut*.

This can be summarized as follows: *gut* is not an end in itself but a medium that can allow the *hanpuri* to occur; *hanpuri* is the manifestation of the power of liberation that happens at the moment of *gut*. Liberation (or exorcism) is, in short, the good news being incarnated through the imperfect medium of the religious ritual called *gut*. It is what Tillich would call a religious symbol that becomes demonic when absolutized. Hence, if one questions the validity of *gut* or similar cultural activities in Christian life and worship, one may put such concerns to rest. For *gut*, like any other religious ritual, is not itself the ultimate purpose but a medium through which a greater power becomes manifest in concrete life. The *mudang* performs the ritual to liberate people from their han-ridden ghost of oppression. The *mudang* in this liberating activity, according to Ahn Byung-mu, plays the role of the Christ. (1988: 291) This, he says, is an important point the Church should no longer overlook. Hence, in a discussion of shamanism it is necessary for us to distinguish between negative and positive elements in that tradition. We will begin with the negative.

In the history of *gut*-related activities in Korea, there have been demonic distortions of the ritual. There has been an element of fear on the part of participants for whom the *gut* is performed. This has resulted in an imbalance of power between the *mudang* and the participants, giving the priest(ess) enormous power to abuse his/her "clients" (participants). *Mudang* becomes the end to the ritual rather than a medium through which a greater power can be made manifest. This danger has always been present in all the religious rituals in Korean shamanism, and, for that matter, any religious rituals. In this negative aspect people became subjected to the religion.

There are, however, important positive elements in this tradition, which I call the "shaman ethos." There are two points to consider here.

First, the emancipatory *gut*s have replaced the fear mentioned above with what can properly be called faith. The participants are led to trust the power that will deliver them from their present unfortunate life situation. What was previously beyond their reach has now suddenly become available to them. Fatalism is replaced with hope.

Second, the experiences of *gut* have given people the assurance that the status quo does not need to continue without being challenged. There has followed from this an impetus for culture-critique. It is also to be noted that such a "shaman ethos" provided the cultural spirit for many popular uprisings in the later part of the Josôn (Yi) dynasty, of which the Donghak Farmers' Revolt, discussed above, is the most well-known.

**Syncretism and the Multi-religious Encounter.** We now turn to the issues of syncretism and religious dialogue in the Korean context. The methodology for many in the discussion of such subjects tends to be highly conceptual and metaphysical. However, without denying the value of some of these approaches, the way of Minjung Theology is to deal with issues in the light of the concrete and historical events that occur in the "social biography" of minjung. Hence, it is noteworthy that Suun, the founder of Donghak, felt the importance of this sense of historical actuality long before the Minjung theologians.

The term "syncretism" carries certain negative overtones in theological circles. For most Christians the reason for this has to do with the issue of Christian identity. What is Christian identity? What are the values of nominal Christians, those who are conscious of being Christian without the Christ necessarily being reflected in their lives, and of "anonymous Christians," those non-Christians who live in such a way that they are considered by other Christians to have been "touched" by God's grace? Is there any constant element in Christianity that must always remain the same regardless of historical or cultural circumstances? Even if Christianity is a dynamic religion, is there any limit to its willingness to accommodate other cultural and religious elements? In short, what makes one a Christian and who is to decide? These questions are as difficult as they are important. Although this book is not an attempt to answer any of them directly, it is, nevertheless, in part a consideration of them.

Any discussion of syncretism in Christianity must include a consideration of the nature of the Bible and the history of Church doctrines. In relation to such a consideration, the question is, is

Christianity or any part of it free from syncretism? We must begin by defining syncretism itself?

For Andre Droogers (1989: 7), "syncretism" is a difficult ("tricky") term, because it has been used with great variation in its meaning. First, the basic "objective" meaning, viewed from outside of the religions involved, would be the mixing of religions. Second, the "subjective" meaning, viewed from inside any of the religions involved, would necessarily involve a value judgment. Since syncretism is the blend of two or more culturally different elements in one belief-system, and since such blending suggests the likelihood of impurity, it has by and large been seen as a threat to the integrity of Christianity. The assumption underlying such a view is that there is an essence in a religion which is eternal and unchanging, regardless of its spatio-temporal context. The underlying philosophical framework of this would be essentialism: a belief that "ascribes ultimate reality to essence embodied in a thing perceptible to the senses."[7]

Those who warn against the mixing of a religion with 'impure elements' presuppose that whatever they believe to be the ultimate reality can be expressed only in certain specific ways and not in others. But can there be any religious language that does not need to be adapted to the medium of a particular cultural-linguistic expression? God as Father of Jesus shows the role and authority of patriarchy in the Judaeo-Aramaic culture of the first century C.E. As feminists have argued, the cultural assumptions built into such religious language can be demonic when the language endorses repressive patriarchy. Moreover, in a culture in which a father's role is less significant or even negative, such language needs to be replaced with more appropriate language that can at the same time provide an analogue to the father-image Jesus used in his time. The relationship between religion and culture, following Tillich, is that of "substance" and "form." Religion, according to Tillich, is the substance of culture; culture, the form of religion.(1959: 42) The gospel, then, must take a certain form, *gestalt,* from the culture in which it is first heard. "The Word became flesh," says the author of John's Gospel. The "flesh" here was a first century Jew! Therefore, he spoke the language and lived according to the culture of his time. Is this too difficult to accept? How about the Bible?

Biblical scholars have found that from the beginning of its formation the Bible—both the Old and the New Testaments—was mixed

---

7  Webster's Ninth New Collegiate Dictionary.

with diverse "pagan" cultural elements.[8] The Bible, then, is a syncretic book. Church history is the history of Christian syncretism with various western philosophies. Augustine and Thomas Aquinas, for example, based their theologies on the philosophical foundations of Plato and Aristotle, respectively. Scientists such as Newton and Galileo forced the Church to abandon its old cosmological dualism of heaven and earth. The Enlightenment has radically altered the course of Western theology by renewing the importance of reason in the process of understanding reality for many theologians. Our understanding of God, nature and reality is shaped and conditioned by the environment in terms of which we find suitable linguistic-cultural expressions. Robert J. Schreiter contends that the reason for the often incomplete encounter between church and culture "could well be that the church does not adequately understand the culture." He hence proposes to start "from the culture's perspective."(1985: 152) According to this approach, in incorporating the "new datum," i. e., Christianity, there are four "syncretistic possibilities" for a culture to take: (1) playing upon the *similarities* between the sign systems of the culture and that of Christianity; (2) *filling gaps*, in which the "invading culture provides signs and often codes for dealing with a problem not adequately accounted for in the dominant sign system of the receiving culture"; (3) *indiscriminate mixing*, which happens when "the receiving culture is at a low level of social and cultural organization"; and (4) *domination*, in which "the sign system in local culture has been so weakened that the sign system of the invading culture takes over completely, replacing the local sign system."(1985: 152-4) This last point, Schreiter notes, has been considered the ideal form of evangelization in the history of Christianity. It was also the way Protestant mission work was carried out in Korea from the late nineteenth century on.

Charles A. Clark recalls an "interesting incident" which happened at the time of the Independence Movement of 1919 when he was a missionary professor in the Presbyterian Theological Seminary of Korea in Seoul:

> One Sunday morning a young Korean Christian... came to see me and said that he had been asked by certain members of the Chuntokyo to sound out some of the missionaries on the possibility of combining the Chuntokyo organization and the Christian Church... He said... that they were all good members in good standing in their own organization, that they were willing to

---

8   M. M. Thomas (1985: 387–397).

consider joining in a body with us, but that they were unwilling to enter as raw new believers, and pass one by one through probation, and have to make a public confession of sin, professions of faith, etc. I called his attention to the fact... that many of them were drinking men... The young man was unconvinced ... I have no doubt also that he talked with many leading Koreans also, but I heard nothing further of the matter, so judge that he met an *impasse* everywhere and gave the matter up. (1981: 170–1)

It is not surprising that the young Korean Christian was not convinced by the reasons this American missionary gave him for rejecting the proposal. As Clark himself notes, the "strict rules for entrance into the Christian Church" in Korea then were "far more rigid than those required for Western churches."(1981: 170–1) The missionaries made genuine efforts to change Koreans in accordance with their ideals. In other words, conversion into Christianity at the time required almost a complete shift from one culture to another.

Although Clark does not mention the term "syncretism" here, the purity of the Gospel, for him, is identical with that which the Western churches have always known in their own cultural contexts; thus any cultural alteration must be guarded against. Evangelization, then, is a transplantation of one culture into another's soil. Significantly, Schreiter argues that this is also one kind of syncretism. He says that this amounts to a "less than successful coming together of these two realities," i.e., the gospel (note the small "g"—see the Introduction), or the church, and the culture.

For Schreiter, then, it is important to start from the perspective of the receiving culture. "Syncretism," he says, "is not an isolated phenomenon;" from the perspective of the receiving culture it "is a way of reading the incorporative attempts" of the local culture. (1985: 155) This point of Schreiter's is an important insight in the discussion of the gospel and culture. After all, who are the subjects in such discussions? Who is theology to serve? Certainly, theology is not a self-satisfying activity of the invading culture. Among the people of the receiving culture, then, whose perspective is to be considered? There is no uniform perspective in the receiving culture itself. What are the criteria? Which of the cultural perspectives is to be primary? In the case of Korea, what are the criteria of theology? How do the Minjung theologians reconstruct the nature of the "divine-human encounter" in the person of Jesus?

## Social Context: Methodological Present

In this section I shall attempt a brief social analysis of contemporary Korean society. I cannot, of course, offer a full or adequate political and socio-economic analysis, which is far beyond the scope of this book. However, a glimpse of this dimension is essential for understanding the rise of Minjung theology. As Suun's thought had been the fruit of his dialogue with his time, Minjung theology arose as the theological reflection of some theologians upon the circumstances of their time. This section, therefore, is the social setting of Minjung theology.

As shall be mentioned again below, one of the most important contentions of liberation theologies is the validity of human experience as a source for theology. Stories, in particular, are an important source for Minjung theology. Thus, instead of listing some "facts" and figures of socio-economic analysis, I shall introduce my story and the story of Chun Tae-il, "the igniter of minjung-consciousness in the 1970s."

**My Story.** I attended six elementary schools. The reason I had to change elementary school 5 times before graduating provides an illustration of how the government maintained its oppressive policy. We, my family, were in the midst of the massive migration that occurred during the 1960s; we moved from Kyunggido to Seoul in 1968, shortly after I became a second grader in public school. This was the time of the rise of Minjung theology. At that time there were about 3 million people in the suburban area of Seoul who were living in destitute poverty. These people provided cheap labor for industry to suit the needs of the export-oriented economy designed by the military government. The 3 million plus people who lived in the suburban area of Seoul were quasi-illegal refugees, for the land on which they lived was owned by the city. This was the case whether they had built their shelters or paid for them. The government would pick certain places where the shelters would be bulldozed in the name of the "modernization" of the city. So when people tried to rent or buy a shelter, they had to depend on guesswork or rumor as to the possibility of becoming the next target. In this situation there was no way people could live a decent life, let alone save any money to plan for their future.

My parents and their five children had to pack and find a new place whenever rumors arrived about the coming of the bulldozers. At the time, I could not understand why we had to move around so frequently, and I doubt whether my parents themselves did either.

When I was in grade 5, I could not remain idle, knowing the financial situation of my family. I guess I wanted to take my share of the burden. So I asked my friend to introduce me to a small newspaper-depot, which he did. The delivery hours were between 5 and 8 o'clock in the morning before school: I got sick a few times and was late for school frequently, before I quit the job in less than two months. How fortunate I was compared to many of my friends who could not afford to get sick!

Besides selling or delivering newspapers, other jobs that children my age then did were things like shoe-polishing. One of the better known stories about the many young children who could not afford to go to public school and had to begin working before they reached the age of ten was that of Chun Tae-il.

**The Story of Chun Tae-il.**[9] By the time Tae-il was eight he was already working as a shoeshine boy. When he reached sixteen, he became a sewing-machine operator, which was likened to a hen-house. His co-workers were mostly young people in early to mid-teens like himself. They worked fourteen to fifteen-hour days, with only two days off a month to earn a daily wage of seventy to one hundred Won,[10] which was barely enough to keep them going on the cheapest instant food. The typical lunch at this time for the factory owners was around 200 Won.

Like other young persons of his age, Tae-il also had dreams and visions about his future and worked hard. But no matter how hard he worked the future he had dreamed of was becoming unreachable, at least in this life anyway. Alas, it was not only him; all these young workers around him were also without a bright future. Tae-il once thought that knowledge was power. Thus he picked up the books and studied the labor law. But he could not go very far; he was devoid of any formal education, and his memoirs later show how much he wanted to have a university student as a friend. But university students?

Traditionally, Korea has perhaps dramatized the idea of student-power more vividly than any other country in the world. Whether it was foreign domination, such as that during the Japanese occupation of Korea at the beginning of this century, or military dictatorship, it was almost always the students who had been in the forefront of the protest movement. However, students were not greatly conscious of the

---

9   This story is also introduced in Suh Nam-dong (1983: 351–3).
10  Won is the Korean currency. The exchange rate at this time was around six hundred Won for U.S. $1.00.

oppressive and inhuman labor situation until the late 60s. They were not yet greatly conscious of the economic system. All they wanted was a typical Western-style liberal democracy. Until this time, at their endless protests and demonstrations, their slogans did not refer to the economic justice needed for laborers and farmers. Hence, Tae-il could not find the friend he longed for so much.

It seemed now that there was nothing he could do to change the oppressive labor situation. He tried to organize unions, but with the military dictatorship behind the shop owners, every attempt was frustrated. What more could he do to get some attention from other people, from the literati, the students, the religious leaders? After many frustrations, he came to the realization that there was nothing more he could do to change the situation and to give hope to his junior co-workers.

On the 13th of November, 1970, Tae-il and 500 other laborers peacefully marched into the Peace Market with a placard saying, "We are not machines." As usual, a special police unit was dispatched, and it dispersed this lawful demonstration with brutal force. In Korean we have an expression appropriate to this type of situation: "It is like hitting a rock with an egg." Seeing the incredible odds against himself and his fellow workers, Tae-il immolated himself—he set himself ablaze. While dying, he cried aloud, "Do not exploit the young lives! Do not make my death futile!"

Tae-il was 22 years old when he immolated himself. However, the flames that burned his body also ignited a labor-consciousness among many students and theologians alike.

**The Military Government Policies.** The military dictatorship began at the beginning of the 1960s with General Park Chung-hee. Park wanted to induce the migration of young labor from the rural population into big cities, especially Seoul, where there was a heavy concentration of major industries. The following are some of the oppressive policies enforced by his government: firstly, it dropped the prices of agricultural products so that most families could not survive unless their children made extra income; secondly, in order to implement this policy, the government imported rice from the United States, abandoning much of the domestic farm industry; and thirdly, the companies were allowed to pay their workers any wage they wanted to. As the exodus from the countryside into Seoul began in the 1960s, many foreign and domestic companies opened factories to absorb this cheap labor. The military government used force to maintain its policy of a low rice-price and cheap labor. "In short," says Chun Chul-hwan, "exterior and unbalanced development-oriented economy, centered around foreign companies, was maintained under the strict control of the government."(1984: 114)

Chun, of course, does not object to the idea of development. What he objects to is the superficial "exterior" development. By "exterior" he means the type of development shown only in figures and numbers, especially the amount of export. The export-oriented economy, at least in the way the Korean government maintained it in the 1970s, for Chun, did not take essential factors for the life of the people into account. There should be, for example, more fundamental aspects to be considered for the people and the nation, such as the quality of labor, technology, pollution, and others, which not only have lasting effects on the people and the nation but constitute the more fundamental realm of human life. Chun calls the latter the "interior development." For him, the interior must accompany the exterior. Otherwise, government policies become inhuman, as was the case in Korea during the 1970s. The concern for human rights and the quality of labor, and for pollution simply were not given consideration by the government at this time.

The shift in population from rural to urban places, which occurred as a result of the oppressive policies of the government as mentioned above, further stimulated individualism, which had already been becoming more and more evident in Korean society. Hong I-seop traces the root of the contemporary economic system and individualism to the advancement of Christianity in the nation. Christian influence among Koreans, argues Hong, is most visible in their ideas on the economic system and in individualism.(1983: 14) An average Western academician would advise Hong to distinguish between capitalism and Christian faith, and between a particular Western cultural inclination, viz., individualism, and the Christian gospel. However, sadly enough, that was, to a large degree, the way the Christian message was proclaimed in Korea. The development of individualism and capitalism coincided with the activities of Western missionaries.

Hence, behind the "success" of the contemporary Korean capitalist economy, there was the "sweat and blood" of minjung. Although a great increase in prosperity for a large middle class came about, there is continuing poverty among a substantial minority. Whereas the export-oriented economy produced some multinational corporations, such as Samsung and Hyundai, the minjung slums around the suburban areas of Seoul—which were the targets of bulldozers—continue to draw the attention of mission workers. The "success" story of Korean capitalism also accompanied that of mega churches. Their "success" stories coincide with, and are largely based on, the common social phenomenon: individualism. During the 1970s, when the political oppression was so intense that many Minjung theologians were imprisoned and lost their teaching jobs, many congregations in Seoul became mega churches, teaching individualistic and other-worldly doctrines. The development of capitalism under such a politically oppressive situation provided a suitable climate for the rise of "evangelical" and pentecostal mega churches with individualist doctrines.

Harold Wells observes that the success of the capitalism of some of the East Asian nations, including Korea, is due in part to the communal, especially Confucian, ethos of the culture of the same region.(1996: 93–98) That capitalism is also culturally/religiously shaped is an important point social scientists should not miss. This view is also shared by some social scientists in Korea. Park Young-shin, for example, argues that Korean capitalism is based on the family-centered morality of Confucianism.(1987: 151–169) As such, Park says, Korean capitalism, on the one hand, stimulates the anxiety for success, diligence, and faithfulness, much like the aristocratic social atmosphere of the Yi dynasty (1392–1910), except that in the case of the latter, the aristocratic pursuit of success was mainly for the fame and the integrity of their families, rather than for their material advancement. The "success" of Korean capitalism is, in part, due to the highly competitive nature of the family-centered morality. Such a family-centered social norm, however, warns Park, ultimately leads into a self-centered morality, for it does not go beyond the immediate family boundary and refuses to see the entire society as a communal entity.

Furthermore, as the nation is increasingly becoming more liberal, individualism is stretching its roots more and more deeply into the life of the Korean people. Minjung theology is, in part, an attempt to deal with this situation.

## The Past and the Present in Minjung Theology

In this section I shall deal with some salient points of the Minjung theologians Suh Nam-dong and Ahn Byung-mu. Before going on to their theologies, however, we need some discussions on the "minjung

# Minjung Theology

perspective." I shall, therefore, begin with the contention of Kim Chi-ha on minjung perspective.

**The Minjung Perspective.** "Minjung," again, is a Korean word, which can be translated as "common people." However, due to the dynamic nature of this term, many prefer not to translate it, nor do they attempt to define it. Kim Chi-ha, a representative protest-poet in Korea since the 1970s, for example, likens the term, "minjung," to the "tao" of the *Tao Te Ching*, which begins with the following words:

> The Tao (the Way) that can be expressd is not the eternal (real) Tao.[11]

According to the author of this ancient literature, Tao cannot be defined, nor can it be spoken of adequately. Likewise, says Kim, one should not attempt to find a precise meaning of the term "minjung." Minjung, he continues, is a dynamic living entity and, hence, cannot be objectified as one thing or another. For as soon as it is defined as something, it may cease to be so. As a living entity minjung moves and changes continuously. Suffice it, for Kim, to list some of the main characteristics of minjung in terms of the two classifications as follows: definition by species (*Jong gaenyôm*) and definition by types (*Ryu gaenyôm*). (1984: 486–538)

The first classification of "minjung" is definition by species. There are two characteristics of minjung by this definition. Firstly, minjung are the subjects of history. They constitute the backbone of human civilization, taking care of all the labor necessary for the maintenance of society. Secondly, contrary to the importance of their work, they do not possess power to control the outcome of their own labor. Hence, they become subject to frequent exploitation and abuse in the face of the constant threat from poverty. In short, according to this classification, minjung are, positively, the subjects of history, and yet, negatively, they are oppressed people.

The second classification of "minjung" is definition by types, or kind. There are also two characteristics in this classification. Firstly, in relation to the Buddhist notion of *jung saeng* 衆生, "myriad creatures," minjung are at the centre of labor and, hence, represent life in its fullness. Defined this way, "minjung" is distinguished from the "proletariat," which, Kim points out, may become a collectively selfish group, as

---

11   道可道 非常道

exemplified in the corruption of the Communist Party in the former Soviet Union. Thus, no particular group should be glorified. In this minjung are no exception. If minjung were to be identified with specific groups, such as laborers and farmers, at the same time they would be a part of human evil, participating, for example, in the production or use of dangerous chemicals to produce more crops. Defined this way, minjung would also be a selfish group.

Secondly, however, minjung are to be more dynamically defined as those who continue to create and sustain life, defying all attempts to destroy life, human and nature alike. In the past, Kim points out, "minjung" has been defined as an historical notion, i. e., simply as "oppressed people." Now, however, he insists, it must be understood as an organic notion. Viewed this way, possessing minjung-consciousness does not lead us to an anthropocentric attitude. On the contrary, it calls for human responsibility to care for the entire organic life-system. A "minjung perspective," then, is one which addresses the issue of oppression/destruction, in search of liberation/salvation through organic union.

**Theologies of Ahn Byung-mu and Suh Nam-dong.** Among the circle of the "first generation" Minjung theologians—those who espoused their theologies explicitly from a minjung perspective—I shall focus on the theologies of Ahn Byung-mu and Suh Nam-dong, who are considered the "founders" of Minjung theology. The central points of these authors, I suggest, are that "Jesus is an event" for Ahn, and that "'diachronic christology' is to be balanced by 'synchronic pneumatology'" for Suh.

There seems to be a possible point of juncture between Ahn's treatment of Jesus as an event and Suh's pneumatological approach. The present struggle of minjung for their identity and subjectivity finds expression in both authors. For both, the past and the present are inseparably connected. The apparent contradiction between the two is seen in their hermeneutical starting points: Ahn begins with the minjung in the Bible, and Suh with the minjung in Korea.

**Jesus as an Event in Minjung Culture.** Who, asks Ahn, is Jesus for Koreans? In the case of Ahn, the interrogative pronoun "who" can be replaced with "what"; Jesus is interpreted more as an event than a person by this biblical scholar. For Ahn, Jesus was the most minjung-centered saviour among the religious founders (or saviors) of the world. The search for Jesus, Ahn says, has been his "life-long objective." Though this search was inevitably academic, it was for him not due to academic curiosity. Rather, he adds, it was an existential search for himself. For Ahn the interpreter is not an onlooker but a historical participant.(1993, vol. 3: 3) When he went to Germany for post graduate study, Western, especially German, theological (biblical) academia had already abandoned the search for the historical Jesus. Hence, Ahn too had become an agnostic about the historical Jesus by the time he completed his study in Germany.

A turning point of his agnosticism came with his awareness of the seriousness of the military dictatorship in Korea, which began in the early part of the 1960s. The oppressed minjung in Korea enabled him to open his eyes to the neglected word in the Gospel of Mark, namely, *ochlos*. *Ochlos* is usually translated as "crowd." Until Ahn met the oppressed minjung in Korea during this period, this term, he says, had been read so lightly that its existence in the Gospel was like an objectless shadow; it was there but not recognized. However, in the face of such an intense political situation in Korea, Jesus and his *ochlos* came alive for Ahn. The situation of first century Galilee coalesced with that of contemporary Korea for him. The *ochlos* in the Gospel of Mark are none other than the Korean minjung now. For Ahn, Jesus was there because of the *ochlos*, and the *ochlos* because of Jesus. Who, then, was Jesus? Or rather what was he?

Jesus, Ahn contends, should not be made a heroic figure, nor a charismatic revolutionary leader—though he certainly opened a new era for humanity. It is, for Ahn, wrong to treat Jesus as the subject who exerted his power over his "crowd," the object. Jesus, for Ahn, was not such a leader in the sense that Moses was the leader of his people. On the contrary, Ahn argues, the course of action Jesus took was shaped by the situation of his minjung. That is, the association of Jesus with the minjung is the core of his behavior. For Ahn christology has been too religious (or conceptual) and speculative. In a sense, Ahn is in the same camp with those who call for "back to Jesus." The miracle stories in the synoptics, in contrast to those in the gospel of John, are concerned little with the question of *who Jesus was*. Rather, they concentrate on *what he did* for, and *how he lived* with, the minjung. In this sense, the biblical account of Jesus is not a personal biography; rather, it is a minjung-event. Herein, claims Ahn, lies the greatness of Jesus; Jesus was thoroughly minjung-centered. Therefore, the minjung of Jesus, Ahn concludes, are not mere objects of Jesus' ministry but the great "power-container" that made Jesus Jesus. The perspective of heroism, Ahn argues, which treats Jesus as the subject and the crowd as the object is a hermeneutical mistake. Hence, for Ahn, the call for "back to Jesus" is in fact a call for "back to the original event."

Consequently, Ahn has insisted that Jesus is the minjung and the minjung is Jesus. This aspect of his theology would be the least acceptable to the traditionalists.[12] The identification between Jesus and minjung, however, is not a logical outcome of metaphysical speculation. Nor does one come to such an identification through propositional logic. But interpreting Jesus as an event rather than as a person certainly makes it possible to understand him as the prototype of subsequent liberation movements. It is to be noted here that the traditional christological formulae centered on Nicene-Chalcedonian creeds are by and large moved to the background of Asian theological debates. For those are but the best expressions of the historical cultural understanding of the time.

Hence Ahn makes a shift in epistemological norms—from who Jesus was then to who (what) Jesus is today. The interesting feature in Ahn is that, to make his point, he begins with the historical Jesus as he appears in the Gospel of Mark. For him, two contrasting terms stand out in Mark: "ochlos" and "laos." The former describes the oppressed people, the outcasts such as tax-collectors, prostitutes, etc, and the latter denotes the chosen people of God, who always distanced themselves from the former. It is always the ochlos, Ahn finds, with whom Jesus associated. Ahn's eyes gaze at this Jesus of Mark's Gospel without relying on the Nicene-Chalcedonian lens.

As a biblical scholar, however, Ahn knows much about the problem of the historical Jesus. Hence, for him, what is important is *what happened* with Jesus and the minjung of his time rather than *who* Jesus really *was*. Whoever Jesus was two thousand years ago according to Nicene-Chalcedonian statements, Ahn indicates, is not in itself of any interest to him.(1988: 25-6) This surprising statement, however, should not be misunderstood. For Ahn believes that the quest for the historical Jesus, however difficult such a task might be, should not be abandoned. Ahn wants to emphasize here that it is more important to continue today

12   Even such a progressive theologian as Moltmann says that the former, i.e., "Jesus is minjung," is acceptable, but he wonders how the latter, i.e., "minjung is Jesus," is possible—this has been the major point of the theological debates between the two theologians. Ahn, who also received his theological education in Germany, accepts that the statement can generate confusion for Westerners. For Ahn (1988), it is wrong to be preoccupied with the *persona* side of Jesus. The theological training he received in Germany, Ahn realized, "did not work for him in Korea."

what happened then than to maintain the traditional doctrines about the *persona* of Jesus.

Ahn departs from most form-critics, beginning with Bultmann, in that, for him, kerygma does not precede the actual activity of Jesus as witnessed in the Gospels, especially in that of Mark. "In the beginning," says Ahn, "there was the Jesus-event, not the kerygma."(1984/5: 27) Contrary to Bultmann, therefore, Ahn insists on moving from the original event to the kerygma.

For Ahn a distinction needs to be made between the letter and its spirit in a given text. The latter presupposes the former, but not vice versa. He insists on not being preoccupied with the words of the Bible, which are expressed through the medium of the culture-bound language of first-century Palestine. All languages are cultural expressions. What must be retained from them is the spirit of those expressions and not the expressions themselves. The spirit of the biblical account of Jesus, for Ahn, can best be preserved when Jesus is interpreted as an event. As a "political event," he says, this is not a matter of past history. It is not a completed event, but continues to happen today in the lives of the minjung. That is, Jesus as an event continues to meet the event of today's minjung. "Jesus is the great stream of volcanoes in the minjung event."(1988: 26) What happened then was minjung-Jesus, and what continues to happen today is Jesus-minjung (with the prefixes as adjectives). For those who are mainly preoccupied with the *persona* of Jesus, however, this view will always be problematic.

Accordingly, for Ahn, the two Asian christological formulations that Aloysius Pieris describes, namely, the "return to Jesus," and "the new Asian formula,"[13] are not mutually exclusive. For Ahn's Jesus is non-personal or *a*personal, and in this connection we need here to deal briefly with Ahn's philosophical analysis of Western thought.

He identifies three essential elements of Western thought: dualism, *jugaek dosik* (subject-object dichotomy), and *persona*. These three are closely related. The first, dualism, needs no explanation. The second, *jugaek dosik*, has been an important philosophical methodology in Western academia. It denotes the ways in which subject and object are divided, text and context are separated, and I and thou are alienated. (1993, vol. 2: 81–2) The Western preoccupation with the third element, *persona*, Ahn contends, neither originated in nor is supported by the Bible. Nor, he says, is it such an important concept in the East.

---

13   See Chapter V.

Originally, *persona* had the meaning of "mask" in the theatre, an artifice by means of which actors and spectators are clearly separated. As such, this notion has encouraged dualism and has divided the sacred from the profane, this life from the after-life, and history from nature.(1993, vol. 2: 5) Ahn asks, "if God were forever separated from humanity like two parallel lines, what use would such a God be for us"?

Thus, he argues, Jesus and Christianity need to be distinguished. "Christianity," he says, "presupposes Jesus, but in its content it excludes him."(1993, vol. 2: 3) In the words of W. C. Smith, "Christianity—for some, Christian theology—has been our idol."(1987: 61) "Christianity," Ahn continues, "is not a necessary condition for Jesus."(1993, vol. 2: 3) The implication of this for Ahn's christology is that the interpretation of the Jesus-event cannot be limited to the scope of Christianity when this is seen as something conditioned by a certain culture. However, this does not mean that Ahn is attempting to formulate a non-Christian christology. Rather, his attempt is to de-westernize Christianity.

Ahn's meeting with the minjung in Korea enabled him to overcome the dualistic framework which the Korean Church had inherited from the Western Christian mission. It was his involvement with the Korean minjung in the political struggle that gave him this perspective (he is one of those who were frequently imprisoned because of their political views). As mentioned above, after returning from Germany he had to make a significant adjustment in his theological perspective in the light of his experience with the oppressed people of Korea, among whom he discovered the Jesus that *happens*.

This leads us to the hermeneutical tools Ahn employs in his system. There are at least three elements in his hermeneutical approach: a materialist reading of the Bible, a sociological consideration of the early Christian community, and Ahn's own experience with the minjung in Korea. His argument on the primacy of Jesus's deeds as opposed to his words (Apophthegma) is clearly illustrated in his interpretation of the story of plucking the ears of wheat on the sabbath (Mk. 2:23-28). Whereas form critics have generally argued that the passage "the sabbath was made for man, not man for the sabbath" is the kerygma for the purpose of which the whole story is told, Ahn warns that without any consideration of the hungry people in the story as its social context, the statement by itself becomes "very abstract."(1984/5: 35) Only when the whole event of the story is interpreted in a materialist way in the light of a certain type of sociological analysis do the words of Jesus become clear. That is, Jesus actually sided with the hungry people for doing what any hungry people might do in that situation.

In interpreting such biblical passages as this, all three elements described above are at work for Ahn: a materialist reading of the Bible, and a sociological analysis of the given passage, in the light of Ahn's experience with the minjung in Korea—all these without any resort to the Nicene-Chalcedonian faith statements. Ahn's rejection of those historical doctrines is, in fact, the rejection of the preoccupation with the *persona* of Jesus as suggested by those doctrines. What, then, gives Ahn the confidence to trust the Jesus-event at all?

Ahn's confidence in the Jesus-event comes from his experience with the struggling minjung in Korea. For the question is related to the question of who the bearers of the Jesus-event were. Ahn's thesis is that it was not the kerygma but the the minjung and their rumors that were the faithful transmitters of the Jesus-event. The underlying premise here, of course, is that Jesus was a victim of political violence. Ahn gained his insight on "rumor" through his involvement with the minjung in Korea in the political struggle. In the intense political situation in Korea during the 1970s and '80s people trusted the rumors more than the mass-media, because the government-controlled media were but the means of propaganda for the ruling group. Ahn and many others in Korea found that rumors in such a situation are more trustworthy. Since the stories of Jesus, who was a victim of political violence, were transmitted by the minjung in this way, the Jesus-event, especially as it is described in the Gospel of Mark (Ahn's favourite text), is credible. This is the reason why Ahn insists on not abandoning the quest for the historical Jesus. After all, the political rumors of the minjung of Jesus are trustworthy.

In so far as the issue of the contextualization of the gospel in Korea is concerned, Ahn argues, it must be discussed in the cultural dimension. (1985: 306) He supports Park Bong-bae's analogy of gospel and culture as yeast and dough as a suitable model for contextualization. The task of Korean theology, then, for Ahn, is a new creation of Korean culture. The presupposition here, of course, is that culture is not static, but changes constantly. A distortion of the so-called "purity" of the gospel, he contends, should not be a matter of concern for Korean Christians. It has been an issue, he says, for the West, where Christianity is culturalized, and therefore where it is felt necessary to distinguish between Christ and culture in the way that Westerners have done. The history of Western Christianity, for him, however, does not need to be repeated in Korea.

The task of Korean theology as culture-creation does not mean the Westernizing of Korean culture. Nor does it simply mean illuminating an old Korean tradition. The task of Minjung theology, he asserts, is to discern, or to discover, Christ-the-transformer-of-culture *in* Korea.

In this connection, Ahn's first premise, that the relationship between the gospel and culture is that of yeast and dough, is questionable, for yeast is a definite, identifiable element with a concrete form and substance at the time of mixing. It is something that comes from outside already made. As he himself realized, any given tradition, such as the Jesus-story in the Bible, needs to be interpreted for each cultural context that encounters it. That is, the gospel messages (note the small "g") must first be culturally reconstructed to make any sense at all. This implies that a mutual influence occurs between the received gospel and the culture. The traffic on this road goes both ways at once: the gospel is interpreted and reconstructed in accordance with the needs of the people, and the people are challenged and reshaped by the interpreted *Gospel* (large G). The gospel must become the *Gospel*. For people are not mere receivers of foreign doctrines, nor are they objects to be preached to, but are at the centre of theological concern. Hence, Ahn's support of the analogy of the gospel and culture as yeast and dough (or powder) does not seem to be fully compatible with his own version of Minjung theology.

**"Confluence of the Two Stories."** "Now," says Suh, "the task for Korean minjung theology is to testify that in the Mission of God in Korea there is a *confluence* of the minjung tradition in Christianity and the Korean minjung tradition [italics mine]."(1983: 176) The Korean term for "confluence" that Suh originally uses is *haplyu*, which indicates the meeting or merging of two streams, as in a river-system.

There are, Suh explains, three paradigms[14] for Minjung theology: the Bible, Church history and Korean history. The first two, the Bible and Church history, form one stream, and the paradigm of Korean history forms the other. Since the first stream comes from outside and the second is indigenous, a confluence must occur for theology to have any significance in Korea. These two streams come together to form the reservoir of meaning, which in turn provides the theologian resources to

---

14   Suh's term, in Korean, is *jôn'gô* 典據, which means "referential authority," "paradigmatic reference," or "illustrative precedence." "Paradigm" in this sense, as it is translated into English, can be misleading.

analyze and to challenge the present situation in her/his struggle with the minjung for liberation. This is clearly shown in his treatment of the "text" and the "context" of theology.

According to Suh's theology, the traditional dispute between the Protestant and Catholic Churches on the question of primacy between the Bible and the Church is mistaken. For him it is neither the Bible nor the Church that is the ultimate norm for theology. The Bible, for example, is not the text which can be applied to our situation as its context. Rather, he argues, it is the present context, especially that of the minjung, which should be the text for which the Bible should be understood. In other words, the Bible per se is not a kind of behavioral code for the life of the minjung but is at the service of the transformation of their present situation. Strictly speaking, then, the respective functions of the text and the context, as traditionally viewed, become reversed in the thought of Suh.[15] That is, the particularity of the socio-historical condition of the minjung becomes the text, and the tradition, including the Bible, becomes the reference to be considered for the salvation/liberation of the minjung. This is possible, in fact necessary for Suh, on the ground that the liberation of the minjung today is more important than the maintenance of the Christian tradition of the past, which by and large is a Western one. The past is at the service of the present for the betterment of the latter. That is, the Gospel is more a story for the present than that of the past.

***Hyônjang* (Context) and Praxis.** In the case of multi-religious contexts, such as that of Korea, the "confluence" that Suh mentions inevitably leads into the subject of dialogue with the existing traditions. As has been suggested above, in my view, it is by starting from the historical cultural situation of the minjung, rather than from abstract philosophical or doctrinal concepts, that we can draw the most constructive theology of religions. The praxis of Donghak, again, is the case in point here. A keen analysis of the cultural/political situation of his time directly influenced the way Suun formulated his doctrines, and these doctrines in turn gave the minjung their historical consciousness. The value of this new religion lay, no doubt, in the way it contributed to the transformation of the culture of its time. Suun's task of the conceptualization of his new found teaching was itself a part of the holistic attempt to meet the needs of his

---

15  This later point became a major thesis for Chung Hyun Kyung's thesis-turned book *Struggle to be the Sun Again* (1990).

time. In the face of a multireligious situation, his way of dialogue was thoroughly praxis-oriented: for him, the concrete life situation of minjung was the hermeneutical key that guided his dialogue with the various traditions.

The debate over praxis reminds us that *hyônjang*, the concrete life place of the minjung, is to be the centre of dialogue. Comparing dogmas may be a useful mental exercise and may even be an inevitable part of any religious dialogue. A dialogue centered on it, however, can easily fall into the area of a "supra-structure" of ideas far removed from the historical condition of the minjung in the "material infra-structure," as Suh Nam-dong warns with respect to the approach Song Choan Seng takes.(1984/5: 12–15) Suh's concern is that when theological discussions are transplanted from the soil of *hyônjang*, the place of minjung, to the religions themselves, such discussions cannot reflect the spirit of minjung. As Schreiter points out, when the encounter between the invading culture and the receiving culture is incomplete, "the two never come into serious contact" and the "invading sign system remains 'foreign.'"(1985: 155) The "invading" Christian sign system still remains foreign in Korea. Dialogue taking place between the Christian religion and other traditions, in this sense, would not be a genuine dialogue because the Korean people have not been able to make Christianity penetrate their own cultural sign system. Our concern here is with where, how, and from whose perspective, theological discussions on culture are to be undertaken.

**The Spiritual Precursor of Minjung Theology—Donghak.** Donghak is a good theological paradigm in Korea not so much because of the beauty of the final outcome of its dogmas formulated out of different religious doctrines, but because of its consideration of *how* such religious doctrines came to be, i. e., the very way Suun accommodated the various religious traditions in light of the life of the minjung of his time. In this praxis-oriented theologizing/philosophizing, the life situation of people becomes the signpost showing the direction to be taken by theological formulations and discernment. As has been demonstrated thus far, Donghak was born in *hyônjang*. This made it possible to transfer the "shaman-ethos" into a power to transform the culture of the Yi dynasty. The life of the minjung here was the source and motivation of the religion in which the minjung became the controllers of their own destiny.

There is a clear continuity between Donghak and Minjung theology in the very way they were formulated. Suh's suggestion that Donghak and Christianity might be unified can be accepted in the light of this understanding. Such a unification of the principles of revolution and salvation gives both spiritual meaning to Donghak and a prophetic revolutionary impetus to Christianity in the context of Korea. Praxis becomes the point of juncture for the two different religions. Interpreting the gospel and formulating its messages occurs as a result of the confluence of the two traditions, one from outside and the other indigenous, *from the perspective of the minjung*. Whether something foreign is good news in Korea or not is for the Korean minjung to discern. The gospel, in the way it came from the outside, is not Good News until it is joined by the spirit of the minjung.

When one starts, as Schreiter does, from the perspective of the indigenous culture, in this case, the Korean culture, one becomes able to observe that the contact between the incoming and the indigenous has been "incomplete." As Schreiter observes, in many former "mission fields," "the invading sign system" has remained "foreign" in that it has not penetrated "either the world-view or the group-boundary-formation process of the receiving culture."(1985: 155) The right to discern the rights or wrongs of the Korean culture has always been taken for granted by the incoming foreign culture. By and large, the culture-change that occurs as a result is a shift from one into the other, rather than the transformation of the old culture. And, naturally, this results in the glorification of the incoming culture, in this case, the Western culture. As Suh indicates, power remains in the "supra-structure" of foreign ideas rather than in the "material infra-structure" of the life of the minjung. Such power can result in an abusive situation such as that stated in "Problems" at the beginning of this book.

The transference of power from the supra-structure of ideas to the infra-structure of the life of the minjung that Suh calls for, then, can be interpreted as a transference of authority from the foreign (biblical) stories that came to Korea, to the outcome of a "successful coming together" of the two realities, the gospel-stories and the life-stories of the minjung. This is the paradigmatic praxis which can give us a clue to the meaning of the thematic phrase describing the minjung as "the subjects of history." The gospel stories, reinterpreted and reformulated in the light of the minjung's "shaman-ethos," in turn give a critical judgment as well as a positive acceptance of the minjung culture. Donghak, therefore, is viewed as a paradigmatic forerunner—one which provided an ideological framework—for Minjung Theology, and Suun as a prototype Minjung theologian.

This, of course, is my interpretation of Minjung theology. Ahn, for example, does not explicitly acknowledge his indebtedness to Donghak. The influence of Donghak on Ahn is, therefore, indirect, i.e., through minjung movements in the modern history of Korea. In my view, Ahn is much more influenced by the Korean minjung cultural tradition epitomized by Donghak than he himself realizes. In the Korean Buddhist tradition, for example, "Buddha is *jung saeng* 衆生 (people or myriad creatures) and *jung saeng*, Buddha." Suun, again, also wrote that *o shim jûk yo shim*, "my (God's) mind is your mind." There is no doubt that this cultural ethos was operative in Ahn's thought, as reflected in his contention, for example, that "Jesus is minjung and minjung, Jesus."

Suh, however, is more explicit in his opinion about Donghak. Suh says,

> [t]he Donghak Revolution in many ways represents the peak of the Korean minjung movement in history. With the ideology "humanity is heaven," it fought, on the one hand, the feudal social system in Korea and, on the other, the invasion of Korea by foreign capital. (1983: 170-1)

Suh here alludes to both Donghak the revolt (1894) and Donghak the religion founded by Suun. The revolt is acknowledged by Suh as the "peak of the Korean minjung movement" and the Chôndogyo (Donghak's later name) doctrine of "humanity is heaven" (*in nae chôn*)[16] as the driving force and the motivating ideology of the movement. Moreover, for Suh, the minjung consciousness raised by Donghak has always been the kernel of Korean minjung movements. He continues,

> [I]t is evident that those who participate in the human rights struggle see their genealogy beginning with the Donghak movement,... The historical consciousness which has this genealogy of the minjung movement needs to be manifested and realized as an appropriate political hermeneutic for today. (1983: 171)

---

16   *In nae chôn* 人乃天 is espoused by Sohn Uiam (1861–1922), the third leader of the religion, which name he changed from "Donghak" into "Chôndogyo" in 1905. Hence, although Uiam developed this notion based on Suun's doctrine of *Shichônju*, "bearing God," "nurturing God," or "serving God," it comes later than the revolt of 1894.

## Minjung Theology

There is, for Suh, a clear continuity of Donghak with Minjung theology. This continuity in the case of Ahn, however, is my interpretation. In other words, in my view, Ahn's theology is more culturally relevant than it is often recognized. His contention that Jesus is an (pneumatological) event, in particular, can be a suitable point of contact with the theology of Suh.

Since this book is not about christology, I cannot deal with this subject adequately here. However, one christological implication of their theologies should be mentioned. For both Ahn and Suh, the (*persona*) Jesus of the past should not be our main preoccupation. Instead, the focus is on the activity of the Spirit through the particular historical event of Jesus. For them, Jesus Christ is not the once-and-for-all revelation of God for the whole world. A shift of focus occurs here from the christological to the pneumatological. In my view, the latter, the pneumatological, takes account of the present reality much more helpfully than the former, the christological. The shift of focus from the christological to the pneumatological enables us to view the past (the story of Jesus *then*) in the light of the present (the story of minjung *now*).

I shall now turn to a dialogue with a similar religious formulation from the Buddhist circle, namely, Minjung Buddhism, followed by yet another dialogue with theologies from other parts of the world, noting that for them too there is a clear emphasis on the needs of the present, and that the demands of context and praxis are fundamental for theological method.

# Chapter IV

# Minjung Buddhism

## The Case of Wonhyo

Does Korean Buddhism have a suitable paradigm for the minjung movement in the nation? To begin with my own opinion, it is not an easy task to find one. Those who attempted to search for coherence in Buddhism realize how quickly they can be discouraged by the tradition's diverse and complex system of thought. One of the peculiarities of Buddhism is its adaptability to different geographical and cultural contexts, more so than any of the other major religions of the world. Another characteristic of this tradition is its immense number of scriptures. To this Korean Buddhism is no exception; it is both contextualized and diverse. Among the many different sects of Buddhism which exist in Korea, perhaps, Sôn (Ch'an; Zen) is the most well-known in the West—thanks to the efforts of such scholars as D. T. Suzuki.

For that reason, I will not deal with Zen as much as other less well-known traditions, such as the Pure Land and the Maitreya beliefs here. My search will be centered on a historical figure, Wonhyo (617–686), who was both erudite and minjung-centered.[1] Although not adequate, for now, I have settled with Wonhyo for the paradigm of Minjung Buddhism in Korea. He lived about one hundred years after the arrival of Buddhism in his nation, which is comparable to Minjung Theology, developed also around one hundred years after the arrival of Protestantism in Korea. One cautions, however, any attempt to make an ancient figure like Wonhyo a

---

1   Again, I use this term "minjung-centered" as a notion characteristic of the minjung of the society. A philosophy, for example, would be minjung-centered if it is thought out from the perspective and the benefit of the minjung, the common people who are often oppressed. Although there is a debate among scholars whether an intellectual, as a member of the elite of the society, is by definition a minjung, there is no doubt that her/his thought can be minjung-centered. See the section on "the Minjung Perspective" in Chapter III.

contemporary revolutionary. Wonhyo was not a leader of a social movement; he was a monk, a thoroughly religious one. The basis of my argument, then, is not the existence of a social transformation which may be detectable after the life of a revolutionary; there was no such discernable social change after Wonhyo's life. I will argue on the basis of the overall observation that he stood against the Buddhist current of his time, which current may be generally characterized as an ideologization of Buddhism for the ruling groups, by being, to put it briefly, a friend of the minjung of his time.

Buddhist schools may be classified in terms of the different emphases in attaining their goal of enlightenment/deliverance. Those who stress personal devotion and dedication do so on the basis of their belief in the "self-power" in attaining enlightenment. Theravada and Zen belong to this group. In these traditions, the adherents are expected to follow the intense discipline of monastic life.

Other Mahayana schools, especially Pure Land, stress the necessity for faith for their deliverance. Genuine seekers are said to be guided by the power of Buddhas and Bodhisattvas, who will eventually deliver them into the "Land of Ultimate Bliss" in their rebirth. This approach became popular among the common people who could not abandon everything to seek the Way. It is said that even the most wretched sinner will achieve rebirth in the Pure Land if s/he recites earnestly the name of the Buddha one to ten times at her/his deathbed. It is also maintained that reciting the name of Kuan-Yin, "the Goddess of Mercy," can offset previously committed bad karma; the power of Kuan-Yin will counterbalance our bad karma and save us from calamity.

In reality, however, "self-power" and "other-power" are not separated. "Other-power" does not become manifest without one's own genuine desire and effort for a rebirth in the Land of Ultimate Bliss "Pure Land" is the purity of inherent mind, our buddha-nature. As J. C. Cleary (1988) explains, the confluence of the two distinct teachings of Zen (Sôn) and Pure Land was an attempt to guard the Zen followers from the "lip-service Zen" of the pseudo-Zen schools during the Mongol period in the thirteenth century in East Asia, especially in Korea. Hence, genuine meditative mind in Buddha-recitation became important in the Pure Land schools, and trusting certain sutras to guide the seekers to a right path to meditation became essential for Zen schools.

Throughout the history of Buddhism in Korea, frequent attempts were made to unite Sôn (Ch'an; Zen) with Kyo, a collective term for the sects emphasizing the importance of studying sutras—Hwaôm (Hua Yen in Chinese), which upholds the Avatamsaka sutra as the central teaching of Buddhism, is the representative scripture in Korea. Since all these Kyo sects invariably practiced the Pure Land faith, such unity meant a combination of faith in Buddha and meditation. One of the most important attempts for such unity was made when the division between the two was at its height in the twelfth century by Jinul who taught that meditation and the Buddha-recitation are not two but one and the same.

## The Pure Land and Wonhyo

Pure Land is probably the most influential school among the Buddhist adherents in East Asia, due to the relative simplicity of its approach to the Way. Pure Land, like all Mahayana schools, aspires to attain Buddhahood for the benefit of all sentient beings. The first step, of course, is to possess the Bodhi Mind. According to the Avatamsaka Sutra, the Bodhi Mind is born from great compassion, and it also leads one to the perfect enlightenment. It is commonly acknowledged that Wonhyo is the most important early evangelizer and systematizer of this Pure Land faith in Korea. Before we discuss some of the salient thoughts of Wonhyo, we need to have a brief look at his historical context.

At the time of Wonhyo, Korea was divided into three kingdoms: Koguryo (37 B.C.E.–668 C.E.), Baekje (18 B.C.E.–660 C.E.) and Silla (57 B.C.E.–935 C.E.). Each of the three kingdoms wanted to establish its own supremacy in the peninsula. After some "tug-of-war" which also had drawn in Chinese and Japanese armies, Silla conquered Baekje in 660 and Koguryo in 668 with the help of the Tang Chinese armies. In these tumultuous times Wonhyo devoted much effort to developing a spiritual ideology out of Buddhism for the unified nation.

**Silla Society.** Silla maintained a caste system of its own based on the *golpum* 骨品, or the "bone ranks". According to Andrew C. Nahm, Silla bureaucracy was patterned after that of China since the seventh century, and it had a total of seventeen ranks.(1988: 32) On the top of the society there was the class of *sônggol* 聖骨, or the "sacred bone" group, which was occupied by the members of the Pak clan, the founding family of the Silla kingdom who maintained the monarchy until the middle of the seventh century. After that time the throne was occupied by the Kim clan until the end of the dynasty. The members of the Kim clan whose mothers were from the Pak clan also belonged to the sacred bone group, and those Kims whose mothers were not of the Pak clan belonged to the next sacred bone group in the caste called *jin'gol* 眞骨, or the "true bone" group. The common people, mostly farmers, were classified into the lower three ranks in the caste. At the bottom of the society there were *chônmin* 賤民, or the "low born", who were not included in the commoner class. There were also slaves who were captured during the wars with the neighboring states. The *chônmin* and the slaves were engaged in manual labor to produce the goods to support the aristocracy. In this beginning stage of feudalism in the kingdom, when systematic oppression against the common people was becoming more and more obvious, what was the role of Buddhism vis-à-vis the oppression?

Unlike the other two kingdoms, Koguryo and Baekje, where Buddhism made smooth inroads by royal approval and blessing from the beginning, there was some resistance among Silla's ruling groups and the people against this new religion. According to Ahn Kye-hyon, Buddhism could not gain acceptance among the people because the indigenous shamanistic beliefs and customs were powerful and deep-rooted.(1989: 3) It was only after the martyrdom of Ichadon, a court official and devout Buddhist, that Silla accepted Buddhism.

**Buddhism and the Royalty in Silla.** The first king in the Buddhist Silla, Bophung (r. 514–540), attempted to solidify monarchy by using the Buddhist Dharma and then identifying it with royal decrees. Sakyamuni, who is regarded as a representative of all Buddhas, is likened to royalty, and Maitreya to the aristocrats. Such a move proved useful for harmony and collaboration between the king and the aristocratic class. Originally, Buddhist concepts were used for royal order in India. The concept of Cakravartin king (cakra: "wheel" and vartin: "turner"), was used to espouse the notion of an ideal king. King Cakravartin is one who rules with the might of Buddhist Dharma instead of that of the sword. The identification of the king with Sakyamuni and the aristocrats with Maitreya, the future Buddha, in Silla, however, is to be seen more as an attempt to strengthen the royalty, holding the powerful aristocrats in check, than as a desire to serve the nation with the Buddhist ideals.[2] This can be argued from the fact that Silla society did not loosen its caste system after its acceptance of Buddhism—one recalls that Sakyamuni

---

2   Kim Jae-young (1990: 357), however, maintains that the Silla kings' efforts were sincere attempts to make Silla an ideal Buddhist state.

opposed the caste system in India.[3] Lee also contends that even the Buddhist notions of transmigration, namely birth and rebirth (samsara), were used to favor the social status of the aristocratic class. The present state of affairs were to be accepted as the result of their karma from previous lives.

Such was the way Buddhism became the religion of the monarchs in the Silla society. The priests who won the favor of the royalty devoted their efforts to developing ideal monarchical order using Buddhist ideals in a way similar to the activities of the royal prophets in the ancient Israelite society. It would be presumptuous to regard the efforts of these Silla priests as succumbing to the power for material gain, a form of flattery. However, their works indeed turned Buddhism into an ideological tool to strengthen the monarchy, and thereby systematized oppression.

Wonhyo was critical of this Buddhism at the service of the powerful. Buddhism, for him, was to deliver the most helpless sentient beings, such as the common people of the Silla society, out of their misery into the place of the Buddha. Kim Chon-choon speculates that Wonhyo "was so keenly aware of such social maladies and defects [as 'unmitigated prejudice and provincialism against all outside the hierarchy of nobility centered around Kyongju (Capital city of Silla)'] that he was motivated to place himself on the side of the common people."(1982: 127) Hence he turned to Pure Land. Why the Pure Land faith? As Lee Ki-baek says, "[a]mong the lower classes, the Pure Land teachings were taken up as a protest against the concept of transmigration and rebirth,"(1989: 180) which were used by the ruling group to legitimize the "bone-rank" system mentioned above. The strong presence of the Pure Land sect at the time of Wonhyo is shown in the following poem entitled *Prayer to Amitabha* by a monk named Kwangdok (?–681).

> O Moon,
> Go to the West, and
> Pray to Amitabha[4]

---

3   For this subject of Sakyamuni's social views, see Kim J. Y. (1990: 314–319); Kang Kon-kee (1988: 108). According to Kim, the Buddha was an ardent supporter of human rights, including the equality of women. See Lee Young-ja (1988) for this particular view of the Buddha on women.
4   Quoted from Nahm (1988: 50–51).

**Enlightening Experience.** One day, Wonhyo and his friend Uisang were on a journey to China (T'ang) to get more education. At dusk they sought a place to spend the night and found what seemed to be a cave. At night Wonhyo woke up from thirst. Fortunately, he saw a gourd-like dipper which contained some water in it. He drank the water and went back to sleep. In the morning while they were packing to leave the place, Wonhyo was dismayed to find a human skull around where he drank the water only a few hours ago. Suddenly, he felt nauseous and had spasms in his stomach. As he attempted to vomit the liquid out of his stomach, a sudden realization came to his mind. What was the difference? Why does the liquid which he thought was quite tasty water turn to attack him this way? Was it the liquid he drank or was it something else in himself that was at work? This became a moment of enlightenment and the kernel of his thought, namely, the centrality of the mind in grasping reality. Wonhyo thus no longer felt the need to get more education, for everything was already in his mind. He parted company with his friend Uisang and went back to Silla.

**Corpus Operandi.** Wonhyo was interested in all of the scriptures, such as Samnon (Madhyamika), Songsil (Satyasiddhi), Hwaôm (Avatamsaka), Bôphwa (Saddharmapundarika), Jôngto (Pure Land), Chôntae (T'ien-tai), Sôn (Ch'an; Zen), Sôpnon (Makayanasamgraha), Chiron (Bhumaka), Bôpsang (Dharmalaksana), Yul (Vinaya), etc. As Rhi Ki-yong puts it, "[t]he remarkable thing is that Wonhyo expostulated his own creative views in treating them."(1977: 197-207)

In his extensive commentaries on the various sutras Wonhyo was not interested in the interpretation and translation of words and sentences, but the comprehension of the central and basic spirit of the scriptures for the people of his time. The following words of Rhi illustrate the spirit of Wonhyo well:

> Wonhyo lamented most the tendency toward pedantry. To him, Buddhism was no longer Indian or Chinese. It was his, the religion of a Silla subject... It was painful for him to see, a hundred years after the transplantation of Buddhism in the country, the triumph of false truth clad in dignity and prestige."(1977: 201-202)

Truth for Wonhyo was not transmitted through words or phrases. Whatever helped Gautama some thousand years ago was not the truth for Wonhyo until it became his own. The ultimate eternal reality as the source and power of our "truly human" life makes our enlightenment possible. How does Wonhyo describe the ineffable nature of reality and enlightenment?

The term Wonhyo employs in Korean/Chinese for the ultimate eternal reality is *bon-gak* 本覺. For him the world itself is in everlasting enlightenment. Rhi (1977) translates *bon-gak* as "Original Enlightenment," "Fundamental Enlightenment," and "Enlightenment a priori," noting that according to Wonhyo's understanding, *bon-gak* is nothing but the *Bôpshin* 法身 (*Dharmakaya*). This Body of Buddha lies beyond the ordinary physical experience of mere mortal beings. What of the problem of the finite human capacity in grasping the ever-transcending nature of the ultimate reality? The mind plays the key role here. Although this reality is the Absolute, it is not so in the sense of Kantian notion of *noumena*. For it is always available within the reach of the common people as that which is to be realized and (re)cognized, a thing to be grasped and experienced of its seed (*Tathagatagarbha*).

The full realization of the *Bopshin*, however, is not attainable until death which becomes a door to the world of true life. Rhi finds that Wonhyo's notion of *bon-gak* is comparable to Teilhard's "Omega point," except, perhaps, in the latter's highly eschatological implications. What, then, can the common people attain through the purification of their minds?

*Shi-gak* 始覺 in Korean/Chinese is translated by Rhi as "Enlightenment a posteriori," which is "the Enlightenment in its realization; this is the *Popshin* in its active aspects as a seed becoming a tree which begins across the ocean of suffering to arrive at the final goal—the Fruit."(1977: 203) *Shi-gak* arises from, or as a result of, *bul-gak* 不覺 ("not" *gak* or non-*gak*, i.e., "not" enlightenment or non-enlightenment). We see here Wonhyo's version of dialectic at work among the three *gak*s (two *gak*s plus one non-*gak*): *bon-gak*, *bul-gak* and *shi-gak*. *Bon-gak* gives rise to *bul-gak*; *bul-gak* begets *shi-gak*; *shi-gak* leads one to *bon-gak*. These three pairs suggest a certain triangular relationship among the three *gak*s. For Wonhyo each of the three *gak*s alone has no characteristics; it is to be considered in relation to its corresponding *gak*, which is in a cyclical relationship to itself. There is a rather fluid continuity between being and non-being for Wonhyo. Dharma, he explains, is neither nothingness 無, nor existence 有, nor both nothingness and existence, but relational in nature.(1990: 100)

In his *Awakening of Faith in the Mahayana[5]: a Commentary*, Wonhyo explains four stages or levels (四位) for the spiritual maturity toward this "Enlightenment a posteriori": non-enlightenment (不覺位), apparent (or semi-) enlightenment (相似覺位), advanced enlightenment (隨分覺位), and the ultimate enlightenment (究竟覺位).

The first stage, non-enlightenment, is when one becomes aware of one's own existential predicament in the state of being wrongful. Aside from this awareness, no concrete measures are taken to correct one's own misdeeds yet.

The second stage, apparent enlightenment, is the stage of legalistic behaviorism. In this stage people become deeds-centered, without a clear mind that can correspond to their deeds. Since they do not possess the clear self-less mind, their actions are usually self-centered.

The third stage, in which one is "gradually coming close," is when these deeds-conscious people come to possess the Bodhi-mind, which does not merely explain their deeds but actually influences them. In this "advanced Bodhisattva" stage their behavior becomes generally altruistic. Their state of enlightenment, however, is not yet complete, because they still retain their ego-consciousness, marked by ignorance of self.

The fourth stage, the ultimate enlightenment, is none other than the state of *bon-gak*, the "original enlightenment." This is the stage of achieving a unity with reality, where one comes to terms with one's One Mind, which is the body of Buddha (Dharmakaya). In this unity the subject-object dichotomy disappears by "overcoming in the depth of our minds the causal process of ego-consciousness."(1977: 205) For Rhi there is a "remarkable coincidence" in language with Jaspers' formula *Subjekt-Objekt* spaltung.

**Subject-Object Non-Duality.** Shin Ock Hee also finds that both Wonhyo's "one mind" and Jaspers' "encompassing" pass beyond the subject-object duality of a monotheistic conception of reality. Nor are their philosophies pantheistic, for they do not "posit a metaphysical substance as the ground of its phenomena, but grasp the absolute in terms of phenomena and not vice versa."(1987: 187) For both Wonhyo and

---

5   Mahayana-sraddhotpada-sastra. Although traditionally attributed to Asvaghosa (c. 80–150 C.E.) around the middle of the 2nd century C.E., the authenticity is generally disputed today. Wonhyo's commentary is 大乘起信論疏.別記.

Jaspers the phenomenon is neither a mere appearance nor a final word for the ultimate.

However, Shin notices a "deadlock" between Wonhyo and Jaspers on this point. While Wonhyo "speaks about the one mind from beyond the subject-object-scheme in the dimension of non-duality of unio mystica with the one mind," Jaspers "comprehends the encompassing that is beyond the subject-object-scheme within the boundary of subject-object-dichotomy, without any hope of direct encounter with it."(1987: 188) While for Jaspers it is possible to comprehend the reality that lies beyond the subject-object split without denying the reality of such a split, for Wonhyo it is necessary to realize that such a split is a false perception by achieving the state of complete union with the one mind (*tathata*, "Suchness"). If we categorize their differences in a conventional way, Wonhyo would be more mystical and Jaspers more philosophically rational, that is, in a Western sense. This point may be due to the immence difference of the cultural environments which shaped the two thinkers.

Shin goes on to expound the soteriological implications of Wonhyo and Jaspers. Although Wonhyo never identified with any particular sect or school, his commentators generally put him in the Pure Land tradition. He is considered one of the most minjung-oriented priests in the history of Korean Buddhism. In line with the truth of Mahayana Buddhist faith, his philosophy seeks to guide sentient beings to attain their liberation and to taste the ultimate bliss. For both Wonhyo and Jaspers, Shin argues, "theory and practice, or being and ethics are inseparably united in their mutual interrelation."(1987: 189) Note that I have argued above that in the thought of Suun, the founder of Donghak religion, ontology and ideology coincide. In this sense, Wonhyo may be viewed as a precursor of minjung-oriented philosophy of Suun. In discussions of minjung-centered faiths in East Asia, one cannot fail to notice this name: Maitreya.

**Maitreya, the Future Buddha.** According to Alan Sponberg, Maitreya, "the future Buddha," is "one of the relatively few elements of the Buddhist tradition that has had some place in every historical and cultural variation of the tradition."(1988: 286) Maitreya also has been one of the most important Buddhist tenets for the common people in East Asia. Daniel L. Overmyer states:

> In a typology of Buddhas, Maitreya shares much with other figures such as Manjusri or Amitabha. He can be an object of contemplation, a revealer of wisdom, or a compassionate savior in paradise. He shares with his model Sakyamuni a concern for life in this world and an easy familiarity with princes and kings. What Maitreya adds to all this is his association with a future age of bliss. He is a symbol of universal and collective hope, beyond individual aspirations, beyond the history of the present age, so that he offers general and transcendent renewal. (1988: 13)

Belief in Maitreya, with its eschatological implications, has been deeply related to various popular revolts in both China and Korea. Sponberg explains the "two basic positions" of the Maitreya cult: On the one hand, there is the postmillenarian core tradition, which focuses on Maitreya's Buddhahood in the distant future and, on the other, there is a repeatedly manifested premillenarian minority view, one often militantly apocalyptic and revolutionary in its expectation of Maitreya's imminent advent. Note, however, that both of these share a concern with what is of this world.

Its millenarian doctrine appealed to people who lost confidence in their rulers and provided a religious ideology for a better world-order with the help of the Buddha who is to come. For example, as Hwang Sun-myong points out, the sporadic activities of the Baeklyôn'gyo (White Lotus) sect in China was based on millenarian Maitreya doctrine since the middle of the fourteenth century. (1980: 134–8)

In Korea also Maitreya has always been a companion of the discontent minjung ever since the inception of Buddhism in Korea. During the Yi dynasty (1392–1910), for example, when Korea was frequently invaded by foreign nations, such as Japan and Ch'ing China, people prayed to Maitreya to appear and to save them from their present predicament. A legendary rebel called Chang Kil-san led a revolt against the local officials with Maitreya belief as his religious ideology. Some of the new religions born toward the end of the dynasty were greatly influenced by the same belief: Jûng San Gyo, for example, is centered on Maitreya doctrine. For Ko Eun, a renown Buddhist poet, the goal of Maitreya belief is the Maitreya world

> where the oppressed people, as the subjects of the world, become liberated from the sufferings of hunger, oppression, disease, submission and persecution which agrarian societies have longed for since antiquity. (1988: 90)

In general the doctrine of Maitreya shares with that of Amitabha the teaching of deliverance by "other power."

The fundamental difference between the two, however, is that while the Amitabha faith is concerned with the place, namely, the "Land of the Ultimate Bliss," the Maitreya doctrine teaches about the one who is to come for the followers who are unable to save themselves. In other words, arguably,[6] the former is more other-worldly, and the latter more this-worldly; in times of political oppression it is easier to pray for messianic help than to attempt to establish an ideal place here. For that reason, Maitreya has influenced the disgruntled people to rise against the oppressive principalities in both China and Korea more than has Amitabha. As Lancaster points out, it is not surprising to learn that "during the Japanese occupation the Maitreya groups were frowned upon by the authorities because they were potential sources of organized opposition."(1988: 148) In fact, most organized religious groups were under constant police scrutiny during the colonial period.

Is Maitreya comparable to a messianic figure of the Judeo-Christian tradition? Sponberg cautions any such quick identification. Maitreya, he argues, should not be understood in the manner the Judeo-Christian tradition has depicted a messiah, for the peculiar characteristics of Maitreya are his "open-ended possibilities" in the core tradition and his humanity, "both the degree to which he is endowed with ordinary human characteristics and the fact that he is so accessible to human understanding and contact as well as emulation." (1988: 287)

Accessibility is also considered the peculiarity of Maitreya by Overmyer. For him, Maitreya is a companion of people in both the future and the present. In the light of Mahayana Buddhism as a whole, which Overmyer calls a "gnostic religion," "Maitreya wandering around as a ragged monk or peasant is about as close to a human, historical savior as one can get."(1988: 132) The political implication of this Buddha is considered superior to that of Kuan-yin (Avalokitesvara) for Overmyer, for the latter is only a bodhisattva, not a world-conquering Buddha. Such open-endedness and accessibility no doubt would have played a role in drawing the common people into the Maitreya-belief.

---

6   For a different view, see Daniel L. Overmyer (1988) who observes that "in the texts themselves his [Maitreya's] role is predominantly otherworldly; he comes to rescue the lost from the profane world by reminding them of their sacred roots and showing them the way home to the Eternal Mother..., chief deity of sectarian tradition" (p. 111).

Some scholars, such as Lancaster, argue that Buddhism came to Korea when the interest in Maitreya cult was at its height in China.(1988: 135) Now we need to consider some of Wonhyo's views on Maitreya.

**Wonhyo on Maitreya.** During Wonhyo's time Pure Land's Amitabha had not yet vigorously set himself against Maitreya, as became obvious in the later Buddhism. Wonhyo's view on Maitreya exhibits his non-elitist philosophy of life. Although he classified the level of enlightenment into the four different stages as we saw above, he viewed that Maitreya was accessible to all beings regardless of their station or vocation in life. The major concern for this savior figure was the deliverance of all sentient beings from their sufferings.

For Wonhyo, then, Maitreya is a soteriological expressway for the great theme of the Mahayana tradition, namely, compassion. All the philosophical insights and the great wisdom of Buddhism must be at the service of this soteriological goal. As subject and object are not separate in reality, a Buddhhood is not out of touch with common people. As original enlightenment (*bon-kak*), non-enlightenment (*bul-gak*) and realized enlightenment (*shi-gak*) are inter-related, the Dharma, the ignorant mass and the enlightened master—no matter how erudite, like Wonhyo, s/he may be—are all relational in nature. As the Buddha nature can be found everywhere, individuality and community are not separate but related together; an individual is understood in the light of the community, and the community is considered the extension of an individual.

## In Search of a Paradigm

There is a debate among Buddhist scholars as to whether they should develop Minjung Buddhism within the dominant Sôn (Ch'an/Zen) tradition or others such as Wonhyo's. The former position is argued by Keel Hee-Sung, who says that the confrontation between the liberationist Buddhists and the Sôn traditionalists is unavoidable. He contends that "like it or not," any liberation theme must ring true to the adherents of the Sôn tradition for it to have some success, because the latter constitutes the largest part of Korean Buddhism. Keel first describes Sôn as a dynamic and "this worldly" religious ideal with an emphasis on facing "things as they are." He further asks whether the movement from "things as they are" to "things as they ought to be" is inherently consistent with Sôn Buddhism. His own answer is reservedly "yes." "Reservedly" because the connection between Sôn and human liberation is not given; it must be worked out. Using the teaching of Chinese Ch'an master Lin-chi Hui-chao (d. 867 C.E.), Keel describes Sôn as an iconoclastic humanism, which for him is distinguishable from the secular humanism of modern society. At the centre of Lin-chi's teaching, Keel argues, lie human values. For Keel, *in* (humanity, *ren* in Chinese) is Lin-chi's central notion, before which all other values become relative. Moreover, Keel notes, there is a consistent rejection of idolatry in Lin-chi. Even Buddha can be an obstacle to enlightenment, and, therefore, one is constantly reminded to kill Buddha if he appears. Such an iconoclastic spirit puts everything in question, giving rise to a revolutionary mood in the mind of the seeker. Now the problem: the reality of Sôn is far removed from such an ideal goal of revolutionary mood-making; for the average Korean Buddhist Sôn is a remote and riddle-filled belief-system. Knowing this situation well, Keel contends that the iconoclastic human subjectivity and freedom which Lin-chi emphasizes must find a way to a theorized objective social expression in order for Sôn to avoid such harsh criticisms as the following:

> Sôn sect provides the pathological atmosphere to a society by limiting freedom within one's inner subjective sphere without eliciting a change in a broader society for a social liberation.[7]

Indeed, self-enlightenment seeking Buddhists must consider this challenge seriously.

However, against the contention of Keel, one wonders how deeply the Chinese Master Lin-chi penetrated into the mainstream Korean Sôn tradition. Keel himself admits that Lin-chi's influence in Korea is more implicit than explicit. This means that Keel is attempting to import a religious ideology for the minjung from outside, which is against the very aspiration of minjung movements in Korea. As Kenneth L. Richard notes, Korean Buddhism is "predominantly doctrinal rather than meditative,"(1977: 224) even though the Sôn tradition is at its centre. This is so because, unlike Ch'an and Zen, its Chinese and Japanese counterparts, which stress meditation, Korean Sôn also values diligent learning of scriptures. We will not go through the historical details as to how it came to be so[8] except to say that both Pure Land and meditative

---

7   Bôpsông (1989: 33); Keel (1991: 43).
8   Interested readers should consult M. Cho (1977), or Keel (1984).

Sôn are prized by most Korean Buddhists. This may be due to the fact that the Avatamsaka sutra, which has been important in Korean Buddhism from its formative period, is considered essential by both traditions. It is also due to the various attempts for unity since the mid-Koryo dynasty (918–1392 C.E.). Keel's insistence, then, that the protagonists for Minjung Buddhism in Korea confront the dominant Sôn sect does not seem to have been well thought out.

For that reason, Mok Woo, a Minjung Buddhist monk, insists that Minjung Buddhism in Korea must be theoretically based on Boddhisattva doctrine rather than on Sôn.[9] The great virtue of Boddhisattva tradition, namely the deliverance of all the sentient beings from their sufferings, provides a better framework in which a minjung-centered Buddhist philosophy may be constructed.

Many scholars agree that Wonhyo gave permanent shape to the Buddhism in Korea. In the formative period of one hundred years or so after the reception of Buddhism in his nation, Wonhyo played a vital role in contextualizing the otherwise alien belief-system. Moreover, what is remarkable, especially for our purpose here, is his inclination toward minjung-centeredness, which was against the Buddhist current of his time. Suh Kyung-soo states: "Wonhyo made efforts to establish popular Buddhism by bringing Buddhism down to the level of the common people at a time when it was highly susceptible of becoming aristocratic." (1982: 127)

Furthermore, although Wonhyo did not see the beginning of full-blown Ch'an (Sôn/Zen) tradition in China, scholars already see the signs of Sôn in his thought. In fact, considering his influence in China, especially through his commentary on *Gumgang Sammaegyông*, it would be true to say that he provided an important source of the ideological framework for the maturation of the Ch'an tradition.[10] The "iconoclastic" nature of Ch'an, which Keel prizes highly, is lived out by Wonhyo; scholars describe Wonhyo as both "great master" and "eccentric"[11] monk. Wonhyo is philosophically sophisticated and, yet, at the same

---

9    See Keel (1991: 44–5).
10   For English readers, see Robert E. Buswell (1989), who argues forcefully that the author of the apocryphon *Vajra-samadhi Sutra* 金剛三昧經 [*Gumgang Sammaegyông*] must have been a Korean monk named Pômnang].
11   Alan Sponberg (1988: 96). Wonhyo is described as an eccentric figure with mysteriously superior knowledge/wisdom and power in 高僧傳(四) [*Biography of Eminent Monks*, Vol. 4] (新羅國 沙門元曉傳), written during Sung dynasty (960–1279) in China; Rhi. (1990: 47–8)

time, soteriologically plain; he is both erudite and non-elitist. Beginning with Wonhyo, then, seems to be appropriate for the minjung context of Korean Buddhism.

# Chapter V

# Ecumenical Implications

In this concluding chapter, I shall provide some ecumenical implications of the book. It is often said that a good theology must possess both particularity and universality. It needs to be specific enough to come out of a particular historical context, and general enough to have some universal significance. Hence, this chapter seeks to demonstrate the ecumenicity of the religious thought of Suun and his heirs in the Minjung theology movement.

## Normativity and Experience

This section is a brief survey of the epistemological approach of various liberation theologies, of which Minjung theology is one. My attempt here is to situate Minjung theology within the larger global theological context. It is also to show how epistemological approaches are reflected in specific areas of theology. Epistemological questions are also related to the issue of the norm in theology. What are the discerning criteria in theology? The new theological expressions such as "God is Black" and "God is Mother" are not a logical outcome of traditional theology. They are rather the outcome of the experience of people who have been marginalized. This imperative begs certain questions, such as "Can theology be neutral, objective, or supracultural?," "Who does theology and for whom?," and "Between the past tradition and the present situation, which is the determining factor in theology?"

I shall, therefore, attempt to survey the general approach of the liberation theologies. Generally, in these approaches "experience," especially that of the oppressed, is not treated as a theological category secondary to the "tradition" of the Church. What is primarily normative in theology is what reflects the experience of the oppressed, and contributes to their liberation. Using Stanley J. Smartha's expression, "*tarka* (logic)" is "less helpful than *anubhava* (experience, intuition),"

(1981: 51) especially in traditionally non-Christian cultures. That is, theology is liberative only when it becomes culturally relevant. To clarify and test this proposition, I shall deal with the arguments of some theologians from diverse liberation theologies, and then focus on an Asian (Aloysius Pieris) perspective, and finally relate it to some Korean Minjung theological perspectives. In ranging widely among liberation theologies, I cannot, of course, deal with any of them thoroughly.

For theologians like Raimon Panikkar there is no value-free theology. Any theology which makes such claims can easily be oppressive. "As much as," he says, "we may abhor apartheid, we practice it theologically under other names and more subtle attitudes." (1991: 9) Hence, Tissa Balasuriya asks, "can the self-understanding of churches that legitimized sexist, racist, classist, and religious oppression be theologically true?"(1985: 202) Generally, in liberation theologies there is an emphasis on listening to the context before attempting to open the "pre-packaged gospel." Samuel Rayan stresses the importance of listening as a theological method. Listening here is not confined to spoken words, for when "communication was wordless," it "was better." "We listened," Rayan says, "to things and to people, to unspoken words, to silences, to tears both shed and unshed."(1980: 53) He is reflecting on his experience of living for four days among the city slums in the city of Colombo.[1] The situation of the slum-dwellers was felt by Rayan before any explanatory words were spoken to him. Listening to the stories of people, some spoken but mostly unspoken, he felt, was fundamental to any attempt to assess and analyze the situation.

Listening to the stories of people is also considered important by the Minjung theologians in Korea. According to Suh Nam-dong, stories of people, especially the oppressed, are more powerful and self-explanatory than didactic religious statements or propositional truths. Those stories carry with them the *han* of people. Since literary activities were confined to the dominant elite males until the turn of the century, storytelling has been an important medium of cultural ethos for the majority of Korean people. For this reason, Minjung theologians, such as Suh, see storytelling as the hermeneutical methodology of people. Stories have been the source of inspiration for the common people of Korea. Simple narrations as meaning-carriers for oppressed people have provided the impetus for their struggle for authenticity. It is fair to say that Suh's

---

[1] This "live-in" arrangement was part of the Asian Theological Conference held in Wennappuwa, Sri Lanka, January 7–20, 1979.

theology is a theology of storytelling. Storytelling as a theological method has also influenced some younger theologians, such as Chung Hyun Kyung.

"Storytelling," says Chung, "has been women's way of inheriting truth in many Asian countries because the written, literary world has belonged to privileged males."(1990: 104) "The power of storytelling," Chung continues, "lies in its *embodied truth*." Women's bodies receive, record, and remember the historical reality of their lives. Chung calls this truth about women's bodies "epistemology from the broken body."

"Epistemology," which can be defined as "the study or a theory of the nature and grounds of knowledge especially with reference to its limits and validity,"[2] has been a crucial subject in Western philosophy. It asks such questions as "What, if any thing, can we know?," "How is knowledge possible?," and "Is our knowledge absolute or is it relative?" The complexity and diversity of modern society as well as the influence of the Enlightenment forced the Church to reconsider its centuries-old claims of absolute certainty on many issues. Hence epistemological questions have now become more important in theology than ever. Chung speaks of Asian women as knowers of a certain reality because they are women in Asia. Can a certain group of people have the privilege of certainty because of their existential predicament? If so, what gives them such privilege? What do they have that others do not?

Gregory Baum, using the notion of the sociology of knowledge theorized by Karl Mannheim, states that

> it is impossible to grasp the meaning and power of ideas until their relationship to the social context has been clarified. Ideas, symbols, moral imperatives and theological concepts do not float above history; they are uttered by people who wrestle with the concrete conditions of their existence. (1986: 49)

Baum and many liberation theologians today stress the importance of the awareness of one's social context in doing theology. For Baum, the neo-orthodox affirmation that "faith is pre-political" is itself a political statement that perpetuates the status quo. Such theology, Baum says, "is no longer adequate for the present age." (1986: 50)

Proponents of liberation theologies, such as Baum, maintain the importance of historical context in theological epistemology. Emilio J.M. de Carvalho calls for a praxis-oriented epistemology through dialogue

---

2  *Webster's Ninth New Collegiate Dictionary.*

between theologians of the Third and the First Worlds. "Hence," he says, "the need felt for an honest and open dialogue on how the concrete struggles and dreams of the oppressed and of the poor against all forms of injustice can lead to a *better understanding of God* and *of God's salvific action in history* and in different global contexts" (1985: 6; italics mine). For this reason, the necessity of contextual analysis became recognized in theology.

Although each of the liberation theologies has its own analytical priority, all these approaches are concerned in varying degrees with the use and abuse of power as well as the allocation of human and material resources. I shall briefly sketch four major currents in contemporary theology, specifically with "liberation" themes: Latin American, Feminist/Womanist, African, and Asian theologies.

**Latin American Theologies.** In this section, I shall identify some of the most salient methodological points of Latin American theologians, such as Gustavo Gutierrez and Juan Luis Segundo, since the late 1960s. Of course, Latin American theologies are very diverse, and here we can only glimpse some major points made by those two important authors.

Liberation theologians have made an important challenge for the primacy of context and praxis over theory in theology. Gutierrez argues that the engagement in the socio-historical context is the "first act" out of which reflection as the "second act" arises. This is a significant shift in theology in which action was commonly considered as the application of principle. The problem of pre-liberation theology was that the experience of the oppressed was not taken seriously. Perhaps this was the outgrowth of spirit/matter dualism; there was a profound mistrust of human experience. When reality was divided into the domains of the sacred and the profane, physical experience was resisted as being untrue, or a thing to be overcome. This shift, in my view, is the most important contribution of the liberation theologies to theology.

The recognition that there is oppression in the world naturally calls for a tool of social analysis. Some turned to the class analysis of Karl Marx. According to Marx, society is divided essentially into two clearly distinguishable classes—those who control the means of production, and the workers. The elite ruling class is constantly designing ideology to maintain the social structure in its favor. "The ideas of the ruling class," says Marx, "are in every epoch the ruling ideas."[3] The lower class, which

---

3 Marx, *German Ideology*, in Robert Tucker (1978: 172).

is controlled by the ruling class, actually labors, producing goods and services for society. The suspicion, then, is that, traditionally, theology has in fact usually sided with the ruling class, thereby sanctioning its oppressive ideology. In order to rectify this situation, liberation theologians look to the experience of the oppressed as a source of insight for their theology.[4] Hence, theology follows praxis as the "second act." The growth of the Base Ecclesial Communities is a logical development of this shift of focus in liberation theology.

What, then, of the method of interpretation? For this I select Segundo's "Hermeneutic Circle" for our consideration here. The "fundamental difference," he says, "between the traditional academic theologian and the liberation theologian is that the latter feels compelled at every step to combine the disciplines that open up the *past* with the disciplines that help to explain the *present*." (1975: 7–39; italics mine) For Segundo, the liberation theologian is in search of an ideology to critique the underlying ideologies of academic theologies, which somehow "hold the naive belief that the word of God is applied to human realities inside some antiseptic laboratory that is totally immune to the ideological tendencies and struggles of the present day."

The "hermeneutic circle," for Segundo, therefore, is based on two preconditions: questions about our situations and a new interpretation of the Bible. These two preconditions are further comprised of "four decisive factors": (1) our experience which leads to ideological suspicion; (2) application of that ideological suspicion to theology and to the whole ideological superstructure; (3) exegetical suspicion; and (4) a new way of interpreting Scripture. But what Segundo does not seem to take into account adequately enough, at least not immediately within his discussion of the hermeneutic circle, is that both our experience and Scripture—which, for him, is "the fountainhead of our faith"—are shaped by certain cultural assumptions. That is, both suspicion and a new interpretation are pre-determined to a certain extent. Questions about the socio-economic conditions of our reality, for example, are also culturally conditioned. This, of course, does not mean that the issues of hunger and poverty are not problems for peoples in some cultures. However, how we diagnose such problems may be different from culture to culture, for

---

4  On this particular point, however, Gutierrez is more "dialectical," perhaps ambiguous too. At times he speaks of the experience of the oppressed as the "starting point" in theology. At other times, however, he says that "Jesus Christ is the "starting point" and the "point of departure." See his book, for example, *The Power of the Poor in History* (1984), pages 4, 13, 15, etc.

there is no one objective analysis which will suffice for us all. We cannot expect a common solution if our diagnoses of the problems are different.

The Latin American liberation theologians have made an enormous contribution in their identification of theology as a "second act" which follows practical commitment, and by their emphasis on social/contextual analysis. However, by privileging "Christ" and "Scripture" as they do in their methodology, they do not go as far as Suun in relativising classic texts, nor as far as Minjung theology in implicitly relativising Jesus Christ.

**Feminist/Womanist Theologies.** In this section, I shall identify some of the major methodological points of leading feminists/womanists in North America, such as Rosemary Radford Reuther, Elizabeth Schussler Fiorenza, and Delores S. Williams. Again, there exists a wide spectrum of feminist theologies, and we have to be very selective here to make our methodological point.

The most conspicuous aspect of the feminist challenge to theology, which is consistent with other liberation theologies, may be found in its effort to validate the experience of the oppressed, especially of women. At the heart of the problem of human oppression lies the "dualism" of patriarchy. Hence, for Ruether, patriarchy is an encompassing notion of oppression. The underlying principle is that whatever denies the full humanity of women is not redemptive. (1985: 18–19) That is, the hermeneutical key in understanding biblical passages is centered not on metaphysical truth claims but on the ability to "pass" the test on the basis of that principle. Thus, the idea of "canon within the canon" becomes a useful notion for Ruether. The premise here is that there are liberative elements within the biblical Christian tradition.

Fiorenza, however, criticizes Ruether as "neo-orthodox" for not going far enough in recognizing the male-dominated context of the world of the Bible itself. When the Bible is written in such a patriarchal climate, the method of "pick-and-choose" is not good enough, for, according to feminist theory, "the way we frame our texts and choose our rhetorical strategies raises issues of power that need to be made explicit." (1993: 334) Feminist theology should be a critical theology,[5] making explicit the basic cultural power-structure of the Church and the society at large. The locus of divine revelation, then, is neither the Church nor

---

5 Fiorenza acknowledges her indebtedness to the critical theory developed by the Frankfurt school, especially by Jurgen Habermas.

the Christian tradition as a whole but the *ekklesia* of women. The following statement is worth quoting:

> Moreover, historical-critical studies and hermeneutical theological reflection have shown that not only theology but also the revelation of God in Scripture is expressed in human language and shares culturally conditioned concepts and problems... This hermeneutical insight is far-reaching when we consider that Scripture as well as theology are rooted in a patriarchal-sexist culture and share its biases and prejudices. (1993: 61–62)

Among all the culturally biased issues, argues Fiorenza, "the 'maleness' and 'sexism' of theology is much more pervasive than the race and class issue." (1993: 64)

However, not all women theologians agree with her on this point. A group of black women, called "womanists," part ways with white feminists. The term "womanist" was first used by Alice Walker in her book, *In Search of Our Mothers' Gardens: Womanist Prose*, where she defines it as a woman who "loves other women...and prefers women's culture, ... Loves struggle. *Loves* the Spirit. Loves herself. *Regardless*. Womanist is to feminist as purple is to lavender."[6] One important factor which distinguishes womanists from other feminists is the consideration of the history of slavery and the experience of racism. Unlike the feminist movement in general, therefore, womanists maintain a strong identification with their male counterparts. Like feminists, for whom the experience of sexism is an important source for theology, womanists value their experiences of sexism and racism as authoritative sources for their theology.

Recognizing that the present social structure clearly exhibits the interconnection between race and class, Williams is also attentive to "folk culture"—developed by Alice Walker—as a source of theology. The interesting aspect of Williams (and Walker) is the recognition of the oppressed "culture" within the dominant culture. In this sense, womanist theology exhibits continuity with American Black theology in general and certain theological developments in Africa in the insistence on their own culture. Again, we find basic structural similarities between Suun's and Minjung methods, on the one hand, and feminist/womanist theologies, on the other, especially the more radical forms of the latter.

---

6   Walker, p. xii; source from Linda Hogan (1995: 122).

## Chapter Five

**African Theologies.** When we shift our attention away from the Euro-American continents to the continents of Africa and Asia, the context changes dramatically. Here we can only glimpse African theologies for the sake of seeing their similarity and difference from Asian theologies. Africa "appears essentially as a land of domination and exploitation, quartered, torn apart, divided, atomized, trampled underfoot."[7] Domination has been so anthropologically thorough that tracing Africa's cultural heritage has become an extremely difficult task. The lack of resources has also been a cause of the "poor quality and lack of vision in creating alternatives."[8] Some theologians describe it as an "anthropological poverty." Independence from colonialism has not helped much. The "greatest tragedy of Africa" is that more than "twenty-five years after colonial times, most African countries have recovered neither their languages, their history, their art, nor the huge wealth of their spiritual heritage."[9] In this context, no amount of socio-economic-racial-gender analysis is adequate for an authentic African theology. How, then, can Africans profess their faith in God in a liberative way? How can they have theological certainty? What are appropriate sources of theology in Africa?

Authentic faith in Africa is said to begin by making connections with the traditional ethos of African people. The African lack of resources, the result of the exploitation of the continent, has been a major influence on theology for some theologians. The glimpse of hope is that, even after such enormous oppression, there is a culture "which refuses to die." It is "the foundation of our identity, our historical path to salvation, and the best African vehicle for the gospel."[10] The identity of Africans also includes their religious heritage. John Mbiti wants to replace the term "only" with "also" in discourses about God's self-revelation. For example, God's self-revelation occurred *also* "in the line of Abraham, Isaac, Jacob, Moses, Samuel and other personalities of the Bible." Finding the term *also*, in this case, for Mbiti, was "extremely liberating." (1986: 200–1) The God who is *also* revealed in the Bible has never been absent in the history of African peoples. Hence, asserts Mbiti, Christian missionaries did not bring God to Africa; it is the same God who brought them to that continent. Given such a view, an inevitable charge against

---

7 "African Report," in K.C. Abraham, ed. (1990: 28).
8 Mercy Amba Oduyoye (1990: 245–6).
9 "African Report," p. 35.
10 "African Report," pp. 43–44.

African theology (and against most Third World theologies) is the "danger of syncretism." However, for African theologians,

> what is called, in different contexts, "Christian tradition," is exactly the same experience carried on in communion with our ancestors in faith. The Christian tradition is neither closed, nor achieved, nor fixed. It is continuously in the making, and through it the gospel becomes historically incarnated in a people. From its sources flow any theological elaboration which is an articulation of the lived experience of the faith of the people of God, hic et nunc.[11]

These theologians continue to argue that myth and symbol are properly cultural language, and the truth of God is something no culture could exhaust, or imprison, or monopolize. Hence sharing the myths and symbols of African traditional worldviews with the rest of the world would be an African contribution to make.

The voices of the African theologians are clear: they are vehemently opposed to the theological/methodological hegemony of the West. Engelbert Mveng writes:

> For example, a vocabulary—a discourse—is now formed that seeks to impose itself upon the Third World. Methodologies and systems of analysis are proclaimed that are said to be "universal." Appeal is made to humane sciences, to structuralism, and to the new exegesis, in order to "teach" us, everlasting school children that we are. All these things are fine, of course—for *their* schools. The only problem with them is they contribute nothing to the solution of *our* problems. We have not gone that far. That is, we have gone much farther than that. (1983: 219; Mveng's italics)

The implication of this is the importance of contextuality and praxis in theology. Theology should be done by those who "have their feet firmly planted on this earth even when they claim to be standing in the council of God." (Mveng: 146)

Generally, in African theologies, there seems to be more emphasis on Jesus the Christ and Scripture than in Minjung theology. For Emmanuel Martey (1993: 55), inculturation and liberation must be considered together. "Africanization" (i.e., "indigenizing in the sense of replacing the Western cultural incidents with African cultural elements"), he says, and "liberation" (which sets "Africa's political and economic struggle within theological contexts and therefore emphasizes the sociopolitical and economic realities of the continent") then can be

---

11   "African Report," p. 50.

described as hermeneutic procedures that seek both *understanding* of the African cultural-political reality and *interpretation* of this reality in the light of the gospel stories, so as to bring about *transformation* of the oppressive status quo. Nevertheless, the hermeneutical approach of African theologians, like Martey, is still closer to Segundo's "Hermeneutic Circle" than, for example, Suh Nam-dong's "Confluence of the Two Stories."

**Asian Theologies.** Though Christianity is a small minority in most parts of Asia, which has many profoundly different contexts, it is possible to make some broad generalizations about method in Asian theologies to see the relevance of Suun and of Minjung theology for their further development. Since we are very limited in space here, one Asian theologian, Aloysius Pieris of Sri Lanka, may be taken as a representative of Asian theologies outside Korea. Again, we find the paramount importance of culture, praxis, and context for theological method.

Aloysius Pieris is critical of the "dialectical fame" of the two Western Karls:

> Marx's dialectical materialism set religion against *revolution*; Barth's dialectical theology opposed it to *revelation*. In their systems, religion was a major obstacle to liberation and salvation, respectively. (1988: 91)

The reductionism of these two Karls, for Pieris, is continued in the "liberation" theologies. The influence of the former is shown in the model of "liberation against religion," and that of the latter in that of "Christ against religion."

Although such reductionism is checked by the "inculturationists," in Asia, for Pieris, the debate between "liberationists" and "inculturationists" is "futile." Liberation and inculturation in Asia are the two sides of the same coin. For Pieris, the contribution of the Latin American liberationists to theology cannot be exaggerated; what the European theologians have achieved through their dialogue with contemporary philosophies until the 1960's is "only a mild reform compared with the achievements of Latin Americans from the 1960s onward."(1988: 82) One important epistemological shift the liberationists made in theology is that they grounded it on theopraxis. "What was formerly revolving around a Kantian orbit," says Pieris, "was made to rotate around a

Marxian axis." Latin American liberation theology, in this sense, is more a new theological methodology than a new theology. (1988: 82)

Theology in Asia, argues Pieris, is "a discovery rather than an invention," much less an importation. It can be seen "as a Christian participation in and a christic explicitation of all that happens at the deepest zone of a concrete ethos where religiousness and poverty, each in its liberative dimension, coalesce to forge a common front against mammon."(1988: 88) Doing theology in Asia is, therefore, the discovery of the ever-present liberative religious/cultural ethos of Asia. Where, then, do we discover this ethos?

The locus of theology in Asia, according to Pieris, is to be found not among Christians in the midst of non-Christians, but among "God's own people living beyond the church." For Pieris, the praxis of God-experience in Asia is none other than the non-Christian experience of liberation. What, then, does the church become? The church in Asia, Pieris contends, must lose itself "in total participation," being "humble enough to be baptized in the Jordan of Asian religion and bold enough to be baptized on the cross of Asian poverty."(1988: 85) The cultural context of Asian traditional religions is a locus for the Latin American theme of liberation to be discovered.

Social analysis in Asia, however, must be complemented by religious analysis. Asia boasts diverse cultures, many of which maintain religious plurality. This plurality also includes the possibility of diverse views within the same religion. Buddha's simile of the blind and elephant shows such possibility well: one day, when asked of the truth, Buddha said that it is like the blind touching different parts of an elephant. Though the same element, each describes differently how an elephant must look like.[12]

This simile depicts both the finitude of human knowledge, and the possibility, or rather the necessity, of different opinions. This is a typical pluralism in Asia. How, then, can we guard ourselves against the danger of relativism? For not all views are equally good. Neo-nazism, for example, should not be considered as good as other contemporary political ideologies. What are the theological criteria for this judgment?

---

12  This story appears in *Udana* (69f), a collection of eighty stories in eight Vaggas. As this well known story traveled throughout Asia, it produced some variations as to the details of the blindmen's touching and their descriptions. But the main thrust of the message is clear: Each description is accurate—but only partially.

Reason alone is inadequate to find this criterion for theological certainty. As liberation theologians rightly argue, reason must be guided by experience—not the opposite! In the discussion of oppression, for example, those who experienced oppression are better able to describe oppression than those who did not. For example, during the Japanese occupation of Korea in the first half of the century, the early missionaries in Korea declared that it was not desirable for Koreans to seek liberation. Was it that the missionaries enjoyed seeing the enormous oppression Korean people were going through? I do not think so. Did they not know, then, that Korean people were being oppressed at all? This too I do not hold. However, one thing is said to be clear: the vested interest of the missionaries was the success of their mission, and they found the right moment for their objective. For they believed that such social crisis can be an aid to their mission: in times of oppression, the disillusioned people turn to religious messages to find refuge. This they did. The period of Japanese occupation in Korea witnessed one of the most rapid periods of growth in church membership in the history of the Christian mission. The theological certainty of the missionaries, however, did not meet the needs of the context in which they preached. The missionaries did not *know* something essential about human reality: the experience of oppression.

What is the most appropriate tool for the oppressed to use in describing their oppression? As mentioned above, Minjung theologians find storytelling the most effective and powerful medium of expression. The stories of Asian women, as Chung H. K. argues, are "embodied truth" because their *bodies know*.(1990: 104) For this reason, their bodies' acquaintance with the reality of the oppressed has been the precondition for a minjung perspective for urban mission workers in Korea. The result of such acquaintance is, in the words of Suh Kwang-sun David, a "somatic incarnational experience." Suh writes:

> Anyone who wished to work in Industrial Mission had to become a laborer for six months to a year so that there would be a somatic identification with the life of the worker. Without such involvement the missioner could not share in the emotional and perceptual experiences of the workers—their fatigue, pain, and anger. (1983: 38).

What began as a traditional type of evangelism in the 1960s, turned into an activism, this time by Koreans, taking up the issues that affect the life of the laborers in the 1970s. What happened to the "certainty" of the gospel message the mission workers possessed only a decade or so ago?

Had the salvation message of Jesus of Nazareth lost its power to save these workers? Either the original certainty of the missioners was no longer there, or it seemed irrelevant to the context after their participation in hard labour. Their experiences led them to realize that, in the words of Kim Yong-Bock, "the 'pre-packaged gospel' could not be communicated to the people."(1992: 4) A profound adjustment had to be made from preaching the Jesus of the Bible to "finding the body of Jesus Christ among the workers themselves." The new conviction incarnated among the missioners is that there is reality which is properly theological, and which is known only to the oppressed. Such realization calls for a new christology which is both relevant and radical at the same time.

According to Pieris, there are two christological perspectives in Asia today: "return to Jesus," and "the new Asian formula." Both approaches are centered around the notion of "baptism." The former approach, according to Pieris, stresses the life of Jesus, who sided with the "*politically dangerous* brand of *prophetic asceticism* practiced by John the Baptizer."(1988: 63) From the moment of Jesus' own vocational discernment at the Jordan, which Pieris calls "his first prophetic gesture," to Jesus' last such gesture on Calvary, Jesus clearly showed where he stood. Both Jordan and Calvary, Pieris notes, are designated as points of "baptism" in the Gospels. Through Jesus' full immersion into the "opted poverty," he became the "victim-judge." In Asia, argues Pieris, the event of Jesus is, "preeminently, the trajectory that *today* links the Jordan of Asian religions with the Calvary of Asian poverty."(1988: 63) When this happens, states Pieris confidently, the "Asian cultures will open their repertoire of titles, symbols, and formulas" for Jesus such as those used by the early Christians, namely, "Christ," "Son of God" and "Lord." For Pieris, there is no Christ for Asians outside of the religio-cultural tradition of Asia.

We have thus far seen that the experience of the oppressed is basic for theological activity, and a fundamental criterion for discernment, in the liberation theologies. Now let us note the significance of Suun's thought, and that of its heir, Minjung theology, for the issue of interreligious dialogue. We shall see that here, too, experience, culture, and context are primary for theological thought.

## Suun and Paul Knitter: a Dialogue

The American pluralist theologian Paul Knitter has been engaged in dialogue with various groups with a desire to listen to the voices of the "religious Other" and of the "suffering Other." Knitter says,

> [s]o people and events in my life have led me, sometimes lured me, to what has become for me a moral obligation to join "pluralism and liberation" or "dialogue and global responsibility." ... I have to speak with and learn from both the voice of the religious Other and of the suffering Other. (1995: 11).

Thus, the two "Others" have profoundly influenced Knitter in shaping his theology.

**The "Religious Other."** The first encounter which changed Knitter's theological outlook was that with the "religious Other." Knitter has been engaged in dialogue with various religious traditions of the world with the conviction that global peace would not come without harmonious co-existence among peoples of different religious beliefs. After his dialogue with many people in other religious traditions, he came to the realization that Christian traditional absolutist claims no longer serve their purpose of conveying the gospel message in today's pluralistic society. Hence, Knitter began to challenge Christians to cross the "theological Rubicon." By this he means that the traditional christocentric absolutism must now be abandoned in view of establishing global peace. The first move Christians are encouraged to make, therefore, is from either exclusivism or inclusivism to pluralism.[13] What is entailed here is that one's theological orientation is to possess a "non-normative, *theocentric*" (1985) approach rather than christocentric or ecclesiocentric ones. It is precisely the actual experience of the "religious other" in his or her religio-cultural context, and the "praxis" of dialogue which is methodologically primary.

**The "Suffering Other."** The second encounter which has altered Knitter's theological outlook was that with the "suffering Other."[14] For

---

13 Knitter follows the classification made by Alan Race (1983), *Christians and Religious Pluralism*.
14 In his book (1995), *One Earth Many Religions*, he extends his theological scope to ecological consciousness by including the ecologically suffering Earth in his term "suffering Other."

him, the challenge of (Latin American) Liberation theology should not be ignored. The widening gap between the rich First World and the poor Third World, the exploitation of the poor by the rich, and various oppressions, are devastatingly clear. Thus, the second move Christians are challenged to make is to shift their attention from the rich and powerful to the poor and the suffering. As an American middle class white male, Knitter calls them the "suffering Other." In dialogue, those on the underside of history have the "hermeneutical privilege" in searching for the true and the good.(1995: 91) Knitter concurs with liberationists like Gregory Baum, who says that liberation is the precondition for dialogue and mutual understanding.

What theological criterion can a pluralist seeking liberation have? Did Knitter not say that there should not be an absolute criterion in dialogue? The criterion Knitter wants to maintain is "eco-human justice," which is not absolute nor relative but a *"relative absolute criterion."* He proposes to be assertive in seeking eco-human justice without being aggressive or dominating. Hence, the second major proposal Knitter made recently, after his "non-normative *theocentric*" approach is a "multi-normative, *soteriocentric*" approach.(1995) In the midst of conflicting truth claims among different religions and ideologies, Knitter is cautious in selecting words to be "globally responsible." Hence, he "prefer[s] the term 'relational' rather than 'complementary' or 'inclusive uniqueness'" of Jesus, and of Christian truth claims. (1996: 81–82)

**Critics of Knitter.** Among the many voices of, in Knitter's term, the "large chorus" of the critics of the pluralist model for interreligious dialogue, Knitter takes the "song" of the so-called postmodernists seriously. These critics rightly claim that we human beings are all contextually shaped, and, accordingly, our knowledge and experience are thus historically filtered. It seems that there are as many perspectives to arrive at this conclusion as there are "postmodernists." Whether we look at it from the perspective that we are "thrown" into our historical situation (Heidegger) or that our knowledge is the construct of our "language game" (Wittgenstein), "postmodernists" argue, we must realize that our views are conditioned by our own historical/cultural/linguistic lens. How, then, they ask, can anyone insist that there can be a common ground in which all cultures and religions can meet for dialogue? For these critics pluralists like Knitter are but self-appointed judges. Thus, they warn, any attempt to draw guidelines or rules for dialogue will turn out to be "anonymous imperialism." The concern for "justice," for example, is not equally shared by all religions (Cobb).

Knitter concurs with his critics that no attempt should be made for quick and easy methods or guidelines for dialogue. This, however, for Knitter, should not mean that we all become religious agnostics. Such solipsism would be theological anathema. Another anathema, for him, is to participate in dialogue with a certain hidden agenda, which he detects from both exclusivists and inclusivists who claim to possess the "absolute truth." Dialogue is not monologue (Lochhead); no dialogue is genuine if either party has a preconceived "final answer" or hidden agenda to win the other over to his/her own side. What many, including the above "postmodernist," critics often forget is that most wars in human history were religiously motivated; if the religious slogans for the wars were politics in disguise, at least, they were religiously disguised. That is, dialogue is no longer an option when one realizes that no one tradition can provide complete solutions for all cultures and peoples. Raimon Panikkar is to the point when he says:

> We can no longer say "that's your problem!" Hinduism will not survive if it does not face modernity. Christianity will disappear if it does not meet Marxism. Technocratic religion will destroy itself if it does not pay heed to, say, the Amerindian tradition, and so on. (1995: 175)

The concern here is clear: without dialogue there is no future for humanity.

**Suun and Knitter: a Comparison.** In my opinion, Suun's theology exhibits a comparable passion for liberation through dialogue implicit in the "relative absolute criterion" of Knitter. The difference between Suun and Knitter is that, unlike the latter, for whom dialogue with the "religious Other" is a theological responsibility for those who have been conditioned by mono-religious cultures, for the former, the "others" for dialogue are not competing religions but the cultural and philosophical mentors of the past whose teachings have been the very fabric of being and meaning of his time. Suun's mentors themselves lived in and dealt with inherently pluralistic cultures. The advance of Christianity in Korea, therefore, was itself not so much a threat. On the contrary, it could simply have been welcomed as a new addition, except, of course, by those few ruling elite who were preoccupied with the maintenance of the state-ideology (Neo-Confucianism). The real threat, for Suun, was the powerlessness of the traditional religions of Asia in the face of the military and political assault of the Western nations armored with this "foreign doctrine" (Christianity). At least, the pluralistic situation has not been a threatening factor for peoples in most part of Asia.

In this connection, I argue, some of the concerns the critics raise to Knitter and to other "pluralists" stem from their traditionally mono-religious context. Some critics, for example, warn of the danger of a subtle imperialism under the guise of "pluralism."

The context in which Suun was shaped leaves no room for any doubt about pluralism. Peoples in East Asia have freely drawn upon their favorite classics for ethical/spiritual insights. In China, for example, the two religious/philosophical traditions, Confucianism and Taoism, were maintained by groups of people called *yuga* 儒家 and *doga* 道家, followers of the two traditions, respectively. That one belonged to any one of those traditions, however, did not mean that one ought to make a wholesale rejection of the other. Even though there were some who were more dogmatically inclined than others, the overall spiritual culture was still very much pluralistic and syncretic.[15] Hence, those who belonged to one were not shut to the other tradition, and vice versa.

What is significant about Suun is that he was not so much interested in faithful maintenance of one or another tradition. At the center of his religious quest was his concern for the oppressed people (the "suffering Other"); at the center of his life as a minjung was the quest for connection with the rich spiritual resources of the past (the "religious Other"). Suun, again, sought a past that was useful for the present.

## "Ghandian Liberation Theology"

This section is a comparative glance at the Gandhian liberation theology attempted by Ignatius Jesudasan(1984) and Antony Kozhuvanal (1987) and the Donghak theology—my own designation of the theology implicit in the thought of Suun as demonstrated in this book.[16] The

---

15   I cannot help feeling uneasy about using this term, "syncretism," in Asian cultural context. It seems clear to me that this term is more appropriate in a traditionally mono-religious context, such as that of the West, where the question of orthodoxy was indeed a life-or-death matter. However, if one can treat this term, syncretism, without its pejorative ideological/theological baggage, it is still useful for describing certain religious phenomena.

16   I want to make it clear that my insistence on proper contextualization in Korea

obvious similarity between the former and my own is that both are attempting to construct a Christian liberation theology on the basis of other religious thoughts. In dealing with other religions Christians have attempted to formulate various approaches for constructive dialogue.

For Gandhi the transformation of the Indian society was to be accomplished through the reformation of Hinduism. There have been persistent tensions in Hinduism, as in other religions, between other-worldly and this-worldly tendencies. The former resulted in the life-style of ascetic denial of the world for individual liberation and the latter in concerns for the maintenance and the welfare of society at large. Throughout the history of Hinduism, various attempts have been made either to emphasize the importance of one over the other or to bridge the gap between the two.

According to David R. Kinsley (1982), due to the increasing contact with the West, there have been some important developments in the Hindu tradition in the modern period (1800 to the Present). One such development, Kinsley explains, is the Independence movement of the nineteenth and twentieth centuries. The tension between other-worldly and this-worldly tendencies is clear in the movement.[17] The peculiar aspect of Gandhi is that he combined the two in his struggle against the foreign domination. He became an ascetic for the society; "he wore little clothing and lived on a very restricted diet" not simply for personal *moksha*, liberation, but for national *swaraj*, independence.

**A Gandhian Theology of Liberation.** For Jesudasan, *Swaraj* is a key term in understanding Gandhi's way of liberation theology. According to Jesudasan, the term *Swaraj* was favoured by Gandhi because of its wide usage among the native people in India. Unlike some English terms such

---

should not be confused as reading Christianity into Donghak. While the latter can be viewed as an inspiration and impetus of indigenous spirituality for Christians and Buddhists alike, the distinct integrity of Donghak as a religion must be recognized as such.

17 Kinsley compares the major themes of the "two most famous leaders": Bal Gangadhar Tilak (1856–1920) and Mohandas Karamchand Gandhi (1869–1948). While they both "took the *Bhagavad Gita* and its teachings concerning *loka-samgraha*, supporting the world, as central to their positions, and both were considered *karma-yogis*, masters of disciplined action," they "differed considerably" in their styles. Kinsley describes Tilak as a militant leader, who wanted no compromise, for whom violence was permitted in a just cause. Gandhi, however, "chose to read the *Gita* as a nonviolent text and refused to permit violence in his various political campaigns..." (1982: 22)

as "independence," "freedom," and "liberation," which carried Western connotations, and, hence, did not touch the minds and hearts of Indian people, *swaraj*, Jesudasan explains, suited the socio-religious context of India as Gandhi saw it. For *swaraj* includes the meanings of those English terms as well as the religious connotation of "salvation" of *moksha*, a key term in Hindu spirituality. Although both are holistic terms, encompassing all aspects of life, the difference between *swaraj* and *moksha* is that the former carries more political implications than the latter. Hence, says Jesudasan, "that Gandhi's theology is actualized in political terms accounts for the fact that he chose to focus specifically on *swaraj* rather than *moksha*. Thus the choice of *swaraj* over against *moksha* is as significant in Gandhi's theology as is the choice of "liberation" over against "salvation" in the post-Medellin theology of Latin America."(1984: 48) For this reason, for Jesudasan, Gandhi's is a political theology.

***Satyagraha.*** If *swaraj* is Gandhi's central notion of liberation, Jesudasan argues, *satyagraha* is his method, a "theo-political theory of action" for achieving *swaraj*. *Satyagraha*, explains Kinsley, which literally means "seizing the truth," came "to characterize all Gandhi's later campaigns and was a powerful blend of fearlessness, truthfulness, and non-violent resistance to laws that Gandhi thought oppressed his fellow Indians." (1982: 98) Hence *Satyagraha* was both the faith of Gandhi at work and a means to God-realization, or the perfection of incarnation. In such God-realization the personal and the collective are not two separate paths to truth, for the search for truth evolves one's own will from within as well as one's desire to actualize it from without. There are both personal and social dimensions to such notions as sin, righteousness, vice, and virtue. Through numerous incarnations in human history, human beings are constantly informed of the right paths to truth. In this sense, salvation can never be *a*political or *a*social. What is personal is always social, and vice versa. Gandhi made an arduous attempt to show that a holistic life is the way of religious life. How, then, did Gandhi resolve the problem of oppression, which was clearly sinful and anti-religious? In order for subjugated people to achieve their liberation, should they use all possible means available to them, including violence, which is itself also anti-religious? For this reason, Gandhi "advocated the dual paths of non-violence and non-attachment."(1984: 73) For Gandhi, God-realization was liberative and non-violent. That is, the quest for truth involved the resistance to oppression and to violence. Nor should one surrender before the insurmountable force of evil in the world; pessimism is also anti-religious. Thus, one possible way to avoid these anti-religious attitudes is noncooperation with any of the oppressive, violent, and escapist forces. Noncooperation, in this sense, is not passive; rather, it is an active and aggressive resistance. It was, for Gandhi, "the only alternative to an armed rebellion."(1984: 75) How about the human limitation of those who are engaged in the struggle for freedom? Would they not turn aggressors themselves once their nation became free from foreign domination? How would Gandhi resolve this problem?

One of the basic tenets of Hinduism is its insistence on detachment from all kinds of obsession, greed and anxiety. Gandhi saw non-attachment as a way to solve the problem of the ever-recurrent evil of power-abuse. The revolutionary must refuse to cling to any desire to be powerful, without submitting to the external power. Hence, s/he must continue to resist both the evil outside her/himself (subjugation; power-abuse by others) and that within her/himself (desire to cling to power; power-abuse by self). The latter evil can often lead to dictatorship. Non-attachment, therefore, is an effective way to fight against both evils. One should continue one's quest for God-realization by resisting evil without the desire to enjoy the fruit of one's own labor.

**"Different Paths" and the Untouchability.** One of the most serious problems in India, which Gandhi recognized as a religious problem was the existence of the untouchables. The philosophical rationale behind the social caste system is the Hindu idea of *karma*, the law of cause and effect which governs personal destiny in the life to come in an endless chain of rebirths called *samsara*. Thus one is to strive to attain liberation, which is called *moksha*, from such endless rebirths through proper paths to truth.

According to Hinduism, the different paths to truth are based on the stages of life, which are generally divided in terms of age. There are four such stages: student, householder, spiritual seeker, and spiritual/holy wanderer. The ideal life is one which faithfully follows these stages. In youth, one's basic obligation is to learn how to lead one's life properly within one's own tradition. When married, one is to fulfill one's duty in the family and in the society. By the time one becomes a grandparent, one leaves one's family and social duty to the next generation, and begins to live a contemplative life in search of spiritual meaning. Then in the final stage, one is to live as a wanderer begging food and striving to attain the knowledge to terminate the endless chain of rebirths. The renunciation of the world, therefore, is how one is to end one's life.

Another aspect of Hinduism in relation to the social caste system is its emphasis on the personal aptitude according to which one is to practice *yoga*. It is said that there are, generally, four different aptitudes among people: the contemplative *(raja)* philosophical *(jhana)*, the devotional *(bhakti)*, and the work or action-oriented *(karma)*. What is ideal is that one find whichever of these one is most suited to and follow the spiritual practice *(yoga)* accordingly.

What is implicit in this philosophy is the possibility of social harmony. If only each person can function properly according to his/her aptitude in his/her station of life, the society as a whole will be harmonious. The problem, however, is that this otherwise ideal philosophy has brought about the present social caste system in which people's caste is decided at birth, and not by the station of their life or by their aptitudes, as it was originally meant to be. The most serious problem, among others, for Gandhi, was the existence of the untouchables. For him, again, this was a religious problem. However, Gandhi did not solve the problem by denouncing the indigenous religion, Hinduism, or by taking recourse to foreign religious ideas. On the contrary, he attempted to solve it by reforming the Hinduism from within which gave rise to the social caste system.

**The Significance of Gandhi in Theology.** Unlike Jesudasan, who focuses on Gahdhi's social and political thought in constructing a liberation theology, Kozhuvanal emphasizes Gandhi's method for his theology. Kozhuvanal himself contrasts his own approach to that of Jesudasan:

> Gandhi's significance for Catholic liberation theology in India could be studied from the point of view of his theology and from that of his method. Jesudasan's study of Gandhi is from the perspective of his theology... [However,] our thesis will maintain that in order to develop a relevant and authentically Indian liberation theology, the Indian [Christian] Church may adopt the Gandhian method and benefit from it. (1987: xi-xii)

Kozhuvanal is conscious that a liberation theology should be praxis-oriented. For him, Gandhi is important because of the way he lived rather than because of the way he philosophized. The issue here is between how to think and how to act. In order for us to be more consistent with Gandhi, and with the holistic Hindu tradition as a whole, however, one wonders whether such a distinction is a useful exercise. Perhaps, what Kozhuvanal wants to argue is the importance of actual participation with the oppressed in their struggle for liberation. For him, Gandhi did just that. That Gandhi took the concrete life situation of the oppressed seriously is shown by his notion of "God-realization." We will see now how Kozhuvanal interprets this notion of Gandhi differently from the way Jesudasan views it.

**God-Realization.** For Kozhuvanal, Gandhi's search for God-realization is thoroughly praxis-oriented. Gandhi did not take recourse to anything else but the oppressed part of humanity to meet God. Kozhuvanal quotes Gandhi: "If I could persuade myself that I find Him in the Himalayan cave, I would proceed there immediately. But I know that I cannot find Him apart from humanity."(1987: 92) Moreover, Kozhuvanal continues, "he (Gandhi) stated that God appeared to him in many forms but was most evident in the poor, the oppressed, the frightened, the untouchable." (1987: 92) Herein lies the most striking similarity between Gandhi and Suun, the founder of Donghak. That is, for Gandhi, Kozhuvanal says, "the secularization of religion involves a consecration of the profane; and the service of humanity becomes the place of encounter between God and man."(1987: 92) For Suun, too, humanity was where the Ultimate resided. In fact this has been a general tendency among religious teachings of Asia; one is reminded of one of the most celebrated sayings of Confucious: "it is not the Tao/Dao that makes humans great but humans that make the Tao/Dao great." (*Analects*)

**"Discovered, Borrowed and Transformed."** How did Gandhi deal with the diverse and often contradictory nature of traditional religious scriptures? Kozhuvanal describes Gandhi's theology as highly eclectic. And the well-being of humanity was the criterion for Gandhi's eclectic activity. "His (Gandhi's) policy," Kozhuvanal says, "was... reject anything that was dehumanizing." (1987: 94)

As mentioned above, Hinduism has produced an oppressive structure in India in the social caste system and the existence of the untouchable. Gandhi, however, did not discard the tradition of Hinduism altogether as a degenerate form of religion. On the contrary, he attempted to solve the problem in an intra-traditional way: Kozhuvanal explains, he "discovered, borrowed and transformed" traditional resources available to him. That is, he sought liberative elements within the indigenous tradition itself. Through this eclectic activity, which Kozhuvanal calls "selective assimilation," Gandhi "reinterpreted traditions in such a way that revolutionary ideas, clothed in familiar expression, could be readily adopted and employed towards revolutionary ends."(1987: 98) Hence, Gandhi used some of the key concepts of Hinduism, such as *ahimsa, satya, moksha, tapas, satyagraha* and *swaraj*. It is noteworthy that all these terms are widely recognized as significant by the general populace in India. Gandhi used old and familiar ideas for the betterment of the present society. It seems that, for Gandhi, the past is at the service of the present. What is important is not the maintenance of certain doctrines of the past, but the transformation of the present situation of the oppressed people. Such transformation, however, was attempted by Gandhi within the tradition.

**Politics and Religion.** According to Kozhuvanal, for Gandhi, "politics is not merely a secular activity. When it is directed to the service of humanity it is a religious activity."(1987: 93) Kozhuvanal quotes Glyn Richards who describes Gandhi's view as a "realized eschatology." "The Kingdom of God," for Gandhi, Richards writes, "is here and now and is established through political activity in the service of humanity."[18] "Rather than making religion a tool for liberation struggle," Kozhuvanal says, "Gandhi declared that the struggle for liberation itself is religion, because that is the only means to God-realization." (1987: 97)

As shall be mentioned below, this thought of Gandhi is different from that of Suun, the founder of Donghak. For the latter religious transformation was the way of social transformation. What is similar to Gandhi in Suun is that such religious transformation was thoroughly "from below." We are now going to make some comparisons between Suun and Gandhi.

**Suun and Gandhi: A Comparison.** It is a general perception among scholars of Donghak that according to its philosophy, politics and religion are like the two wheels of a wagon; the two are distinguishable but not separable. Hence, the political realm of a society cannot be thought of separately from its religious aspect. As mentioned above, there is in Donghak's worldview a coincidence of ideology and ontology. The prescriptive feature of politics must be consistent with the way of Heaven. That is, the way things ought to be must be consistent with the way things are meant to be. Proper management of things (politics) is to

---

18  Richards, quoted by Kozhuvanal (1987: 93).

be undertaken in the light of a sincere search for the permanent truth (religion). Conversely, one should not be a solipsist; one's search for the truth is not to be done apart from human society. For Suun, Heaven (God) and the earth (human beings, especially the oppressed) are one. The immanent and the transcendent are inexorably bound together. Hence, for Suun, as for Gandhi, humanity is where God is to be found. All forms of degradation, therefore, are to be resisted, for they are defamatory to the very nature of God.

Thus far we have seen some of the salient points of Gandhi, especially aspects of his liberation theology as presented by Jesudasan and Kozhuvanal in relation to the thought of Suun, the founder of Donghak. I conclude this with some comparisons between Gandhi and Suun to see how a Donghak liberation theology is possible.

First, both Gandhi and Suun attempted to revive indigenous traditions; neither wanted to make his nation a Christian state. This is significant when we consider that Gandhi received his formal education in the West. His experience outside of India taught him the value of maintaining his own tradition. In the case of Suun, his contact with the Christian religion was indirect, through his fellow Korean Catholic converts. For this reason, Suun was more threatened by Christianity than Gandhi was.

Second, Gandhi was more politically active than Suun. That is, theologically, he was a more praxis-oriented liberation theologian than the latter. The activity of Suun must be viewed in light of the then Confucian feudalistic society of his time. The only possible way to protest against the government and change the society was an armed rebellion, which had been common even before his time. Even without such activities, Suun was executed by the central government for "agitating the public with impure thoughts." For him, the religious or the spiritual is what constitutes the most basic realm of humanity. Since Confucianism was the ideology of the ruling group, Suun's attempt to revitalize and reform the old traditions, including Confucianism, by introducing his own, was itself viewed as a dangerous political activity.

They both "discovered, borrowed and transformed" the traditional materials. They discarded anything that was not liberative. And their criterion for such eclectic activity was the situation of the oppressed people. They both were seriously engaged in (inter)religious dialogue "from below," i. e., from the perspective of the poor and the oppressed. The religious, in this sense, must have a direct implication in the political arena. The difference between Suun and Gandhi would be that, while

Gandhi plunged himself right into political activity, Suun attempted to do so by influencing the oppressed people to find their religious, and therefore political, meanings. For this reason, while in the case of the liberation theology of Gandhi, his ideas are important because of his activities, in the case of Donghak, Suun's activities are to be understood in the light of his thought. There is, here, a different emphasis between the two liberation theologies. This difference would largely be due to the difference in the socio-political as well as the historico-cultural settings of the two nations.

Third, both are seriously engaged in religious analysis. In Asia, again, religion is neither opium (Marx) nor unbelief (Barth).

## Donghak-Minjung Theology and "Oikoumene"

In this concluding section, I shall attempt to locate Donghak-Minjung theology in the context of the "Oikoumene" of the WCC. Since there is no theology that is *a*historical or *a*cultural, that is, if theology can only be local[19] or contextual,[20] then, we must start not from traditional doctrines but with and from the perspective of people, especially the oppressed, the "minjung." The main objective in the Christian ecumenical movement, then, should be unity of action rather than that of ideas. Perhaps these two kinds of unity usually go together, but the shift of emphasis makes a profound difference. Another related shift of emphasis urgently needed in theology is that from the past to the present. In this section I shall develop this contention in the following way: first, Konrad Raiser's observation of the transitions in the ecumenical movement of the World Council of Churches up to the end of the 1980s will be discussed in conjunction with Alan Race's (1983) classification of the attitude of Christians toward other religions; second, I shall then make my own statements as to what all this means for the way we do theology.

There is no need to elaborate on the idea that we all write from our own particular historico-cultural perspectives. "The time has come,"

---

19   R. Schreiter (1985). Schreiter argues that theology be local partly because *"old answers* were being urged upon cultures and regions with new questions." (p. 3)
20   Stephen B. Bevans (1992). Bevans says, "The contextualization of theology—the attempt to understand Christian faith in terms of a particular context—is really a theological imperative." (p. 1)

wrote Visser't Hooft in the 1960s, "when the 'multi-coloured' wisdom of God must express itself in new Asian and African expressions of Christian thought and life."(1963: 124) For as Charles Davis also argues, the "growing awareness that other men think and act differently is a factor making for openness and greater freedom." (1970: 14–15) Acquiring "openness and greater freedom," however, is no longer a mere option. Rather, as Paul Knitter insists, it has become a global responsibility.

**A Paradigm Shift in the Ecumenical Movement?** This subtitle is taken from that of Raiser's book (1991). Ecumenism, Raiser says, "is caught in a process of transition."(p. 123) For him the Church is faced with the new "challenges confronting the inherited frame of reference." In fact his book as a whole may be summed up in terms of the question, is our inherited paradigm adequate for the Church in dealing with the present global situation? Raiser believes that perhaps the time is ripe for a transition which may be described as a "paradigm shift."

The painful realization, Raiser notes, that the Church had to accept at the end of the Second World War was that the old idea of Christendom, i. e., of a "Christian world," no longer seemed suitable for the Church to maintain. Such naive and blind optimism would add greater confusion about the new direction in which the Church must now travel. At this time, therefore, there came about a new paradigm to resolve the problem, namely, a "christocentric universalism." An important notion, Raiser argues, that enabled the Church to adapt to this new awareness was historicity. The transition in the self-understanding of the Church in the first half of the twentieth century vis-à-vis its mission was from the spatial to the historical. Raiser says: "The 'Christian world' gave way to a vision which sought to understand the human condition from the perspective of the universal history of salvation."(1991: 35) The aggressively exclusivistic paradigm of the Christian mission has now been replaced by a somewhat more tolerant one. For Raiser the shift of paradigm, from the idea of the "Christian world" to the "christocentric universalism," served the Church well in the first half of the twentieth century.

However, the second half of this century has brought yet another challenge, perhaps this time with greater intensity, namely, the reality of the pluralistic nature of the global village. The very idea of "universal salvation" has now become problematic. Salvation from which viewpoint? The transition required of the Church by this challenge of pluralism has become much more serious and radical than that which the Church confronted in the first half of the century.

Hence the seriousness of the challenge of pluralism in the later part of this century has brought a real crisis to the Church. It has been a real threat to some, while it has become a step of growth for others. The shift from an inclusivistic faith to a pluralistic one is not a smooth transition, as well expressed by Paul Knitter, who calls it the "crossing of a theological Rubicon."

# Postscript

# Religious Synthesis and Being at the Present

As I proposed in the beginning, I have shown the development of Donghak as a spiritual root of contemporary Minjung theology. I have also discussed how these two minjung-centered religious formations can be understood within the global theological context. As I suggested above, the outcome of this study leads us to a heightened concern for contextuality and praxis, which, in turn, calls for certain shifts in our theological preoccupation.

The real shift, for me, however, is from the past to the present, or from the doctrines of the traditions to the present needs of the minjung. What does all this mean for current questions about the relationship between the gospel and culture and inter-religious dialogue?

As argued thus far, the two issues are closely related to each other, for in the case of pluralistic societies such as those of Asia, the culture in connection with which the gospel is discussed is itself pluralistic. That is, peoples in Asia already possess a pluralistic orientation. In discussions on religion, any religion, we cannot squeeze the people of the religion out and deal with the rest. As Wilfred Cantwell Smith insists, "religion"cannot be reified as though it has existence of its own apart from human society. Religion is an integral part of human culture. In dealing with the subject of religion, then, we are in fact dealing with the ways of life of certain people. If we do not realize this, we risk reductionism, reducing religion to historical documents, to the manner of organization and its rituals, or to whatever else that may appear as the predominant type of the religion in question. Hence, whether the issue is the theme of gospel and culture, or dialogue with other religions, we need to ask, what does all this mean to the peoples of the corresponding cultures and religions? Dialogue, then, becomes not a mere mental exercise but a challenge to the status quo, a movement for cultural transformation. Accordingly, instead of being an "exchange of ivory-towers," dialogue is brought down to the concrete historical situation of the peoples of the religions in question. This is where formulating criteria becomes particularly important. For what is entailed by such dialogue is serious business; it has direct consequences for people. What criteria are we seeking?

With respect to the subject of peoples and their religions, a perennial question has to do with the problem of suffering, and also therefore with human oppression. This has a bearing on both issues being discussed here. First, on the level of the subject of gospel and culture, the question can be posed as follows: How might the story from outside, the "gospel," help the people of a particular culture discern the good or the right story among the many stories of that culture, so that the unity of these two stories can become the Good News for the people there in their search for salvation/liberation? Again, whether a story coming from outside is good news or not is not for outsiders to say. There cannot be any *a priori* judgment about this. Conversely, the story coming from outside, the "gospel," is at the disposal of the local people, for the gospel is not "prepackaged" at one end to be unpacked at the other end (Kim Yong-bock). That is, the story must be interpreted from the perspective of the people and not from that of the storyteller, i. e., the missionary or the culture of the missionary. This must also happen in such a way that the storyteller him/herself can be affected by it. The storyteller will learn from his/her listeners how the story might be viewed differently. Mission-work, then, becomes an activity of cultural exchange for mutual transformation. For this to happen, both the story coming from outside and the culture to which it is brought must remain dynamic.

Second, on the level of dialogue with other religions, we must consider at least two questions: the first is, just what do we mean by the "other"? The second is, who is undertaking the dialogue? So far as the first question is concerned, again in traditionally pluralistic societies such as those of Asia, the "other" is not in fact other in the strict sense, for each culture has already been deeply shaped by multi-religious encounters. In this context, the inter-cultural activity in the case of the gospel and culture above becomes *intra*-cultural activity, which has in any case been taking place for a long time. Such activity has formed the matrix of the culture, the very texture of the body and soul of its people. Whether the coming of Christianity into Asian societies should radically alter the course of such a dialogical ethos is, again, not an *a priori* judgment to be made by outsiders.

The second question, i.e., that of who is undertaking the dialogue, can be answered by further asking, who is being affected? Again, I contend, dialogue must take place with particular people in mind. If all religions indeed represent in one way or another a quest for salvation/liberation, it is the people themselves who are the subjects of the dialogue and not objects to be preached to or to be indoctrinated. When I say "people" here I mean particular people, those who constitute the underside of history, in Korean terms, the "minjung." It is the minjung for whom, and, as much as possible, by whom, religious dialogue must be undertaken.

In conclusion, the paradigm shift Raiser has in mind, be it that from "christocentric universalism" to a kind of pluralism or something else, must be accompanied by yet another shift: from a doctrinal emphasis—as exemplified in "Christ-centred" theologies—to a minjung-centred,[1] or to use Knitter's term, to a soteriocentric theology. For the acceptance of religious pluralism alone is not enough: dialogue must be carried out in an historically concrete manner *hic et nunc*, i.e., "from below," to be salvific/liberative. Being faithful to the needs of the present moment was the beginning of the religious quest for Suun, the founder of Donghak. Thus, the real shift, for me, is from the past to the present, and from classic texts to context and praxis, in our theological preoccupation.

Thou shall be at the present moment, for it is the most decisive, religious moment!

---

[1] Recently, some Korean theologians have proposed "life-centred" theology to include ecological concerns. Although the move seems to be promising, the term "life" still needs to be refined. See, for example, Kim Chi-ha (1992), *Saeng Myông* [*Life*].

# Glossary of Names and Terms*

Analects: see Lun yü
Baeklyôn'gyo (白蓮教): White Lotus Sect
bon-gak (本覺): enlightenment a priori (Wonhyo)
Bôpshin (法身): Dharmakaya. Body of Buddha/Truth
bul-gak (不覺): non-enlightenment (Wonhyo)
*Bulssi Japbyôn* (佛氏雜辨): "Various Confusions of Buddhism"
Ch'an (禪): see Sôn
Chang Kil-san (張吉山, fl. 17th c.): A rebel leader who robbed the rulers to feed the poor. He is said to have led thousands people at the height of his influence.
Chang Tsai (Jang Jae, 張載 or Heng-ch'u 橫渠): 1020–1077
Ch'eng Brothers: Ch'eng Hao (Jông Ho, 程顥 or 程明道: 1032–1085) and Ch'eng I (Jông I, 程伊川: 1033–1107)
Ch'eng–Chu: School of Ch'eng I–Chu Hsi
Ch'ien Mu/Qian Mu (Jôn Mok, 錢穆)
Chiki (pron. "ji-gi," 至氣): Ultimate Reality (Suun)
Choe, Chi-won (崔致遠, 857–?): Pseudonym/penname is Goun (孤雲).
Choe, Je-U (崔濟愚, 1824–1864): Founder and the first leader of Donghak. Pseudonym is Suun (水雲).
Choe, Nam-sun (崔南善, 1890–1957): Pseudonym is Yukdang (六堂).

Choe, Shi-hyung (崔時亨, 1827–1898): The second leader of Donghak. Pseudonym is Haewol (海月).
chôn (天; in Chinese, t'ien/tian): H/heaven
chôndo (天道): heavenly way
Chondogyo (天道教): Donghak's later name, changed by Son Uiam, the third leader of the religion, in 1905
Chong, Do-jon: 鄭道傳, 1342–1398
Chong, Yak-yong (丁若鏞, 1762–1836): Scholar official during the Yi Dynasty in Korea. Pseudonym is Dasan. As a representative figure of the Silhak, Practical Learning, he espoused a reform movement, including the abolishment of the slave law and the equal distribution of land.
chôn-in-hap-il (天人合一; in Chinese, t'ien-jen-ho-yi/tian-ren-he-yi): unity of Heaven and human(ity)
Chônju (天主): literally, "the Sovereign of Heaven": Catholic rendering for "God"
Chou, Tun-i/Zhou Dunyi (Ju Don-i, 1017–1073): Pseudonym is Yômgye.
Chu Hsi/Zhu Xi (Ju Hûi, 朱熹): 1130–1200
chuan hsin (jôn shim: 傳心): transmission of the mind
Chuang Tzu/Zhuang Zi (Jangja, 壯子): Refers both to the man (Chuang Chou?) and the work attributed to him. 4th c. B.C.E.
Chung Yung/Zhongyong (Jungyong, 中庸): "Doctrine of the Mean" (James Legge); "Centrality and Commonality" (Tu Wei-ming)

---

* Korean pronunciations are given in parentheses for those names/terms written in Wade Giles or Pinyin system of Chinese.

Confucius (Gongja, 孔子): 551–479 B.C.E., in Chinese, K'ung Tzu/Gongzi, original name is 丘仲尼

Dae Jong Gyo (大宗敎): Indigenous religion of Korea established upon the authority of Dan'gun, the mythic founder of the nation.

Dan'gun (檀君): The mythic founder of Korea. According to Samguk Yusa, compied by the scholar monk Il Yôn (1206–1289), he is born between Hwan Ung and Ung Nyô, the bear-turned woman, and founds Korea in the year 2333 B.C.E.

Dôk (德): virtue or power; see te/de

Donghak (東學): literally, "Eastern Learning"; the religion (and philosophy) founded by Choe Je-U in 1860 C.E.

Donggyông Daejôn (東經大典): The "Great Scriptures of Eastern Learning (Donghak)"; one of two most authoritative books attributed to Choe Je-U.

Eight *kua* (goe, 卦): Eight Trigrams

Five Elements (Ohaeng, 五行): Five elements (Water, Fire, Wood, Metal, and Earth) which form the basis of reality

Four Beginnings (sadan, 四端; ssu tuan, in Chinese): 惻隱 (chûk'ûn, sympathy), 羞惡 (suo, shame), 辭讓 (sayang, concession), 是非 (shibi, reason or judgment)

Four Books (Sa-sô, 四書): Nonô (論語), Maengja (孟子), Daehak (大學), and Jungyong (中庸)

Go-un (孤雲): pseudonym of Choe Chi-won (857–?)

gong li (空理): void li, pure spiritual entity

guishin (鬼神): ghost, spirit

Gumgang Sammaegyông (金剛三昧經): (Apochryphon) Vajrasamadhi Sutra

gunja/kunja (君子; in Chinese, chün tzu/junzi): gentleman, an exemplary person

Haewol (海月): pseudonym of Choe Shi-hyung, the second leader of Donghak

Han (한, philosophy of): one, great, totality

han (恨): a sense of unresolved resentment due to suffering from oppression

Hanalnim (하날님): God, or Supreme Reality

Hananim (하나님, a variation of Hanalnim): Protestant choice for "God" in Korea

Hanûnim (하느님, a variation of Hanalnim): Recently, a Catholic choice for "God" in Korea—traditionally, Catholics used Chônju above.

haplyu (合流): merging of two streams, as in a river system

hobal (互發): alternating manifestation

hsien: an immortal, see sôn (仙)

hsin/xin (shim: 心): mind-and-heart

hsin hsueh/xinxue (shim hak: 心學): (Lu-Wang) School of the Mind

hsing (sang, 象): form, emblems

hsing/xing (sông, 性): nature

hu chôn gae byôk (後天開闢): new heaven and new earth; Suun's millenarian doctrine

Hua-yen: see Hwaôm

*huo jan chih ch'i* (ho yôn ji ki: 浩然之氣): active force, moving force, power inherent in nature (Mencius)

Hwadam: Pseudonym of Suh Kyong-Dok

Hwan In (桓因): The "Sovereign of Heaven (天帝)." (Samguk Yusa)

Hwan Ung (桓雄): The son of Hwan In who, according to Samguk Yusa, receives a permission from his father to come down from Heaven to give blessings to the people on earth. He is given the authority to teach and lead the local people with 360 different tasks to perform. On coming down to the Taebaek Mountains in the northern part of Korea, he marries to Ung Nyô, bear-

# Glossary of Names and Terms

turned woman, who gives birth to Dan'gun, the mythic founder of Korea.

Hwaôm (華嚴; in Chinese, Hua-yen): "Flower Garland" (Buddhism)

Hwaômgyông (華嚴經; Hua-yen ching in Chinese): Avatamsaka (Flower Garland) Sutra

Hwa-rang do (花郎道): literally, "the way of flower boy"; the group of youths, mainly sons of aristocrats, during the Three Kingdoms Period (53 B.C.E.–668 C.E.) in Korea

hyônjang (現場): life-context; the life-situation of people

i/yi (ûi, 義): righteousness

I Ching/Yijing (Yôk Kyông: 易經): Book of Change

ildo (一途): one way, one manner (Yulgok)

Il Yôn (一然, 1206–1289): Scholar monk during the Koryo Dynasty in Korea. Among the works by him the most well-known is Samguk Yusa.

In nae chôn (人乃天): "human(ity) is heaven"; a doctrine of Uiam (義菴, Son Byung-hee, 孫秉熙, 1861–1922), the third leader of Donghak

in ûi ye ji (仁義禮智): "compassion, righteousness, propriety, and wisdom"; the four basic virtues emphasized by Mencius

jayôn (自然; tzu jan/ziran in Chinese): nature, naturalness; things as they are

jen/ren (in, 仁): human-heartedness

jen-hsin (in shim: 人心): human mind

jukiron (主氣論): ki-primary theory

jung saeng (衆生): people; myriad (living) creatures

Jûng San Gyo (甑山敎): Syncretic religion founded by Kang Il-soon in the beginning of the twentieth century. The four major doctrines are: shin-hwa-il-shim (神化一心), in-ûi-sang-saeng (仁義相生), gô-byûng-hae-won (去病解怨), and su-chôn-sôn-gyông (修天仙境).

juriron (主理論): li-primary theory

ki (pron. "gi," 氣): ether, etherial force, breath, matter-energy; ch'i/qi in Chinese

Kim, Bu-sik (金富軾, 1075–1151): Author of Samguk Sagi (三國史記), "History of Three Kingdoms."

Kim, Yu-shin (金庾信, 595–673): As a 12$^{th}$ decendent of King Suro of Gaya Kingdom, Kim joined Hwarang (花郎), a pseudo-military youth league in 609, became the command-in-chief of Silla, and led his troops toward the successful campaign for the unification of the Korean peninsula.

Ko Hung/Ge Hong (Gal Hong, 葛洪, 261–341): Author of Pobakja (Pao P'u Tzu/Baopuzi in Chinese).

kua (goe, 卦): trigrams

Kwon, Kun (權近, 1352–1409): an early proponent of Neo-Confucianism in the Yi Dynasty Korea.

Lao tzu/Laozi (Noja, 老子): The alleged—now refuted—author of Tao Te Ching

li (ye, 禮): ritual, propriety

li (理): principle, noumena

Li Chi (Yegi, 禮記): Book of Rites

li hsueh/li xue (li hak, 理學): (Ch'eng-Chu) School of Principle

Lieh Tzu (Yôlja, 列子: c. 300 C.E.): Work considered an important source of Taoism along with Lao Tzu/Laozi and Chuang Tzu/Zhuangzi.

Lu Hsing-shan (陸象山, or Lu Chiu-yuan 陸九淵, 1139–1193): Contemporary of Zhu Hsi and the philosophical opponent of the latter.

Lun Yü (Nonô, 論語): Discourses or Analects (of Confucius)

lyông (靈): spirit, ghost

Maitreya (Mirûk, 彌勒): future buddha

Mencius (Maengja, 孟子, 372–289 B.C.E.; in Chinese, Meng Tzu/Mengzi): Also refers to his work.

minjung/Minjung (民衆): common people; underprivileged/oppressed people

Mugûk (無極): the Ultimate of Non-being; Wu Chi in Chinese

Daedo (無極大道): the Great Way of the Non-Ultimate; Suun's description of his newly found teaching, Donghak

mudang (巫堂): (female) shaman

muwi (無爲): "non-action" or "inaction"; wu wei in Chinese

nae yu shin lyông (內有神靈): the spirit within

Nonô (論語): see Lun yü

Pao P'u Tzu/Baopuzi (Pobakja, 抱樸子): Work written by Ko Hung.

Principle: see li (理)

Pung lyu do (風流道): literally, "the way of wind and stream"; or the "romantic spirit of spontaneity"

Queen Mother of the West (*Hsi wang mu*, 西王母)

sam shin (三神): three gods: (1) Hwan-in, Hwan-ung, and Dan'gun; or (2) Heaven, Earth, and Humanity

Samgang Oryun (三綱五倫): the Three Bonds and the Five Moral Rules of a Confucian social teaching

Samguk Sagi (三國史記): "History of the Three Kingdoms" (53 B.C.E.–668 C.E.) of Korea, compiled by Kim Busik (1075–1151) in 1145

Samguk Yusa (三國遺事): "Memorabilia of the Three Kingdoms," written by Il Yôn (1206–1289)

san shin (山神): mountain gods, mountain immortals

san shin (産神): fertility god

Sangje (上帝): "God" in Taoism/Confucianism

Seven Emotions (chil jông, 七情): 喜 (hûi: pleasure), 怒 (no: anger), 哀 (ae: sorrow), 懼 (gu: fear), 愛 (ae: love), 惡 (o: hate), 欲 (yok: desire)

Shichônju (侍天主): bearing God, or serving God (Suun)

shi-gak (始覺): enlightenment a posteriori (Wonhyo)

Shih/shi (sa, 事): phenomena, facts, reality

Shih Chi (sagi, 史記): "Records of Historian," compiled by Ssu-ma Ch'ien (司馬遷).

Shim (心): mind-and-heart, see hsin

shin (神): god, spirit

shin sôn (神仙): Taoist immortal, mountain god

Sil Hak (實學): Practical Learning, or Real Learning, propagated by some scholars in the second half of the Yi Dynasty in Korea.

sôn (仙): (Taoist) immortal

Sôn (禪, Ch'an in Chinese; Zen in Japanese): The school of Buddhism that lays a stress on the role of meditation in enlightenmen.

Sohn, Byung-hee (孫秉熙, 1862–1922): A leader of the liberation movement from the colonial rule of Japan. As the third leader of Donghak, Sohn changed its name into Chôndogyo in 1906. Pseudonym is Uiam (義菴).

sôn pung do gol (仙風道骨): stature of immortals

sông (性; in Chinese, hsing/xing): human nature

Sông Lyông/Shin (聖靈/神): Holy Spirit

Ssu-ma Ch'ien (Sa Ma Chôn 司馬遷; c. 145–? B.C.E.): Compiler of Shih Chi, "Records of Historian"

su shim jông ki (修心政氣): discipline mind and right ki (ch'i/qi)

Suh, Kyong-Dok (徐敬德, 1489–1546): Pseudonym is Hwadam. An early proponent of ki-centered monism.

Suun (水雲): the pseudonym of Choe Je-U (1824–1864), the founder of Donghak

Supreme Ultimate (*T'ai Chi*): see Taegûk

Taegûk (太極; in Chinese, T'ai Chi/Taiji): Supreme Ultimate

T'ai Chi/Taiji: see Taegûk

T'ai Chi T'u Shuo/taiji toshuo (Taegûk do sôl; 太極圖說): Explanation of the Diagram of the Supreme Ultimate

Tao/Dao (do; 道): way, path; cosmic principle

# Glossary of Names and Terms

tao chia/daojia (do ga; 道家): the philosophical school of Taoism

tao chiao/daojiao (do gyo: 道教): the Taoist religion

Tao Te Ching/Dao De Jing (Dodôkgyông; 道德經): A short work composed of 81 prosaic chapters or verses. Otherwise known as the Lao Tzu/Lao Zi, the alleged author of the work.

tao t'ung (do tong; 道統): succession of the way; transmission of teachings

te/de (dôk; 德): (1) moral virtue, bounty, to be grateful (D. C. Lau), moral excellence (W. Chan); (2) power (A. Waley, Y.L. Fung) 20

t'ien/tian (chôn; 天): Heaven

Toegye (退溪): the pseudonym of Yi Hwang (李滉; 1501–70)

trigrams: see kua (koe)

tzu jan/ziran: see jayôn

ûi (義; in Chinese, i/yi): righteousness

Uisang (義湘, 625–702): Silla monk. Founder of Hwaôm (Huayen) School in Korea. Surname is Kim.

Wang, Yang-ming (王陽明, or Shou-jen 守仁, 1472–1529): A philosophical opponent—following his mentor Lu Hsing-shan—of the Chu Hsi Neo-Confucianism.

woe yu jôp lyông ji ki (外有接靈至氣): the touch of the spirit from without

woe yu ki hwa (外有氣化): the ki(ch'i)-ization from without 64

Won Bul Gyo (圓佛敎): A Buddhist Sect founded by Park Jung-bin in 1916. Teaches modernization, practical application, and popularization of Buddhism.

Wonhyo: 元曉, 617–686

wu (mu; 巫): shaman

wu (mu; 無): nothingness

Wu Chi/Wuji (Mugûk; 無極): the Ultimate of Non-being, or (the reality of) Non-Ultimate

wu wei (muwi; 無爲): non-action, non-obstruction, or no unreal action

yang (陽): male element of Heaven, or T'ai Chi; activity, sun or sunfulness, maleness

yang-sheng (yang saeng; 養生): preserving life

yin (ûm; 陰): female element of Heaven, or T'ai Chi; passivity, moon or sunlessness, femaleness

yông se mu gung (永世無窮): immortality

Yongdam Yusa (龍潭遺詞 or 辭): one of two most authoritative books written by Choe Je-U (Suun)

Yulgok (栗谷): the pseudonym of Yi I (李珥; 1536–84)

Zen (Japanese pronunciation of 禪; Ch'an in Chinese): see Sôn.

# Bibliography

## Resources in English

Abbot, Imelda and Jager, Alfred (1987). *Weltoffenheit des christlichen Glaubens: Fritz Buri zu Ehren*. Bern: Haupt; Tubingen: Katzmann.

Abe, Masao (1985). *Zen and Western Thought*. Edited by William R. LaFleur. Honolulu: University of Hawaii Press.

——— (1990). "Kenotic God and Dynamic Sunyata" and "A Rejoinder," in *The Emptying God*, edited by John Cobb, Jr., and C. Ives. Maryknoll, NY: Orbis Books.

Abraham, K. C., ed. (1990). *Third World Theologies: Commonalities and Divergences*. Papers and Reflections from the Second General Assembly of the Ecumenical Association of Third World Theologians, December, 1986, Oaxtepec, Mexico. Maryknoll, N.Y.: Orbis Books.

Adams, Daniel J. (1990). "Tillich's concept of time and space in relation to Korean religion" in *Taiwan Journal of Theology* 12: 73–97 (March).

——— (1987). "The sources of Minjung theology" in *Taiwan Journal of Theology*, no. 9: 179–198 (March).

Ahn, Byung-mu (1984/5). "The Transmitters of Jesus-Event," in *CTC Bulletin* Vol. 5 No. 3–Vol. 6 No. 1; December–April.

Ahn. Jae-Woong (1995). "The Wisdom of the Minjung in Korea," in *Ching Feng* 38/2 (May).

Ahn Kye-hyon (1989). "A Short History of Ancient Korean Buddhism," in *Introduction of Buddhism to Korea: New Cultural Patterns*, ed.

by L. Lancaster and Chae-shin Yu. Berkeley, Ca.: Asian Humanities Press.

An, Pyong-ju (1983). "Yi I (Yulgok) and His Thought," in *Main Currents of Korean Thought*. Ed. By the Korean National Commission for UNESCO. Seoul: Si-sa-yong-o-sa.

Ariarajah, Wesley (1985). *The Bible and People of Other Faiths*. Geneva: WCC.

Balasuriya, Tissa (1985). "A Third World Perspective," in *Doing Theology in a Divided World*. Virginia Fabella and Sergio Torres, eds. Maryknoll, NY: Orbis Books.

Barth, Karl (1956). *Church Dogmatics*. Vol. 1/2 sec. 17 (1939). Edinburgh: T. & T. Clark.

Baum, Gregory (1986). "Three Theses on Contextual Theology," in *Ecumenist* 24.

——— (1966). "Christianity and Other Religions," in *Cross Currents* 16.

Bevans, Stephen B. (1992). *Models of Contextual Theology*. Maryknoll, NY: Orbis Books.

Berger, Peter L., ed. (1981). *The Other Side of God: A Polarity in World Religions*. New York: Doubleday.

Bhattacharya, K. (1978). *The Dialectical Method of Nagarjuna*. New Delhi: Motilal Banarsidass.

Bishop, Isabella Lucy (1970). *Korea and Her Neighbors: A Narrative of Travel, with an Account of the Recent Vicissitudes and Present Position of the Country*. Facsimile Reprint of the 1897 edition by Isabella Bird Bishop (New York: Revell). Seoul: Yonsei University Press.

Boff, Leonardo, et. al. (1988). *Theologies of the Third World: Convergences and Differences*. Edinburgh: T. & T. Clark Ltd.

Boff, Clodovis (1987). *Theology and Praxis: Epistemological Foundations*. Maryknoll, NY: Orbis Books.

Bosch, David (1991). *Transforming Mission: Paradigm Shifts in Theology of Mission*. Maryknoll, NY: Orbis Books.

Bruce, Joseph Percy (1973, 1923). *Chu Hsi and His Masters*. New York: AMS Press.

Buswell, Robert E. (1989). *The Formation of Ch'an Ideology in China and Korea: the Vajrasamadhi-Sutra, a Buddhist Apocryphon*. Princeton, NJ: Princeton University Press.

Carey, John J., ed. (1984). *Kairos and Logos: Studies in the Roots and Implications of Tillich's Theology*. New edition. Macon, GA: Mercer University Press.

―――, ed. (1984). *Theonomy and Autonomy: Studies in Paul Tillich's Engagement with Modern Culture*. Macon, GA: Mercer University Press.

Caurus, Paul, compiled (1915). *The Gospel of Buddha*. Chicago and London: The Open Court Pub. Co.

Chai, Ch'u and Chai, Winberg, Intro. and Study Guide of Legge's trans., (1964). *I Ching: Book of Changes*. New York: University Books, Inc.

Chan, Wing-tsit (1987). *Chu Hsi: Life and Thought*. Hong Kong: The Chinese University Press.

―――, trans. and comp. (1963). *A Source Book in Chinese Philosophy*. Princeton: Princeton University Press.

――― (1962). "Syntheses in Chinese Metaphysics," in *The Chinese Mind: Essentials of Chinese Philosophy and Culture*. Edited by Charles E. Moore. Honolulu, Hawaii: University of Hawaii Press.

Chang, Pyong-gil (1978). *Religion*. Seoul: Korean Overseas Information Service.

Chang, Carson (1957-62). *The Development of Neo-Confucian Thought.* 2 volumes. New York: Bookman Associates.

Chang, Garma C. C. (1971). *The Buddhist Teaching of Totality: the Philosophy of Hwa Yen Buddhism.* University Park and London: The Pennsylvania State University Press.

Ch'en, Kenneth (1964). *Buddhism in China: A Historical Survey.* Princeton: Princeton University Press.

Ch'eng, Chung-ying (1991). *New Dimensions of Confucian and Neo-Confucian Philosophy.* Albany, NY: State University of New York Press.

––––––– (1965). "Inquiries into Classical Chinese Logic," *Philosophy East and West* 15 (July-October).

Chesneaux, Jean (1973). *Peasant Revolts in China 1840–1949.* Translated by C. A. Curwen. London: Thames and Hudson.

Ching, Julia (1993). *Chinese Religions.* Maryknoll, NY: Orbis Books.

––––––– (1977). *Confucianism and Christianity: a Comparative Study.* Tokyo & New York: Kodansha International.

Cho, Myong-gi (1977). "Ch'an Buddhist Culture in Korea," in *Korean and Asian Religious Tradition.* Ed. by Chai-Shin Yu. Toronto: Korean and Related Studies Press.

Cho, Wha Soon (1988). *Let the Weak Be Strong: A Woman's Struggle for Justice.* Edited by Lee Sun Ai and Ahn Sang Nim. New York: Crossroad.

Choi, Min-Hong (1983). *A Modern History of Korean Philosophy.* Seoul: Seong Moon Sa.

––––––– (1983). *Han Philosophy and the 21st Century.* Seoul: Seong Moon Sa.

Chon, Sin-yong, ed. (1974). *Buddhist Culture in Korea*. Seoul: International Cultural Foundation.

Choung, Haechang and Han, Hyong-jo, eds. (1996). *Confucian Philosopht in Korea*. Seoul: The Academy of Korean Studies.

Christian, William A. (1972). *Oppositions of Religious Doctrines*. London: Macmillan/ New York: Herder and Herder.

Chu Hsi (1991). *Further Reflections on Things at Hand: A Reader*. Translation and Commentary by Allen Wittenborn. Lanham, New York and London: University Press of America.

——— (1990). *Learning to Be a Sage: Selections from the Conversations of Master Chu, Arranged Topically*. Trans. with Comm. by Daniel K. Gardner. Berkeley, Los Angeles and Oxford: University of California Press.

——— (1973, 1922). *The Philosophy of Human Nature*. Trans. by J. Percy Bruce with notes. New York: AMS Press, Inc.

——— (1967). *Reflections on Things at Hand*. Compiled by Chu Hsi and Lu Tsu-Ch'ien. Translated, with notes, by Wing-Tsit Chan. New York and London: Columbia University Press.

Chuang Tzu (1968). *The Complete Works of Chuang Tzu*. Trans. by Burton Watson. New York: Columbia University Press.

——— (1964). *Chuang Tzu: Basic Writings*. Trans. by Burton Watson. New York: Columbia University Press.

Chung, Byung Jo (1990). "International Seminar on Buddhism and Christianity" in *Buddhist Christian Studies* 10: 227–229.

Chung, Chai-Sik (1982). "Korea: the continuing syncretism," in *Religions and Societies*, ed. by C. Caldarola.

——— (1991). "Confucian-Protestant encounter in Korea: two cases of westernization and de-westernization" in *Ching Feng* 34: 51-81(Ja).

―――― (1991). "Humanizing modernity: notes on the agenda for Confucianism and Christianity" in *Ching Feng* 34: 118-120 (Ja).

Chung, David (1959). *Religious Syncretism In Korean Society*. Ann Arbor and London: University Microfilms International.

Chung, Edward Y.J. (1995). *The Korean Neo-Confucianism of Yi Toegye and Yi Yulgok: A Reappraisal of the "Four-Seven Thesis" and Its Practical Implications for Self-Cultivation*. Albany, N.Y.: State University of New York Press.

Chung, Hyun Kyung (1988). "'Opium or the Seed for Revolution?' Shamanism: Women Centred Popular Religiosity in Korea," in *Theologies of the Third World: Convergences and Differences* (*Concilium 199*); Edited by L. Boff and V. Elizondo. Edinburgh: T. & T. Clark Ltd.

―――― (1990). "Han-pu-ri: Doing Theology from Korean Women's Perspective" in *We Dare to Dream: Doing Theology as Asian Women*. Edited by V. Fabella. Maryknoll, NY: Orbis Books.

―――― (1990). *Struggle to be the Sun Again: Introducing Asian Women's Theology*. Maryknoll, N.Y.: Orbis Books.

Clark, Charles Allen (1980). *Religions of Old Korea*. New York: Fleming H. Revell Company, 1932; Reprinted in New York and London: Garland Publishing, Inc.

―――― (1937). "Some Startling Church Statistics," *The Korea Mission Field* XXXIII.1 (January).

Cleary, J. C. (1988). *A Buddha from Korea: the Zen Teachings of T'aego*. Translation with commentary of *T'aego Hwasang Orok*. Boston & Shaftesbury: Shambhala Publications.

Cobb, John, Jr. (1982). *Beyond Dialogue: Toward a Mutual Transformation of Christianity and Buddhism*. Philadelphia: Fortress Press.

——— (1975). *Christ in a Pluralistic Age*. Philadelphia: Westminster Press.

———. and Ives, C., eds. (1990). *The Emptying God: A Buddhist-Jewish-Christian Conversation.* Maryknoll, NY: Orbis Books.

Confucius (1979). *Lun yü (The Analects)*. Trans. with Intro. by D.C. Lau. Harmondsworth; New York: Penguin Books.

Cohn-Sherbok, Dan, ed. (1992). *World Religions and Human Liberation*. Maryknoll, NY: Orbis Books.

Conroy, Hilary (1960). *The Japanese Seizure of Korea: 1868-1910—A Study of Realism and Idealism in International Relations*. Philadelphia: University of Pennsylvania Press.

Cook, Frank H. (1977). *Hua-yen Buddhism: the Jewel Net of Indra*. University Park: Pennsylvania State University Press.

Covell, Jon Carter (1982). *Korea's Cultural Roots*. Salt Lake City: Moth House; Seoul: Hollym.

Covell, Ralph R. (1986). *Confucius, the Buddha, and Christ*. Maryknoll, NY: Orbis Books.

Coward, Harold G. (1983). *Religious Pluralism And the World Religions.* Madras, India: University of Madras.

——— (1988). *Sacred Word and Sacred Text: Scripture in World Religions*. Maryknoll, New York: Orbis Books.

Cox, Harvey (1992). *Many Mansions: A Christian's Encounter with Other Faiths*. Boston: Beacon Press.

Creel, Herrlee G. (1970). *What Is Taoism? and Other Studies in Chinese Cultural History*. Chicago and London: The University of Chicago Press.

——— (1970). *The Origins of Statecraft in China. Volume One: The Western Chou Empire*. Chicage and London: The University of Chicago Press.

Crossman, Richard C. (1983). *Paul Tillich: A Comprehensive Bibliography and Keyword index of Primary and Secondary Writings in English*. Metuchen, N.J., & London: The Scarecrow Press.

Csikszentmihalyi, Mark and Ivanhoe, Philip J., eds. (1999). *Religious and Philosophical Aspects of the Laozi*. Albany, NY: State University of New York Press.

CTC-CCA, ed. (1983). *Minjung Theology: People as the Subjects of Theology*. Revised Edition. London: Zed Press/ Maryknoll, NY: Orbis Books/ Toa Payoh, Singapore: CCA.

Davis, Charles (1970). *Christ & The World Religions*. London: Hodder and Stoughton.

D'Costa, Gavin, ed. (1992). *Christian Uniqueness Reconsidered: The Myth of a Pluralistic Theology of Religions*. Maryknoll, NY: Orbis Books.

de Bary, William Theodore (1981). *Neo-Confucian Orthodoxy and the Learning of the Mind-and-Heart*. New York: Columbia University Press.

——— (1988). *East Asian Civilization: a Dialogue in Five Stages*. Cambridge, Mass.: Harvard University Press.

——— (1989). *The Message of the Mind in Neo-Confucianism*. New York: Columbia University Press.

———, ed. (1985). *The Rise of Neo-Confucianism in Korea*. New York: Columbia University Press.

de Carvalho, Emilio J. M. (1985). "Opening Statement" of the Sixth International Conference of the Ecumenical Association of Third World Theologians (January 5–13, 1983, Geneva, Switzerland), in

*Doing Theology in a Divided World.* Ed. by Fabella and Torres. Maryknoll, NY: Orbis Books.

De Silva, Lynn A. (1979). *The Problem of the Self in Buddhism and Christianity.* London: Macmillan/ New York: Barnes & Noble.

Deuchler, Martina (1992). *The Confucian Transformation of Korea: A Study of Society and Ideology*, esp. chapt. 6, "Confucian Legislation: The Consequences for Women." Cambridge, Ma.: Council on East Asian Studies, Harvard University.

——— (1983). *Confucian Gentlemen and Barbarian Envoys: The Opening of Korea, 1875-1885.* Seattle and London: University of Washington Press.

Deutsch, Eliot and Bontekoe, Ron, eds. (1997). *A Companion to World Philosophies.* Cambridge, Ma.: Blackwell.

Dharmasiri, Gunapala (1988). *A Buddhist Critique of the Christian Concept of God.* U.S.A: Golden Leaves.

Diaz, Hector (1986). *A Korean Theology: Chu-Gyo Yo-ji. Esseantials of the Lord's Teaching by Chong Yak-jong Augustine (1760–1801).* Immensee: Neue Zeitschrift Fur Missionswissenschaft. Switzerland.

Di Censo, James J. (1990). *Hermeneutics and Disclosure of Truth: Study in the Work of Heidegger, Gadamer and Ricoeur.* Charlottesville: University Press of Virginia.

Dickson, Kwesi A. (1988). "And what of culture: an African reflection on Minjung theology" in *An Emerging Theology in World Perspective.* Edited by J. Y. Lee. Mystic, Connecticut: Twenty-Third Publications.

Droogers, Andre (1989). "Syncretism: The Problem of Definition, the Definition of the Problem," in *Dialogue and Syncretism: An Interdisciplinary Approach.* Ed. by J.D. Gort, et. al. Grand Rapids, MI.: Eerdmans.

——— (1995). "Cultural Relativism and Universal Human Rights?" in *Human Rights and Religious Values*. Ed. by A. An-Na'im, et. al. Amsterdam: Editions Rodopi; Grand Rapids, Mich.: W.B. Eerdmans.

Eno, Robert (1990). *The Confucian Creation of Heaven: Philosophy and the Defense of Ritual Mastery*. Albany, NY: State University of New York Press.

Eliade, Mircea (1964). *Shamanism: Archaic Techniques of Ecstasy*. Trans. from French by Willard R. Trask. Princeton: Princeton University Press.

——— (1974). *Patterns in Comparative Religion*. Translated by D. R. Pocock. New York: Free Press.

———, and Kitagawa, Joseph, eds. (1959). *Essays in Methodology*. Chicago: University of Chicago Press.

Fabella, Virginia, ed. (1980). *Asia's Struggle for Full Humanity: Towards a Relevant Theology*. Maryknoll, NY: Orbis Books.

Fabella, Virginia and Lee-Park, Sun Ai, eds. (1990). *We Dare to Dream: Doing Theology as Asian Women*. U. S. edition. Maryknoll, NY: Orbis Books.

Fabella, Virginia, Lee, Peter, K.H., and Suh, David, Kwang-sun, eds. (1992). *Asian Christian Spirituality: Reclaiming Traditions*. Maryknoll, NY: Orbis.

Fabella, Virginia and Oduyoye, Mercy Amba, eds. (1988). *With Passion and Compassion: Third World Women Doing Theology*. Maryknoll, NY: Orbis Books.

Fabella, Virginia and Torres, Sergio, eds. (1983). *Irrputionof the Third World: Challenge to Theology*. Maryknoll, NY: Orbis Books.

———, eds. (1985). *Doing Theology in a Divided World*. Maryknoll, NY: Orbis Books.

Fenwick, M. C. (1911). *The Church of Christ in Korea*. New York: Hodder & Stonghton.

Ferm, Deane William (1986). *Third World Liberation Theologies: A Reader*. Maryknoll, NY: Orbis Books.

Finazzo, Giancarlo (1968). *The Notion of Tao in Lao Tzu and Chuang Tzu*. Taipei, Taiwan: Mei Ya Publications, Inc.

Fiorenza, Elisabeth Schussler (1993). *Discipleship of Equals: A Critical Feminist Ekkllesia-logy of Liberation*. New York: Crossroad.

Freire, Paulo (1972). *The Pedagogy of the Oppressed*. London and New York: Harmondsworth.

―――― (1972). *Cultural Action for Freedom*. London and New York: Harmondsworth.

Fu, Charles Wei-Hsun (1987). "A Universal Theory or a Cosmic Confidence in Reality? A Taoist/Zen Response," in *Toward a Universal Theology of Religion*, ed. by L. Swidler. Maryknoll, NY: Orbis Books.

―――― and Wawrytko, Sandra A., eds. (1991). *Buddhist Ethics and Modern Society: an International Symposium*. New York: Greenwood Press.

Fung (Fêng), Yu-Lan (1952-3). *History of Chinese Philosophy*. 2 vols. Trans. with introduction, notes, bibliography and index by Derk Bodde. Princeton: Princeton University Press.

―――― (1958). A Short History of Chinese Philosophy. Ed. by Derk Bodde. New York: Macmillan.

―――― (1962). *The Spirit of Chinese Philosophy*. Trans. by E. R. Hughes. Boston: Beacon Press.

Gadamer, Hans-Georg (1976). *Philosophical Hermeneutics*. Trans. and ed. by David E. Linge. Berkeley: University of California Press.

——— (1975). *Truth and Method*. New York: Seabury.

Garvey, John, ed. (1986). *Modern Spirituality: An Anthology*. London: Darton, Longman and Todd.

Gassmann, Gunther, ed. (1993). *Documentary History of Faith and Order 1963-1993*. Faith and Order Paper No. 159. Geneva: WCC Publications.

Geertz, Clifford (1973). *The Interpretations of Cultures*. New York: Basic Books.

Giles, Lionel, trans. (1912). *Taoist Teachings from the Book of Lieh Tzu*. London: John Murray.

Gilkey, Langdon (1982). "God", in *Christian Theology*, ed. by P.C. Hodgson and R.H. King. Philadelphia: Fortress Press.

——— (1981). *Society and the Sacred*. New York: Crossroad.

Gort, Jerald D., et. al. eds. (1989). *Dialogue and Syncretism: An Interdisciplinary Approach*. Grand Rapids, Michigan: Eerdmans.

Graham, A. C. (1958). *Two Chinese Philosophers: Ch'eng Ming-tao and Ch'eng Yi-ch'uan*. London: Lund Humphries.

Grayson, James Huntly (1985). *Early Buddhism and Christianity in Korea: A Study in the Emplantation of Religion*. Leiden: E.J. Brill.

——— (1989). *Korea: A Religious History*. Oxford: Clarendon Press.

Greinacher, Norbert and Mette Norbert, eds. (1994). *Christianity and Cultures: A Mutual Enrichment (Concilium, 1994/2)*. London: SCM Press; Maryknoll, NY: Orbis Books.

Griffis, William Elliot (1971). *Corea: The Hermit Nation*. Ninth Edition, Revised and Enlarged (reprinted from the edition of 1911). New York, NY: AMS Press. [Griffis, "formerly of the Imperial University of Tokio, Japan," dedicates this book to "all Corean

Patriots: ... to rid their land of superstitution, bigotry, despotism, and priestcraft ...]

Griffiths, Paul J. (1990). *Christianity Through Non-Chrisian Eyes*. Maryknoll, NY: Orbis Books.

Grigg, Richard (1985). *Symbol and Empowerment: Paul Tillich's Post-Theistic System*. Macon, GA: Mercer University Press.

Guisso, Richard W. I. and Yu, Chai-shin, eds. (1988). *Shamanism: the Spirit World of Korea*. Berkeley, CA.: Asian Humanities Press.

Gurriere, Daniel, ed. (1990). *Phenomenology of the Truth Proper to Religion*. Albany, NY: State University of New York Press.

Gutierrez, Gustavo (1973). *A Theology of Liberation*. Maryknoll, NY: Orbis Books.

———  (1984). *The Power of the Poor in History*. Maryknoll, NY: Orbis Books.

Habermas, Jurgen (1973). *Theory and Practice*. Trans. by John Viertel. Boston: Beacon Press.

——— (1984). *Theory of Communicative Action*. Trans. by Thomas McCarthy. Boston: Beacon Press.

Habito, Ruben L. F. (1989). *Total Liberation: Zen Spirituality and the Social Dimension*. Maryknoll, NY: Orbis Books.

Haboush, JaHyun Kim (1988). *A Heritage of Kings: One Man's Monarchy in the Confucian World*. New York: Columbia Univeristy Press.

Hall, David L. (1982*). The Uncertain Phoenix: Adventures Toward a Post-Cultural Sensibility*. New York: Fordham University Press.

——— and Ames, Roger T. (1987). *Thinking Through Confucius*. Albany: State University of New York Press.

―――― and Ames, Roger T. (1998). *Thinking from the Han: Self, Truth, and Transcendence in Chinese and Western Culture*. Albany, NY: State University of New York Press.

Hallenkreutz, Carl F. (1977). *Dialogue and Community*. Geneva: WCC.

―――― (1988). "Tambaram Revisited," in *International Review of Mission*, Vol. 78, No. 137 (July).

Hammond, Guyton B. (1993). *Conscience and Its Recovery: From the Frankfurt School to Feminism*. Charlottesville and London: University Press of Virginia.

Han-shan, Te-ch'ing (1993). *Pure Land of the Patriarchs: Zen Master Han-shan on Pure Land Buddhism*. Trans. by Lok To. New York–San Francisco–Toronto: Sutra Translation Committee of the United States and Canada.

Hanson, Eric O. (1980). *Catholic Politics in China and Korea*. Maryknoll, NY: Orbis Books.

Harrington, Fred H. (1944). *God, Mammon, and the Japanese: Dr. Horace N. Allen and Korean-American Relationss, 1884–1905*. Madison: The University of Wisconsin Press.

Hartshorne, Charles (1984). *Omnipotence and Other Theological Mistakes*. Albany, NY: State University of New York Press.

Hebblethwaite, Brian L. (1980). *The Problem of Theology*. Cambridge: Cambridge University Press.

Heim, S. Mark (1995). *Salvations: Truth and Differences in Religion*. Maryknoll, NY: Orbis.

Henderson, John B. (1984). *The Development and Decline of Chinese Cosmology*. New York: Columbia University Press.

Hennelly, Alfred T., S. J., ed. (1990). *Liberation Theology: A Documentary History*. Maryknoll, NY: Orbis Books.

Herbert, Edward (1955). *A Taoist Notebook*. London: John Murray.

Hick, John (1995). *A Christian Theology of Religions: The Rainbow of Faith*. Louisville, Kentucky: Westminster John Knox Press.

——— (1989). *Interpretation of Religion: Human Responses to the Transcendent*. Basingstoke: Macmillan.

——— (1985). *Problems of Religious Pluralism*. New York: St. Martin's Press.

———, and Knitter, Paul, eds. (1987). *The Myth of Christian Uniqueness: Toward a Pluralistic Theology of Religions*. Maryknoll, NY: Orbis Books.

Hogan, Linda (1995). *from Women's Experience to Feminist Theology*. Sheffield, England: Sheffield Academic Press.

Hu, Tse Ling, trans. and annot. (1936). *Lao Tsu: Tao Te Ching*. Chengtu, Szechwan: Canadian Mission Press.

Huang, Tsung-his (1987). *Ming ju hs eh an (The records of Ming scholars)*. Trans. and ed. by Julia Ching. Honolulu: University of Hawaii Press.

Hulbert, Homer B. (1905). *The History of Korea*. 2 Vols. Seoul: The Methodist Publishing House.

——— (1906). *The Passing of Korea*. New York: Doubleday, Page & Company.

Humphreys, Christmas (1951). *Buddhism: An Introduction and Guide*. London: Penguin Books.

Hunt, Everett Nichols, Jr. (1980). *Protestant Pioneers in Korea*. Maryknoll, NY: Orbis Books.

Hyun, Younghak (1985). "The cripple's dance and Minjung theology" in *Ching Feng*, 28 No. 1: 30-35.

Il Yôn (1972). *Samguk Yusa: Legends and History of the Three Kingdoms of Ancient Korea*. Trans. by Ha Tae-Hung and K. Mintz. Seoul: Yonsei University Press.

Inada, Kenneth K. (1987). "Christocentricism-Buddhacentrism," in Toward a *Universal Theology of Religion*, ed. by L. Swidler. Maryknoll, NY: Orbis Books.

International Cultural Foundation, ed. (1982). *Buddhist Culture in Korea*. Seoul: the Si-sa-yong-o-sa Publishers.

——— (1974). *Folk Culture in Korea*. Seoul: International Cultural Foundation.

Isaacs, Marie E. (1976). *The Concept of Spirit*. London: Heythrop College.

Jesudasan, Ignatius (1984). *A Gandhian Theology of Liberation*. Maryknoll, NY: Orbis Books.

Joe, Wanne J. (1972). *Traditional Korea A Cultural History*. Seoul: Jung Ang University Press.

Kalton, Michael C., Kim, Oaksook C., Park, Sung Bae, Ro, Youngchan, Tu, Wei-ming and Yamashita, Samuel, eds. (1994). *The Four-Seven Debate: An Annotated Translation of the Most Famous Controversy in Korean Neo-Confucian Thought*. Albany, NY: SUNY.

Kalupahana, David (1986). *Nagarjuna: The Philosophy of the Middle Way*. Albany, NY: State University of New York Press.

Kane, Margaret (1987). "Minjung theology" in *Theology*, 90: 351-356 (Summer).

Keel, Hee-Sung (1984). Chinul: the Founder of the Korean Sôn Tradition. Berkeley, Ca.: University of California Press.

Kendall, Laurel (1988). *The Life and Hard Times of a Korean Shaman: of Tales and the Telling of Tales*. Honolulu: University of Hawaii Press.

Bibliography 171

Kim, C. I. Eugene and Kim, Han-kyo (1967). *Korea and the Politics of Imperialism, 1876-1910*. Berkeley and Los Angeles: The University of California Press.

Kim, Chi-ha (1978). *The Gold-Crowned Jesus And Other Writings*. Edited by Kim Chong Sun and Shelly Killen. Maryknoll, NY: Orbis Books.

Kim Chon-choon and Suh Kyung-soo (1982). "Korean Buddhism: a Historical Perspective," in *Buddhist Culture in Korea*. Ed. by International Cultural Foundation. Seoul: the Si-sa-yong-o-sa Publishers, Inc.

Kim, Duk-Whang (1988). *A History of Religions in Korea*. Seoul: Daeji Moonwhasa.

Kim, Kyoung Jae (1994). *Christianity and the encounter of Asian religions: Method of correlation, fusion of horizons, and paradigm shifts in the Korean grafting process*. Zoetermeer, the Nethelands: Boekencentrum Publishing House.

Kim, Myung Hyuk (1990). "The Concept of God in Minjung theology and its socio-economic and historical characteristics" in *Evangelical Review of Theology* 14: 126-149 (April).

Kim, Samu (1984). "His Holiness Pope John Paul II," in *Spring Wind: Buddhist Cultural Forum*, 4. 2 (Summer)

Kim, Yong Bock (1987). "Minjung social biography and theology" in *Asia Journal of Theology* 1: 523-530 (O).

───── (1992). *Messiah and Minjung: Christ's Solidarity with the People for New Life*. Hong Kong: Urban Rural Mission, Christian Conference of Asia.

Kim, Yong Choon (1978). *The Chondogyo Concept of Man: An Essence of Korean Thought*. Seoul: Pan Korea Book Corporation.

King, Ursula, ed. (1994). *Feminist Theology from the Third World: A Reader*. London: SPCK/ Maryknoll, NY: Orbis Books.

Kinsley, David R. (1988). *The Goddesses' Mirror: Visions of the Divine from East and West*. Albany, NY: State University of New York Press.

——— (1982). *Hinduism: a Cultural Perspective*. Englewood Cliffs, NJ: Prentice-Hall.

Kirk, J. Andrew (1979). *Liberation Theology: An evangelical view from the Third World*. Hants, England: Marshall Morgan & Scott.

Knitter, Paul (1996). *Jesus and the Other Names: Christian Mission and Global Responsibility*. Maryknoll, NY: Orbis Books.

——— (1995). *One Earth Many Religions: Multifaith Dialogue & Global Responsibility*. Maryknoll, NY: Orbis Books.

——— (1985). *No Other Name? A Critical Survey of Christian Attitudes toward the World Religions*. Maryknoll, NY: Orbis Books.

———, ed. (1991) *Pluralism and Oppression*. Lanham, Md.: University Press of America.

Kohn, Livia, ed. (1993). *The Taiost Experience: An Anthology*. Albany, NY: State University of New York Press.

——— (1991). *Early Chinese Mysticism: Philosophy and Soteriology in the Taoist Tradition*. Princeton: Princeton University Press.

——— and LaFargue, Michael, eds. (1998). *Lao-tzu and the Tao-te-ching*. Albany, NY: State University of New York Press.

Korean National Commission for UNESCO, ed. (1983). *Main Currents of Korean Thought*. Seoul: The Si-sa-yong-o-sa Publishers, Inc.; Arch Cape, Oregon: Pace International Research, Inc.

Kovel, Joel (1991). *History and Spirit: An Inquiry into the Philosophy of Liberation*. Boston: Beacon Press.

Kozhuvanal, Antony (1987). *The Emerging Roman Catholic Liberation Theology in India: The Significance of Mahatma Gandhi.* Th.D. Thesis, Toronto School of Theology.

Kraemer, Hendrik (1938). *The Christian Message in a non-Christian World.* London: Edinburgh House Press.

────── (1960). *World Cultures and World Religions.* London: Lutterworth Press.

Krieger, David J. (1991). *The New Universalism: Foundations for a Global Theology.* Maryknoll, NY: Orbis Books.

Kuhn, Thomas (1970). *The Structure of Scientific Revolutions.* 2nd ed., enlarged. Chicage: The University of Chicage Press.

Kung, Hans and Ching, Julia (1989). *Christianity and Chinese Religions.* New York: Doubleday and Collins Publishers.

Kwok, Pui Lan (1995). *Discovering the Bible in the non-biblical world.* Maryknoll, NY: Orbis Books.

LaFargue, Michael (1992). *The Tao of the Tao Te Ching: A Translation and Commentary.* Albany, New York: State University of New York Press.

Lancaster, Lewis R. and Yu, C. S. (1989). *Introduction of Buddhism in Korea: New Cultural Patterns.* Berkeley, CA.: Asian Humanities Press.

────── (1991). *Assimilation of Buddhism in Korea: Religious Maturity and Innovation in the Silla Dynasty.* Berkeley, CA.: Asian Humanities Press.

────── (1988). "Maitreya in Korea," in *Maitreya, the Future Buddha.* Ed. by Alan Sponberg and Helen Hardacre. Cambridge: Cambridge University Press.

Lao Tzu (1934). *The Way and Its Power.* Trans. by Arthur Waley. London: Allen & Unwin.

——— (1982). *Chinese Classics: Tao Te Ching*. Trans. by D. C. Lau. Hong Kong: Chinese University Press.

Lee Chong-Sik (1991). "South Korea: The Challenge of Democracy," in *Minidragons: Fragile Economic Miracles in the Pacific*, ed. by Steven Goldstein. New York: Westview Press.

Lee, Hee Chung (1992). "Liberation spirituality in Dae-dong Gut" in *Asian Christian Spirituality: Reclaiming Traditions*. Ed. by V. Fabella, et. al. Maryknoll, NY: Orbis Books.

Lee, Jung Young (1996). *The Trinity in Asian Perspective*. Nashville, TN: Abingdon Press.

———, ed. (1988). *An Emerging Theology in World Perspective: Commentary on Korean Minjung Theology*. Mystic, Connecticut: Twenty-Third Publications.

——— (1981). *Korean Shamanistic Rituals*. The Hague, The Netherlands: Mouton Publishers.

Lee, Ki-baek (1989). "Buddhism in Silla Society," in *Introduction of Buddhism to Korea: New Cultural Patterns*. Ed. by L. Lancaster and Chae-shin Yu. Berkeley, Ca.: Asian Humanities Press.

Lee, Peter, et. al., eds. (1997). *Sources of Korean Tradition*. Volume One: From Early Times Through the Sixteenth Century. New York: Columbia University Press.

Lee, Peter K. H. and Chung, Hyun Kyung (1990). "A Cross-Cultural Dialogue on the Yin-Yang Symbol" in *Ching Feng* 33: 136-157 (S).

Legge, James, trans. (1885). *The Yi King* (*Sacred Books of the East*, vol. 16). Oxford: Clarendon.

——— (1880). *The Religions of China: Confucianism and Taoism Described and Compared with Christianity*. London: Hodder and Stoughton.

―――― (1961). *The Chinese Classics*. Hong Kong: Hong Kong University Press. Original edition, Hong Kong: 1861–1873.

Li, Chenyang (1999). *The Tao Encounters the West: Explorations in Comparative Philosophy*. Albany, NY: State University of New York Press.

Lieh Tzu (1960). *The Book of Lieh-Tzu*. Trans. by A. C. Graham. London: John Murray.

Liu, Shu-hsien and Allinson, Robert E., eds. (1988). *Harmony and Strife: Contemporary Perspectives, East & West*. Hong Kong: The Chinese University of Hong Kong Press.

Lochhead, David (1988). *The Dialogical Imperative*. Maryknoll, NY: Orbis Books.

Luk, B., ed. (1992). *Contacts between Cultures*. Volumes 3-4. Selected papers from the 33rd International Congress of Asian and North African Studies, Toronto, August 15-25, 1990. Lewiston: Edwin Mellen Press.

Luzbetak, Louis J. (1988). *The Church and Cultures: New Perspectives in Missiological Anthropology*. Maryknoll, NY: Orbis Books.

Mackie, Steven G. (1989). "God's people in Asia: a key concept in Asian theology" in *Scottish Journal of Theology* 42, no. 2: 215-240.

Macquarrie, John (1985). *In Search Of Deity: An Essay in Dialectical Theism*. New York: Cross Road.

Mair, Victor H., ed. (1983). *Experimental Essays on Chuang-tzu*. Center for Asian and Pacific Studies, University of Hawaii Press.

Mannheim, Karl (1936). *Ideology and Utopia: An Introduction to the Sociology of Knowledge*. New York: Harcourt, Brace & Co.

Marquette, Jacques De. (1949). *Introduction to Comparative Mysticism*. New York: The Philosophical Library.

Martey, Emmanuel (1993). *African Theology: Inculturation and Liberation*. Maryknoll, NY: Orbis Books.

Maspero, Henri (1981). *Taoism and Chinese Religion*. Trans. by Frank A. Kierman, Jr. Amherst: The University of Massachusetts Press.

Mbiti, John (1986). "Christian Faith and African Religion," in *Third World Liberation Theologies: A Reader*, ed. by D.W. Ferm. Maryknoll, NY: Orbis Books.

McCune, George M. (1973). *Korea's Tragic Hours: The Closing Years of the Yi Dynasty*. Edited by Harold F. Cook and Alan M. McDougall. Seoul: Taewon Publishing Co.

McFague, Sallie (1987). *Models of God: Theology for an Ecological, Nuclear Age*. Philadelphia: Fortress Press.

McGuinn, Bernard (1981). "The God Beyond God: Theology and Mysticism in the Thought of Meister Eckhart," *Journal of Religion* 61.

McKenzie, Frederick A. (1908). *Tragedy of Korea*. London: Hodder & Stoughton.

———— (1920). *Korea's Fight for Freedom*. New York: Fleming H. Revell.

McNaughton, William (1971). *The Taoist Vision*. Ann Arbor: the University of Michigan Press.

Meng Tzu/ Mencius (1970). *Mencius*. Tr. by D. C. Lau. Harmondsworth, Middlesex: Penguin Classics.

———— (1963). *Mencius: A new translation arranged and annotated for the general reader*. Tr. by W.A.C.H. Dobson. Toronto: University of Toronto Press.

Miller, John W., ed. (1986). *Interfaith Dialogue: Four Approaches*. Waterloo, Ontario: University of Waterloo Press.

Moltmann, Jurgen (1980). "Christianity and the World Religions," in *Christianity and Other Religions,* ed. by J. Hick and B. Hebblethwaite. Collins Fount Paperbacks.

Moon, Tong Whan (1986). "Doing theology in Korea with reference to theological education: from Minjung theological viewpoint" in *East Asia Journal of Theology* 4 No. 2: 35-45 (O).

Moor, Charles E., ed. (1962). *The Chinese Mind: Essentials of Chinese Philosophy and Culture.* Honolulu, Hawaii: University of Hawaii Press.

Muller-Fahrenholz, Geiko, ed. (1978). *Unity in Today's World: The Faith and Order Studies on "Unity of the Church—Unity of Humankind."* Geneva: WCC.

Munro, Donald J. (1988). *Images of Human Nature: a Sung Protrait.* Princeton, N.J.: Princeton University Press.

Mveng, Engelbert (1983). "Third World Theology—What Theology? What Third World?: Evaluation by an African Delegate," in *Irruption of the Third World: Challenge to Theology.* Ed. by Virginia Fabella, M.M. and Sergio Torres. Maryknoll, NY: Orbis Books.

Nam, Andrew C. (1988). *Korea, Tradition & Transformation: A History of the Korean People.* Elizabeth, N.J. and Chongno-gu, Seoul: Hollym.

Nam, Andrew C. (1988). *Korea, Tradition & Transformation: A History of the Korean People.* Elizabeth, N.J. and Chongno-gu, Seoul: Hollym.

Needham, Joseph (1969). *Within the Four Seas: the Dialogue of East and West.* Toronto: University of Toronto Press.

―――― (1965). Time and Eastern Man. London: Royal Anthropological Institute of Great Britain & Ireland.

Neville, Robert C. (1991). *Behind the Masks of God: an Essay Toward Comparative Theology*. Albany, NY: State University of New York Press.

Newbigin, Lesslie (1961). *A Faith for this One World?* London: SCM Press.

Niebuhr, H. Richard (1943). *Radical Monotheism and Western Culture*. London: Faber and Faber.

——— (1951). *Christ and Culture*. New York: Harper & Row.

Nieuwenhove, J. V. and Goldewijk, B. K., eds. (1991). *Popular Religion, Liberation and Contextual Theology*. Papers from a congress (January 3-7, 1990, Nijmegen, the Netherlands) dedicated to Arnulf Camps OFM. Kampen: Uitgeversmaatschappij J.H. Kok.

Niles, Preman, ed. (1992). *Between the Flood and Rainbow*. Geneve: WCC.

Nishitani, Keyi (1983). *Religion and Nothingness*. Berkeley: University of California Press.

Noh, Jong-Sun (1984). *Religion and Just Revolution, Third World Perspective: Violence and Nonviolence in Minjung's Struggle for Justice in the Tonghak Revolution*. Hamden, CT: Center for Asian Theology.

——— (1992). "Tonghak and Liberation," in *Ching Feng* 35/3-4 (Dec.).

Northrop, F.S.C. (1947). *The Meeting of East and West: An Inquiry Concerning World Understanding*. New York: Macmillan.

Oduyoye, Mercy Amba (1990). "The Empowering Spirit of Religion," in *Lift Every Voice*. Ed. by Susan Brooks Thistlethwaite and Mary Potter Engel. San Francisco: Harper & Row.

Ogden, Schubert M. (1990). "Faith in God and Realization of Emptiness," in The Emptying God: A Buddhist-Jewish-Christian

Conversation, ed. by J. Cobb, Jr, and C. Ives. Maryknoll, NY: Orbis Books.

Oh, Kang-nam (1977). "Philosophical Implications of Hua-Yen Buddhism," in *Korean and Asian Religious Tradition*. Ed. by Chai-shin Yu. Toronto: Korean and Related Studies Press.

Olson, Alan M. (1992). *Hegel and The Spirit: Philosophy as Pneumatology*. Princeton, New Jersey: Princeton University Press.

Oppert, Ernest (1880). *A Forbidden Land: Voyages to Corea*. London: Sampson Low, Marston, Searle and Revington.

Ormiston, G.L., and Schrift, A.D., eds. (1990). *The Hermeneutic Tradition: From Ast to Ricoeur*. Albany: State University of New York Press.

Otto, Rudolf (1950). *The Idea of the Holy.* 2d ed. London: Oxford University Press.

——— (1932). *Mysticism East and West: Shankara and Meister Eckhart.* New York: Macmillan.

Overmyer, Daniel L. (1986). *Religions of China: The World as Living System*. San Francisco: Harper & Row.

——— (1988). "Messenger, Savior, and Revolutionary: Maitreya in Chinese Popular Religious Literature of the Sixteenth and Seventeenth Centuries," in *Maitreya, the Future Buddha*. Ed. by Alan Sponberg and Helen Hardacre. Cambridge: Cambridge University Press.

Paik, George L. (1929). *The History of Protestant Mission in Korea, 1832-1910*. Pyongyang: Union College Press.

Palmer Spencer J. (1967). *Korea and Christianity: The Problem of Identification with Tradition*. Seoul: Hollym Corporation.

———, ed. (1967). *The New Religions of Korea*. Seoul: Royal Asiatic Society, Korea Branch.

Panikkar, Raimundo (1978). *The Intrareligious Dialogue.* New York: Paulist Press.

——— (1979). *Myth, Faith and Hermeneutics: Cross-Cultural Studies.* New York/Ramsey/Toronto: Paulist Press.

——— (1989). *The Silence of God: The Answer of the Buddha.* Maryknoll, NY: Orbis Books.

——— (1991). "Can Theology Be Transcultural?," in *Pluralism and Oppression: Theology in World Perspective,* ed. by P. Knitter. Lanham, Md.: University Press of America.

——— (1995). *invisible harmony: Essays on Contemplation & Responsibility.* Ed. by Harry James Cargas. Minneapolis: Augsburg Fortress Press.

Park, Sung Bae (1983). *Buddhist Faith and Sudden Enlightenment.* Albany, NY: State University of New York Press.

Pathil, K. (1981). *Models in Ecumenical Dialogue: A Study of the Methodological Development in the Commission on Faith and Order of the WCC.* Bangalore, India.

Pieris, Aloysius, S. J. (1982). "Speaking of the Son of God in Non-Christian cultures, e.g., in Asia," in *Jesus Son of God?,* Edward Schillebeeckx and J.B. Metz, eds. *(Concillium,* 53). New York: Seabury.

——— (1983). "The Place of Non-Christian Religions and Cultures in the Evolution of Third World Theology," in *Irruption of the Third World: Challenge to Theology,* Virginia Fabella and Sergio Torres, eds. Maryknoll, NY: Orbis Books.

——— (1989). "Buddhists and Christians on peace and justice: Minjung Buddhism and Minjung theology" in *Dialogue* (Colombo) ns. 16, no. 1-3: 1-96.

——— (1990). *An Asian Theology of Liberation.* Maryknoll, NY: Orbis.

―――― (1996). *Fire and Water: Basic Issues in Asian Buddhism and Christianity*. Maryknoll, NY: Orbis Books.

Pyun, Sun Hwan (1985). "Other Religions and Theology" in *East Asia Journal of Theology* 3:2.

Race, Alan (1983). *Christians and Religious Pluralism: Patterns in the Christian Theology of Religions*. London: SCM Press.

Rahner, Karl (1969). "Reflections on Dialogue within a Pluralistic Society," in *Theological Investigations*. Vol. 6. New York: Seabury.

―――― (1974). "Anonymous Christianity and the Missionary Task of the Church," in *Theological Investigations*, vol. 12. New York: Seabury.

―――― (1980). "Christianity and the Non-Christian Religion," in *Christianity and Other Religions*, ed. by J. Hick and B. Hebblethwaite. Glasgow: Collins Fount Paperbacks.

Rainey, Lee (1992). "The Concept of Ch'i in the Thought of Wang Ch'ung," *Journal of Chinese Philosophy* 19 (Sept.), pp. 263–284.

Raiser, Konrad (1991). *Ecumenism in Transition: A Paradigm Shift in the Ecumenical Movement?* Geneva: WCC.

Rasmussen, David M. (1974). *Symbol and Interpretation*. The Hague: Martinus Nijhoff.

Rayan, Samuel (1980). "Reflections on a Live-In Experience: Slumdwellers," in *Asia's Struggle for Full Humanity: Towards a Relevant Theology* (Papers from the Asian Theological Conference, January 7-20, 1979, Wennappuwa, Sri Lanka). Ed. by Virginia Fabella. Maryknoll, NY: Orbis Books.

Reat, N. Ross and Perry, Edmund F. (1991). *A World Theology: The Central Spiritual Reality of Humankind*. Cambridge: Cambridge University Press.

Reuther, Rosemary R. (1985). *Sexism and God-Talk*. Boston: Beacon.

Rhi, Ki-yong (1977). "Wonhyo and His Thought," in *Korean and Asian Religious Tradition*. Ed. by Chai-Shin Yu. Toronto: Korean and Related Studies Press.

Richard, Kenneth L. (1977). "Translator's Note" at the end of his translation of Myong-gi Cho's article "Ch'an Buddhist Culture in Korea," in *Korean and Asian Religious Tradition*. Ed. by Chai-Shin Yu. Toronto: Korean and Related Studies Press.

Richardson, Alan (1964). *History Sacred and Profane*. London: SCM.

Ricoeur, Paul (1981). *Hermeneutics and Human Sciences*, ed. by J. B. Thompson. Cambridge: Cambridge University Press.

——— (1976). *Interpretation Theory: Discourse and the Surplus of Meaning*. Fort Worth, TX: Texas Christian University Press.

Ro, Young-chan (1989). *The Korean Neo-Confucianism of Yi Yulgok*. Albany, NY: State University of New York Press.

——— (1990). "Symbol, myth, and ritual: the method of the minjung" in *Lift Every Voice: Constructing Christian Thrologies from the Underside*. San Francisco: Harper & Row.

Rosemont, Henry, Jr., ed. (1991). *Chinese Texts and Philosophical Contexts*. La Salle, Ill.: Open Court Pub. Co.

Rousseau, Richard W., S.J., ed. (1982). *Christianity and the Religions of The East: Models For A Dynamic Relationship*. U.S.A: Ridge Row Press.

Roy, Andrew T. (1962). *On Asia's Rim*. New York: Friendship Press.

Rubin, Vitaly A. (1976). *Individual and State in Ancient China: Essays on Four Chinese Philosophers*. Trans. by Steven I. Levine. New York: Columbia University Press.

Russell, L., Kwok, P. L., Isasi-Diaz, A. M., and Cannon, G. K., eds. (1988). *Inheriting Our Mothers' Gardens: Feminist Theology in Third World Perspective*. Philadelphia: The Westminster Press.

# Bibliography

Samartha, Stanley J. (1991). *One Christ—Many Religions: Toward a Revised Christology*. Maryknoll, NY: Orbis Books.

——— (1981). *The Lordship of Jesus Christ and Religious Pluralism*. Park Town, Madras: Christian Literature Society.

Saso, Michael (1978). *The Teachings of Taoist Master Chuang*. New Haven and London: Yale University Press.

Schineller, Peter (1990). *A Handbook on Inculturation*. New York: Paulist Press.

——— (1992). "Inculturation and Syncretism: What is the Real Issue?" in *International Bulletin of Missionary Research* 16 (April).

Schreiter, Robert J. (1985). *Constructing Local Theologies*. Maryknoll, N.Y.: Orbis Books.

——— (1994). "Inculturation of Faith or Identification with Culture?," in *Christianity and Cultures: A Mutual Enrichment (Concilium, 1994/2)*. Ed. by Greinacher Norbert and Mette Norbert. London: SCM Press; Maryknoll: Orbis Books.

Schwartz, Vera (1986). *The Chinese Enlightenment: Intellectuals and the Legacy of the May Fourth Movement of 1919*. Berkeley, Ca.: University of California Press.

Schweitzer, Albert (1951). *Christianity and the Religions of the World*. London: Allen & Unwin, 1922; New York: Holt, 1939; London: Macmillan.

Segundo, Juan Luis (1984). *Faith and Ideologies*. Maryknoll, NY: Orbis.

Seidel, Anna K. (1969–70). "The Image of the Perfect Ruler in Early Taoist Messianism: Lao-Tzu and Li Hung," in *History of Religions*, IX, 2–3.

——— (1984). "Taoist Messianism," in *Numen*, 31, 2.

Setton, Mark (1997). *Chông Yagyong: Korea's Challenge to Orthodox Neo-Confucianism*. Albany, NY: State University of New York Press.

Seung Sahn (1997). *The Compass of Zen*. Compiled and edited by Hyon Gak Sunim. Boston & London: Shambhala.

Shih, Vincent Y. C. (1967). *The Taiping Ideology: Its Sources, Interpretations, and Influences*. Seattle and London: University of Washington Press.

Shin Ock Hee (1987). "'The One Mind and the Encompassing'— Understanding of Reality in Wonhyo and Karl Jaspers," in *Weltoffenheit des christlichen Glaubens: Fritz Buri zu Ehren*, ed. by Imelda Abbt and Alfred Jager. Verlag Katzmann K.G., Tubingen: Verlag Paul Haupt Bern.

Shorter, Aylward (1994). *Evangelization and Culture*. London: G. Chapman.

Slater, Peter (1978). *Dynamics of Religion: Meaning and Change in Religious Traditions*. New York: Harper & Row.

——— (1993). "Other Religion? Other Rationality?," an unpublished paper.

Smart, Ninian (1993). *Buddhism and Christianity: Rivals and Allies*. Honolulu: University of Hawaii Press.

——— (1983). *Worldviews, Crosscultural Explorations of Human Beliefs*. New York: Scribners.

Smith, Wilfred Cantwell (1972). *The Faith of Other Men*. New York: Harper & Row, 1962; New York: Harper Torchbooks.

——— (1964). *The Meaning and End of Religion*. New York: New American Library.

# Bibliography

———— (1987). "Idolatry," in *The Myth of Christian Uniqueness: Toward a Pluralistic Theology of Religions*. Ed. by John Hick and Paul Knitter. Maryknoll, NY: Orbis Books.

Smith, Steven G. (1988). *The Concept of the Spiritual: An Essay in First Philosophy*. Philadelphia: Temple University Press.

Sommer, Deborah, ed. (1995). *Chinese Religion: An Anthology of Sources*. New York & Oxford: Oxford University Press.

Song, Choan-Seng (1986). *Theology from the Womb of Asia*. Maryknoll, NY: Orbis Books.

Spence, Jonathan D. (1985). *The Memory Palace of Matteo Ricci*. London/Boston: faber and faber.

Sponberg, Alan and Hardacre, Helen, eds. (1988). *Maitreya, the Future Buddha*. Cambridge: Cambridge University Press.

Streeter, Burnett H. (1932). *The Buddha and the Christ: An Exploration of the Meaning of the Universe and of the Purpose of Human Life*. London: Macmillan and Co.

Streng, Frederich (1967). *Emptiness*. Nashville: Abingdon.

Suchocki, Marjorie H. (1987). "In Search of Justice: Religious Pluralism from a Feminist Perspective," in *The Myth of Christian Uniqueness*, ed. by J. Hick and P. Knitter. Maryknoll, NY: Orbis Books.

Sugirtharajah, Rasiah S., ed. (1993). *Asian Faces of Jesus*. Maryknoll, NY: Orbis Books.

————, ed. (1991). *Voices from the Margin: Interpreting the Bible in the Third World*. Maryknoll, NY: Orbis Books.

Suh, David Kwang-sun (1991). *The Korean Minjung in Christ*. Hong Kong: CTC-CCA.

———— (1985). "Theology of story-telling: a theology by minjung" in *Ministerial Formation*, no. 31: 10–22 (S).

——— (1983). "Korean Theological Development in the 1970s," *Minjung Theology: People as the Subjects of Theology*. Revised Edition. Ed. by CTC-CCA. London: Zed Press/ Maryknoll, NY: Orbis Books/ Toa Payoh, Singapore: CCA.

Suh, Nam-dong (1984/5). "Cultural Theology, Political Theology and Minjung Theology," in *CTC Bulletin* Vol.5 No.3–Vol.6 No.1; December–April.

——— (1983). "Historical Reference for a Theology of Minjung," in *Minjung Theology: People as the Subjects of Theology*. Ed. by CTC-CCA. Revised Edition. London: Zed Press/ Maryknoll, NY: Orbis Books/ Toa Payoh, Singapore: CCA

Sundermeier, Theo (1987). "Minjung theology of Korea" in *Scriptura*, no. 22: 48-59.

Suzuki, D. T. (1964). *An Introduction to Zen Buddhism*. New York: Grove Press, Inc.

Swidler, Leonard (1990). "A Jerusalem–Tokyo Bridge," in *A Bridge To Buddhist-Christian Dialogue,* by L. Swidler and S. Yagi. New York: Paulist Press.

———, ed. (1987). *Toward a Universal Theology of Religion.* Maryknoll, NY: Orbis Books.

———, et. al., eds. (1990). *Death Or Dialogue: From the Age of Monologue to the Age of Dialogue.* London: SCM Press and Philadelphia: Trinity Press International.

Taylor, John V. (1980). "The Theological Basis of Interfaith Dialogue," in *Christianity and Other Religions,* ed. by J. Hick and B. Hebblethwaite. Glasgow: Collins Fount Paperbacks.

Taylor, Rodney Leon (1978). *The Cultivation of Sagehood as a Religious Goal in Neo-Confucianism: a Study of Selected Writings of Kao P'an-lung (1562-1626).* Missoula, Mont.: Scholars Press.

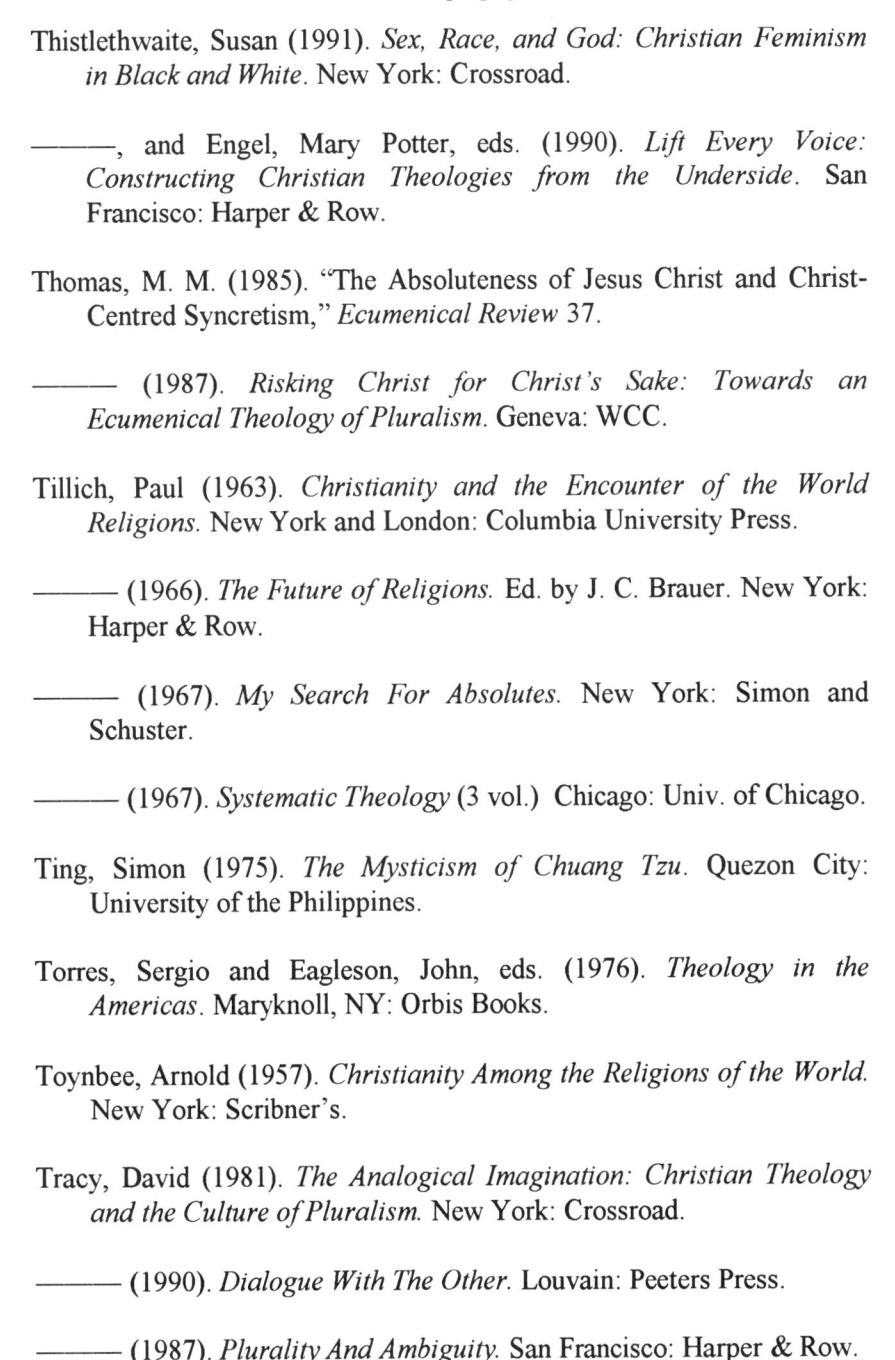

Thistlethwaite, Susan (1991). *Sex, Race, and God: Christian Feminism in Black and White.* New York: Crossroad.

———, and Engel, Mary Potter, eds. (1990). *Lift Every Voice: Constructing Christian Theologies from the Underside.* San Francisco: Harper & Row.

Thomas, M. M. (1985). "The Absoluteness of Jesus Christ and Christ-Centred Syncretism," *Ecumenical Review* 37.

——— (1987). *Risking Christ for Christ's Sake: Towards an Ecumenical Theology of Pluralism.* Geneva: WCC.

Tillich, Paul (1963). *Christianity and the Encounter of the World Religions.* New York and London: Columbia University Press.

——— (1966). *The Future of Religions.* Ed. by J. C. Brauer. New York: Harper & Row.

——— (1967). *My Search For Absolutes.* New York: Simon and Schuster.

——— (1967). *Systematic Theology* (3 vol.) Chicago: Univ. of Chicago.

Ting, Simon (1975). *The Mysticism of Chuang Tzu.* Quezon City: University of the Philippines.

Torres, Sergio and Eagleson, John, eds. (1976). *Theology in the Americas.* Maryknoll, NY: Orbis Books.

Toynbee, Arnold (1957). *Christianity Among the Religions of the World.* New York: Scribner's.

Tracy, David (1981). *The Analogical Imagination: Christian Theology and the Culture of Pluralism.* New York: Crossroad.

——— (1990). *Dialogue With The Other.* Louvain: Peeters Press.

——— (1987). *Plurality And Ambiguity.* San Francisco: Harper & Row.

Troeltsch, Ernst (1980). "The Place of Christianity among the World Religions," in *Christianity and Other Religions,* ed. by J. Hick and B. Hebblethwaith. Glasgow: Collins Fount Paperbacks.

Trollope, Mark Napier (1915). *The Church in Corea.* London & Milwaukee: A. R. Mowbray & Co. Ltd. & The Young Churchman.

Tu, Wei-ming (1989). *Centrality and Commonality: An Essay on Confucian Religiousness.* Revised edition. Albany, NY: State University of New York Press.

———— (1985). *Confucian Thought: Selfhood as Creative Transformation.* Albany, NY: State University of New York Press.

———— (1979). *Humanity and Self-Cultivation: Essays in Confucian Thought.* Berkeley: Asian Humanities Press.

Tuck, Andrew P. (1990). *Comparative Philosophy and the Philosophy of Scholarship: On the Western Interpretation of Nagarjuna.* New York: Oxford University Press.

Tucker, Mary Evelyn (1989). *Moral and Spiritual Cultivation in Japanese Neo-Confucianism: The Life and Thought of Kaibara Ekken (1630-1714).* Albany, NY: State University of New York Press.

———— and Berthrong, John, eds. (1998). *Confucianism and Ecology: The Interrelation of Heaven, Earth, and Humans.* Cambridge, Mass: Harvard University Center for the Study of World Religions.

Tucker, Robert, ed. (1978). *The Marx-Engels Reader.* 2$^{nd}$ ed. New York: Norton.

Van der Bent, Ans J., ed. *Breaking Down the Walls: World Council of Churches Statements and Actions on Racism 1948-1985.*

————, ed. (1981). *Voices of Unity.* Essays in Honour of Willem Adolf Visser't Hooft on the Occasion of his 80th Birthday. Geneva: WCC.

Van Leeuwen, A.Th. (1964). *Christianity in World History: The Meeting of the Faiths of East and West.* London: Edinburgh House.

Visser't Hooft, W.A. (1963). *No Other Name: The Choice Between Syncretism and Christian Universalism.* London: SCM.

——— (1974). *Has the Ecumenical Movement a Future?* Belfast: Christian Journals Ltd.

——— (1982). *The Genesis and Formation of the World Council of Churches.* Geneva: WCC.

Waley, Arthur (1939). *Three Ways of Thought in Ancient China.* London: Allen & Unwin.

Wawrytko, Sandra A. (1981). *The Undercurrent of Feminine Philosophy in Eastern and Western Thought.* Washington, D.C.: University Press of America.

W.C.C. (1979). *Guidelines on Dialogue with People of Living Faiths and Ideologies.* Geneva: World Council of Churches.

Weems, Benjamin B. (1964). *Reform, Rebellion, and the Heavenly Way.* Tucson: Univ. of Arizona Press.

Wehrle, Edmund S. (1966). *Britain, China, and the Antimissionary Riots 1891–1900.* Minneapolis: University of Minnesota Press.

Welch, Holmes (1965). *Taoism: The Parting of the Way.* Rev. ed. U.S.A.: Beacon Press.

——— and Seidel, Anna, eds. (1979). *Facets of Taoism: Essays in Chinese Religion.* New Haven and London: Yale University Press.

Wells, Harold (1987). "The question of ideological determination in liberation theology," *Toronto Journal of Theology* 3: 209–220, Fall.

——— (1992). "Holy Spirit and Theology of the Cross: Significance for Dialogue," in *Theological Studies* 53/3 (Sept).

——— (1996). *A Future For Socialism? Political Theology and the "Triumph of Capitalism."* Valley Forge, Pennsylvania: Trinity Press International.

Whitehead, A. N. (1979). *Process and Reality.* Corrected Ed. New York and London: The Free Press.

——— (1960). *Religions in the Making.* New York: New American Library.

Wiles, Maurice (1992). *Christian Theology and Inter-religious Dialogue.* London: SCM Press; Philadelphia, Pa.: Trinity Press International.

Wilkinson, W.H. (1897). *The Corean Government: Constitutional Changes, July 1894 to October 1895, with an Appendix on Subsequent Enactments to June 30th, 1896.* Shanghai: The Statistical Department of Inspectorate-General of Customs.

Williams, Delores, S. (1993). *Sisters in the Wilderness: the Challenge of Womanist God-Talk.* Maryknoll, NY: Orbis Books.

Won, Yi Beom and Lim, Byeong Ho (1992). *A History of Korean Buddhist Culture and Some Essays: the Buddhist Pure Land & the Christian Kingdom of Heaven.* Seoul: Jip Moon Dang Publishing.

Woods, Richard, ed. (1980). *Understanding Mysticism.* Garden City, NY: Doubleday & Company.

Wu, John C.H., trans. and Sih, Paul K.T. ed. (1961). *Lao Tzu/ Tao Te Ching.* New York: St. John's University Press.

Wu, Kuang-ming (1982). *Chuang Tzu: World Philosopher at Play.* New York: Crossroad.

Yadav, Bibhuti S. (1987). "Anthropomorphism and Cosmic Confidence" in *Toward a Universal Theology of Religion*, ed. by L. Swidler. Maryknoll, NY: Orbis Books.

Yagi, Seiichi, and Swidler, Leonard, eds. (1990). *A Bridge To Buddhist-Christian Dialogue.* New York: Paulist Press.

Yin, Kuang (1992). *Pure-Land Zen/ Zen Pure-Land: Letters from Patriarch Yin Kuang*. Translated by Thich Thien Tam, et. al. and edited by Forrest Smith. Bronx, N.Y.: Sutra Translation Committee of the United States and Canada.

Yoo, Boo-Woong (1988). *Korean Pentecostalism: Its History and Theology*. Frankfurt am Main & New York: Peter Lang.

Yu, Chai-shin, ed. (1977). *Korean and Asian Religious Tradition*. Toronto: Korean and Related Studies Press.

## Resources in Korean

Ahn, Byung-mu (1993). *Jônjip [Collection]*. 6 Vols. [1. *Yôksawa Haesôk*; 2. *Minjung Shinhakûl Malhanda*; 3. *Galilaeaûi Yesu*; 4. *Yesuûi Iyagi*; 5. *Minjungkwa Sôngsô*; 6. *Yôksawa Minjung*]. Seoul: Han'gilsa.

———— (1989). *Minjung Sagôn Sogûi Grisdo [Christ in Minjung Event]*. Seoul: Han'guk Shinhak Yôn'guso.

———— (1988). *Minjung Shinhak Iyagi [Story of Minjung Theology]*. Rev. ed. Seoul: Han'guk Shinhak Yôn'guso.

———— (1985). "Contemporary Situation and the Task of Korean Theology," in KNCC, ed., *Han'guk Yôksa Sogûi Gidokgyo [Christianity Within Korean History]*, Ed. by KNCC. Revised and expanded edition.

Bae, Jong-ho (1989). *Han'guk Yuhakûi Cholhakjôk Jôn'gae [Philosophical Development of Korean Confucianism]*. Vol. II. Seoul: Won Kwang Univ. Press.

Bôpsông (1989). "Minjung Bulgyo Undongûi Inyômkwa Gyorijôk Baegyông [Ideological and Doctrinal Background of Minjung

Buddhism]," in *Minjung Bulgyoûi Tamgu [Studies in Minjung Buddhism]*. Seoul: Minjoksa.

Bulgyo Shinmunsa, ed. (1994). *Han'guk Bulgyosaûi Jaejomyông [History of Korean Buddhism: A Re-illumination]*. Seoul: Bulgyo Sidaesa.

—— (1988) *Bulgyoesô Bon Insaengkwa Segye [Humanity and World in Buddhism]*. Seoul: Hongbôpwon.

Cha, Ju-hwan (1984). *Han'gukûi Dogyo Sasang [Taoist Thought in Korea]*. Seoul: Donghwa Chulpan Gongsa.

Chae, Pil-gun (1992). *Bigyo Jonggyoron [Theory of Comparative Religion]*. Seoul: Daehan Gidogkyo Sohoe.

Chinul or Jinul (1978). *Jinshim Jiksôl [Direct Exposition on True Mind]*. Trans. and Comm. by Rhi Ki-yông. Seoul: Dongguk Daehakgyo Bulgyo Ganhaeng Wiwônhoe.

Cho, Hung-yun (1992). "Mugyo [Shamanism]," in *Han'guk Jonggyo Sasangsa [History of Korean Religious Thought] IV*. Seoul: Yonsei Univ. Press.

Cho, Hung-yun (1990). *Muwa Minjok Munhwa [Shamanism and Korean Culture]*. Seoul: Minjok Munhwasa.

Choe, Dong-hee (1990). "Choe Je-U: Donggyông Daejôn'oe [A Commentary on Choe Je-U's Donggyông Daejôn and Others]," in *Han'gukûi Minsok-Jonggyo Sasang [Korean Cultural-Religious Thought]*. Ed. by Lee Byung-do, et. al. Seoul: Samsung Chulpansa.

—— and Ryu, Byung-dok (1993). *Han'guk Jonggyo Sasangsa III [History of Korean Religious Thought III]: Chôndogyo and Wônbulgyo*. Seoul: Yonsei University Press.

Choe, Gil-song (1994). *Han'guk Musokûi Ihae [Understanding Korean Shamanism]*. Seoul: Yejonsa.

# Bibliography 193

Choe, Han-ki (1857). *Kihak* [*Study on Ki (Ch'i)*]. Translated by Sohn Byung-wook (Seoul: Yogang Chulpansa, 1992).

Choe, Je-U (1860-4). *Donggyông Daejôn* [*Great Scriptures on Eastern Learning*].

────── (1860-4). *Yongdam Yusa* [*Writings at Yongdam*].

Choe, Nam-son (1948). *Josôn Sangshik* [*Plain Truths of Korea*]. Seoul.

Chu, Jae-yong, ed. (1987). *Asiaûi Sanghwangkwa Shinhak* [*Asian Situation and Theology*]. Seoul: The Christian Literature Society.

Chun, Chul-hwan (1984). "Gukje Gyôngjeûi Chejil Byônhwawa 70 Nyôndaeûi Han'guk Gyôngje [Changes in International Economic Climate and the Korean Economy of the 70s]," in Park Hyun-che, et. al., *Han'guk Sahoeûi Jaeinsik I: Gyôngje Gaebale Ttarûn Jôngchi.Gyôngje. Sahoeûi Gujo Byônhwa* [*A New Look at the Korean Society I: Changes in the Social/Economic/Political Structure Due to Economic Development*]. Seoul: Han Ul.

Chung, Dae-hwan (1992). *Josônjo Sônglihak Yôn'gu* [*A Study of Human Nature in Josôn (Yi) Dynasty*]. Kangwondo: Kangwon Univ. Press.

Chung, David (1986). *Christianity and The World of East Asians: Confrontation and Accommodation.* Seoul: Korea Theological Study Institute.

Chung, Suk-jong (1983). *Josôn Hugi Sahoe Byôndong Yôn'gu* [*Studies in Social Change in the Later Josôn (Yi) Dynasty*]. Seoul: Iljogak.

Cubo, Noritada (1990). *Dogyosa* [*History of Taoism*]. Translated by Choi Jun-sik. Seoul: Bundo Chulpansa.

Dolbegae Pyônjipbu, ed. (1980). *Han'guk Gûndae Minjok Undongsa* [Premodern Nationalist Movement in Korea]. Seoul: Dolbegae.

Donghak Yon'guwon, ed. (1991). *Han'gûl Donggyông Daejôn* [*Great Scriptures of Eastern Learning in Korean*]. Daejun: Donghak Yon'guwon.

Gidokgyo Sasang Pyônjipbu, ed. (1983). *Han'guk Yôksawa Gidokgyo [Korean History and Christianity]*. Seoul: Daehan Gidokgyo Sohoe.

———, ed. (1983). *Han'gukûi Shinhak Sasang [Theological Thoughts in Korea]*. Seoul: Daehan Gidokgyo Sôhoe.

———, ed. (1992). *Han'gukûi Munhwawa Shinhak [Culture and Theology in Korea]*. Seoul: Daehan Gidokgyo Sôhoe.

Gohee Committee of Dr. Ahn Byung-mu, ed. (1992). *Yesu. Minjung. Minjok [Jesus. Minjung. Peoples]*. Essays Written in Commemoration of the Seventieth Birthday of Dr. Ahn Byung Mu. Chun An, Chungnam: The Korea Theological Study Institute.

Gohee Ginyom Nonmunjip Chulpal Wiwonhoe, ed. (1993). *Han'guk Jonggyowa Han'guk Shinhak [Korean Religions and Korean Theology]*. Seoul: Han'guk Shinhak Yôn'guso.

Han, Jong-man (1991). "Han'gukûi Yubuldo Samgyo Hoetongron [Mutual Interaction of the Three Traditions Buddhism-Confucianism-Taoism in Korea]," in *Han'guk Dogyowa Doga Sasang [Korean Taoist Religion and Philosophy]*, ed. by Han'guk Dogyo Sasang Yôn'guhoe. Seoul: Asea Munhwasa.

Han'guk Chôlhakhoe, ed. (1987). *Han'guk Chôlhaksa [History of Korean Philosophy]*. Volume II. Seoul: Dongmyongsa.

Han'guk Chôlhaksasang Yôn'guhoe (1995). *Nonjaeng ûro Bonûn Han'guk Chôlhak [Korean Philosophy Viewed Through Debates]*. Seoul: Yemunsowon.

Han'guk Dogyo Sasang Yônguhoe, ed. (1989). *Dogyo Sasangûi Han'gukjôk Jôn'gae [Contextual-ization of Taoist Philosophy in Korea]*. Seoul: Asea Munhaksa.

Han'guk Gidokgyo Hakhoe, ed. (1992). *Changjoûi Bojônkwa Han'guk Shinhak [Restoration of Creation and Korean Theology]*. Seoul: Daehan Gidokgyo Sôhoe.

# Bibliography

Han'guk Jonggyo Hakhoe, ed. (1992). *Jonggyodûlûi Daehwa: Han'gukesô Jonggyoûi Gyoryuwa Jônmang [Dialogue Among Religions: Interchange And Prospect In Korea]*. Seoul: Sasangsa.

Han'guk Minjungsa Yôn'guhoe [Society for the Study of Minjung's History], ed. (1986). *Han'guk Minjungsa [History of Korean Minjung]*. 2 vol. (Premodern & Modern). Seoul: Pulbit.

Han'guk Sahoesa Yôn'guhoe, ed. (1987). *Han'gukûi Jonggyowa Sahoe Byôndong [Korean Religions and Social Transformation]*, Seoul: Munhakkwa Jisôngsa.

———, ed. (1988). *Hyôndae Han'guk Jabonjuûiwa Gyegûp Munje [Contemporary Korean Capitalism and the Issue of Class]*. Seoul: Munhak kwa Jisongsa.

———, ed. (1989). *Hyôndae Han'gukûi Jabon Chukjôkkwa Minjung Saenghwal [Accumulation of Capital in Contemporary Korea and the Life of Minjung]*. Seoul: Munhakkwa Jisôngsa.

Hong I-seop (1983). "Han'guk Hyôndaesawa Gidokgyo [Modern History of Korea and Christianity]," in *Han'guk Yôksawa Gidokgyo [Korean History and Christianity]*, ed. by Gidokgyo Sasang Pyônjipbu Seoul: Daehan Gidokgyo Sôhoe.

Hong, Jang-hwa (1990). *Chôndogyo Gyoriwa Sasang [Chôndogyo Doctrine and Thought]*. Seoul: Chôndogyo Jung'ang Chongbu.

Hwang, Hyun (1985). *Donghaklan [Donghak War]*. Translation and introduction by Lee Min Su. Seoul: Ûlyo Munhwasa.

Hwang, Sun-myong (1980). *Minjung Jonggyo Undongsa [History of Minjung Religious Movement]*. Seoul: Jonglo Sôjôk.

Jangja [Chuang Tzu] (1999). *Jangja [Thinking With Chuang Tzu: A New Translation of the Inner Chapters and Some Reflective Notes]*. Trans. by Kang-nam Oh. Seoul: Hyon'amsa.

Jinul. See Chinul.

Jonggyo Shinhak Yôn'guso, Sokang Daehakgyo, ed. (1988–91). *Jonggyo Shinhak Yôn'gu [Studies in Theology of Religion]: vols 1-4*. Seoul: Bundo Chulpansa.

Kang Kon-kee (1988). "Bulgyoûi Pyôngdûngkwan [Buddhist Notion of Equality]," in *Bulgyoesô Bon Insaengkwa Segye [Humanity and World in Buddhism]*, ed. by Bulgyo Shinmunsa. Seoul: Hongbôpwon.

Kang, Man-kil (1978). *Bundan Sidaeûi Yôksa Insik [Historical Understanding of the Divided Times]*. Seoul: Changjakkwa Bipyôngsa.

Keel, Hee-Sung (1991). "Sônkwa Minjung Haebang [Sôn (Zen) and Minjung Liberation]," in *Jonggyo Shinhak Yôn'gu [Studies in Theology of Religion]*. Vol. 4. Ed. by Jonggyo Shinhak Yôn'guso, Sokang Daehakgyo [Centre for the Study of Theology of Religion, Sokang University]. Seoul: Bundo Chulpansa.

Kim, Bum-bu (1986). *Punglyu Jôngshin [Punglyu Spirit]*. Seoul: Jong'umsa.

Kim, Bu-sik (1977). *Samguk Sagi [History of Three Kingdoms]*. Trans. and comm. by Yi Byung-do. Seoul: Ulyu Munhwasa.

Kim, Chi-ha (1994). *Donghak Iyagi [The Story of Donghak]*. Seoul: Sol Publishers.

────── (1992). *Saeng Myông [Life]*. Seoul: Sol Publishers.

────── (1984). "Saengmyôngûi Damjijain Minjung [Minjung the Authority of Life]," in *Han'guk Minjunglon [Discussions on Minjung Perspective in Korea]*, ed. by KNCC. Seoul: Korea Theological Study Institute.

Kim, Ha-tae (1985). *Dongsô Chôlhakûi Mannam [Encounter of Philosophies East and West]*. Seoul: Jonglo Sôjôk.

Kim, Hong-chul, Kim, Sang-il and Cho, Hung-yun (1992). *Han'guk Jonggyo Sasangsa [History of Korean Religious Thought] IV: Jûngsangyo, Daejonggyo and Mugyo*. Seoul: Yonsei Univ. Press.

Kim, In-hwan (1994). *Donghakûi Ihae [Understanding Donghak]*. Seoul: Koryo University Press.

Kim, Jae-young (1990). *Minjok Jôngtoron 1: Minjok Undong [Peoples' Pure Land Theory 1: Peoples' Movement]*. Seoul: Bulkwang Chulpansa.

Kim, Ki-hyon (1992). "Toegyeûi Sadan Chiljônglon [Toegye on the Four Beginnings and Seven Emotions]," in *Sadan Chiljônglon [Theory of the Four Beginnings and Seven Emotions]*, ed. by Minjokkwa Sasang Yon'guhoe [Society for the Study of (Korean) Peoples and Thought].

Kim, Kil-hwan (1981). *Han'guk Yangmyônghak Yôn'gu [Studies on Wang Yang-ming Thought in Korea]*. Seoul: Ilchisa.

Kim, Kyoung-jae (1994). *Haesôkhakkwa Jonggyoshinhak: Bogûmkwa Han'guk Jonggyowaûi Mannam [Hermeneutics and the Theology of Religions: The Encounter Between the Gospel and the Religions in Korea]*. Chôn An, Chungnam: Han'guk Shinhak Yon'guso.

─── (1985). *Yôngsông Shinhak Sôsôl [Introduction to Theology of Spirituality]*. Seoul: Daehan Gidokgyo Chulpansa.

─── and Kim, Sang-il, ed. (1988). *Kwajông Chôlhakkwa Kwajông Shinhak [Process Philosophy and Process Theology]*. Seoul: Heemangsa.

Kim, Kyung-il (1985). "Donghak Thought from a Humanistic Perspective [Inbonjuûiesô Bon Donghak Sasang]," *Jongshin Munhwa Yôn'gu* 26. Sungnam, Kyunggido: Jongmunyôn.

KNCC, ed. (1985). *Han'guk Yôksa Sogûi Gidokgyo [Christianity Within Korean History]*. Revised and expanded edition. Seoul: Kiminsa.

———, ed. (1984). *Han'guk Minjunglon [Discussions on Minjung Perspective in Korea]*. Seoul: Korea Theological Study Institute.

Ko, Eun (1988). "Mirûkkwa Minjung [Maitreya and Minjung]," in *Mirûk Sasangkwa Minjung Sasang [Maitreya Thought and Minjung Thought]*. Seoul: Hanjin Chulpansa.

Koryo Daehakgyo Minsok Munhwa Yôn'guso, ed. (1982). *Han'guk Minsok Daegwan (Survey of Korean Folk Culture): Min'gan Shin'ang-Jonggyo [Folk Belief-Religion] 3*. Seoul: Koryo Univ. Centre for the Study of Korean Folk Culture.

Kum, Jang-tae (1994). *Han'guk Yuhaksaûi Ihae [Understanding the History of Korean Confucianism]*. Seoul: Minjok Munhwasa.

——— (1990). *Han'guk Gûndaeûi Yugyosasang [Modern Korean Confucian Thought]*. Seoul: Seoul University Press.

——— and Ryu, Dong-sik (1986). *Han'guk Jonggyosasangsa [History of Korean Religious Thought]*. Vol II: Confucianism and Christianity. Seoul: Yonsei Univ. Press.

Kawada, Kumataro (1988). "Bulta Hwaôm: Hwaômgyôngûi Gochal [Hwaôm (Hua-yen) Buddhism: A Study of Hwaôm (Avatamsaka) Sutra]," in *Hwaôm Sasangron [Essays on Hwaôm Thought]*. Ed. by Sok Won-wook. Seoul: Undansa.

Kwon, Jin-kwan (1993). *Sônglyôngkwa Minjung–Silchônjôk Shinhakkwa Shinhakjôk Silchôn [Holy Spirit and Minjung–Praxis Theology and Theological Praxis]*. Chônan, Chungnam: Han'guk Shinhak Yôn'guso [Korea Theological Study Institute].

Lee, Byung-do, et. al, eds. (1990). *Han'gukûi Minsok-Jonggyo Sasang [Korean Cultural-Religious Thought]*. Seoul: Samsung Chulpansa.

Lee, Don-hwa, ed. (1969). *Chôndogyo Changgônsa [History of Chôndogyo Foundation]*. Seoul: Chôndogyo Jung'ang Jongliwon, 1933; Seoul: Gyoung'in Munhwasa.

Lee, Eun-bong, ed. (1994). *Dan'gun Shinhwa Yôn'gu [Study on Dan'gun Myth]*. Seoul: Onnuri.

Lee, Hang-nyong (1982). "Dan'gun Sasangkwa Donghak Sasang [The Philosophies of Dan'gun and Donghak]," in *Shin In Gan [New Humanity]*, 394: 16–23,

Lee, Hyun-hee (1992). *Donghak Sasangkwa Donghak Hyôkmyông [Donghak Thought and the Donghak Revolution]*. Seoul: Chôngha Chulpansa.

Lee, Jong-sul (1997). *Toegye Yulgok Chôlhak Yôn'gu [Studies on Toegye (Yi Hwang) and Yulgok (Yi I)]*. 6 Vols. Ed. by Han'guk Sasang Yôn'guwon. Seoul: Sudôk Munhwasa.

Lee, Jung-yong (1980). *Yôkkwa Gidokgyo Sasang [The (Book of) Change and Christian Thought]*. Seoul: Korea Theological Study Institute.

Lee, Kang-O, et. al. (1994). *Han'guk Gûndaesae Issôsôûi Donghakkwa Donghak Nongmin Undong [Donghak and the Donghak Farmers Movement in the Modern History of Korea]*. Han'guk Jôngshin Munhwa Yôn'guwon.

Lee, Kang-su (1989). *Doga Sasangûi Yôn'gu [A Study on Taoist Thought]*. Seoul: Koryo Daehakgyo Minjok Munhwa Yon'guso Chulpanbu.

Lee, Kwang-lin (1981). *Han'guksa Gangjwa V (Gûndaepyôn) [Lectures on Korean History: vol. V (Premodern)]*. Seoul: Iljogak.

Lee, Man-yul (1981). *Han'guk Gidokgyowa Yôksa Ûisik [Korean Christianity and Historical Consciousness]*. Seoul: Jisik Sanôpsa.

Lee, Nung-hwa (1981). *Josôn Dogyosa [History of Korean Taoism]*. Trans. with notes by Lee Jong-eun. Seoul: Bosông Munhwasa.

Lee, Se-kwon, ed. (1986). *Donghak Gyôngjôn [Scriptures of Donghak]*. Seoul: Jungminsa.

## Bibliography

Lee, Suk-ho and Chung, Byung-jo (1991). *Han'guk Jonggyo Sasangsa I: Bulgyo & Dogyo P'yôn [History of Korean Religious Thought I: Buddhism & Taoism]*. Seoul: Yonsei University Press.

Lee, Ul-ho, et. al. (1990). *Han Sasangkwa Minjok Jonggyo [Philosophy of Han and Korean Religions]*. Seoul: Iljisa.

Lee Young-ja (1988). "Bulgyoûi Yôsôngkwan [Buddhism on Women]," in *Bulgyoesô Bon Insaengkwa Segye*. Ed. by Bulgyo Shinmunsa. Seoul: Hongbôpwon.

Min, Kyung-bae (1993). *Han'guk Gidokgyohoesa [Church History in Korea]*. Seoul: Yonsei Univ. Press.

Minjokkwa Sasang Yôn'guhoe, ed. (1992). *Sadan Chiljônglon [Theory of the Four Beginnings and Seven Emotions]*. Seoul: Sôgwangsa.

Mok, Jong-bae (1989). *Samguk Sidaeûi Bulgyo [Buddhism in the Three Kingdoms]*. Seoul: Dongkug Daehakgyo Chulpanbu.

Moon, Ik-hwan (1990). *Hebree Minjungsa [History of Hebrew Minjung]: Moon Ik-Hwan Iyagi Madang [Moon Ik-Whan's Story Garden]*. Seoul: Samminsa.

NCC Shinhak Yôn'gu Wiwonhoe, ed. (1982). *Minjungkwa Han'guk Shinhak [Minjung and Korean Theology]*. Seoul: Han'guk Shinhak Yôn'guso.

Oh, Ji-young (1974). *Donghaksa [History of Donghak]* (Seoul: Yôngchang Sôgwan, 1940). Trans. with explanatory notes by Jang Hee-lee. Seoul: Pak Yông Sa.

Park, Bong-lang (1991). *Shinhakûi Haebang [Liberation of Theology]*. Seoul: Daehan Gidokgyo Chulpansa.

Pak, Chong-hong (1983). "Historical Review of Korean Confucianism," in *Main Currents of Korean Thought*, ed. by the Korean National Commission for UNESCO. Seoul: The Si-sa-yong-o-sa Publishers, Inc.; Arch cape, Oregon: Pace International Research, Inc.

Park, Hyun-che, et. al. (1984). *Han'guk Sahoeûi Jaeinsik I: Gyôngje Gaebale Ttarûn Jôngch'i/ Gyôngje/Sahoeûi Gujo Byônhwa [A New Look at the Korean Society 1: Changes in the Social/Economic/Political Structure Due to Economic Development]*. Seoul: Han Ul.

Park, Jong-chun (1991). *Sangsaengûi Shinhak [Theology of Sangsaeng (Life of Reciprocity)]*. Seoul: Han'guk Shinhak Yôn'guso.

Park, Se-kil (1988). *Dasi Ssunûn Han'guk Hyôndaesa [Rewriting Korean Modern History]*. 2 vol. Seoul: Dolbegae.

Park, Soon-kyung (1985). "Han'guk Minjokkwa Gidokgyoûi Gwaje [Korean peoples and the Task of Christianity]," in *Han'guk Yôksa Sogûi Gidokgyo [Christianity Within Korean History]*. Revised and expanded edition. Ed. by KNCC. Seoul: Kiminsa.

Park, Young-shin (1987). "Han'gukûi Jôntong Jonggyo Yunliwa Jabonjuûi [Traditional Korean Religious Morality and Capitalism]," in *Han'gukûi Jonggyowa Sahoe Byôndong*, ed. by Han'guk Sahoesa Yôn'guhoe. Seoul: Munhakkwa Jisôngsa.

Pyun, Sun-hwan (1992). *Jonggyo Dawonjuûiwa Han'gukjôk Shinhak [The Religious Pluralism and Korean Theology]*. Publication Committee for the Celebration of Principal Pyun Sun-hwan's Retirement, ed. Seoul: Han'guk Shinhak Yôn'guso.

Rhi, Ki-yông, ed. and trans. (1990). *Han'gukûi Bulgyo Sasang [Korean Buddhist Thought]: Wonhyo, Ûisang, and Jinul (Chinul)*. Seoul: Samsung Chulpansa.

Ryu, Dong-sik (1982). *Han'guk Shinhakûi Gwangmaek [Mineral Vein of Korean Theology]*. Seoul: Heemangsa.

——— (1992). *Pung Lyu Dowa Han'guk Shinhak [Pung Lyu Do (Art of Wind and Stream) and Korean Theology]*. Seoul: Heemangsa.

——— (1965). *Han'guk Jonggyowa Gidokgyo [Korean Religions and Christianity]*. Seoul: Daehan Gidokgyo Sôhoe.

Ryu, Young-ik (1990). *Gabo Gyôngjang Yôn'gu [Studies on the Gabo Reform Movement 1894-1886]*. Seoul: Iljogak.

Sahoe-Minsok Yôn'gusil [Department of Socio-Cultural Study], ed. (1992). *Josôn Hugiûi Gûndaejôk Sahoeûisik [Modern Social Consciousness in the Late Josôn (Yi) Dynasty]*. Kyônggido: Han'guk Jôngshin Munhwa Yôn'guwon [Institute for Korean Psychocultural Study].

———, ed. (1994). *Han'guk Gûndaesae Issôsôûi Donghakkwa Donghak Nongmin Undong [Donghak and Donghak Farmers Movement in the Modern History of Korea]*. Kyônggido: Han'guk Jôngshin Munhwa Yôn'guwon.

Shim, Jin-song (1995). *Shini Sôntaekhan Yôja [Spirit-Possessed Woman]*. Seoul: Baeksông. [An autobiography of a mudang (shaman) who became famous after predicting the death of Kim Il-sung, the arch-leader of North Korea.]

Shin, Bok-ryong (1977). *Jûngbo Donghakdang Yôn'gu [Study of Donghak Group: Revised]*. Seoul: Tamgudang.

——— (1985). *Donghak Sasangkwa Gabo Nongmin Hyôkmyông (Thoughts of Dong-hak Religion and The 1894 Peasants' Revolution)*. Seoul: Pyôngminsa.

Shin, In-chul (1987), "Donghak Sasangûi Dogyojôk Sôngkyôk Munje [The Issue of Taoist Elements in Donghak Thought]," in *Donghak-Chôndogyo*, ed. by Yu Byung-duk. Seoul: Gyomunsa.

Shin, Yong-ha (1987). *Han'guk Gûndae Sahoe Sasangsa Yôn'gu [Study of Pre-modern History of the Korean Social Thought]*. Seoul: Iljisa.

Shukamoto, Geisho, Ueyama, Shunpei and Gajiyama, Yuichi (1989). *Bulgyoûi Yôksawa Gibon Sasang [History and Basic Thought of Buddhism]*. Trans. from Japanese by T. W. Park and Y. K. Lee. Seoul: Daewon Jôngsa.

Sok, Won-wook, ed. (1988). *Hwaôm Sasangron [Essays on Hwaôm (Hua-yen) Thought]*. Seoul: Undansa.

Sokang Daehakgyo Jonggyo Shinhak Yôn'guso, ed. (1991). *Jonggyo Shinhak Yôn'gu [Studies in Theology of Religion]* IV. Seoul: Bundo Chulpansa.

Sol, Wonhyo (1990). "Daesûng Gishinronso. Byôlgi [Awakening of Faith in Mahayana: a Commentary]" and "Gûmgang Sammaegyông [Diamond Samadhi Sutra, or Adamantine Absorption Sutra]" in *Han'gukûi Bulgyo Sasang [Buddhist Thought in Korea]*. Ed. and tr. by Rhi Ki-young. Seoul: Samsung Chulpansa.

Song, Sok-gu (1985). *Han'gukûi Yubulsasang [Confucian-Buddhist Thoughts in Korea]*. Seoul: Sasayôn.

Suh, Nam-dong (1976). *Jônhwan Sidaeûi Shinhak [Theology at a Turning Point]*. Seoul: Han'guk Shinhak Yôn'guso [Korea Theological Study Institute].

―――― (1983). *Minjung Shinhakûi Tamgu [Studies of Minjung Theology]*. Seoul: Han'gilsa.

Suh, Kwang-sun (1985). *Han'guk Gidokgyoûi Saeinsik [New Thinking in Korean Christianity]*. Seoul: Korean Christian Literature Publishing Co.

Theology of Religion Institute in Sokang University, ed. (1988–1991). *Jonggyo Shinhak Yôn'gu [Studies on Theology of Religion]*, 4 vol: 1-4. Seoul: Bundo Publishing Co.

Wonhyo. See Sol, Wonhyo.

Yôksahak Yôn'guso–1984 Nôyn Nongmin Jônjaeng Yôn'guban [Study Group on the Farmers War of the Year of 1894, Institute for the Study of History], ed. (1994). *Nongmin Jônjaeng 100 Nyônûi Insikkwa Jaengjôm [Issues on the Peasants War At Its 100th Year]*. Seoul: Gôrûm.

Yu, Byung-duk, ed. (1987). *Donghak.Chôndogyo*. Seoul: Gyomunsa.

Yu, Jun-ki (1994). *Han'guk Gûndae Yugyo Gaehyôk Undongsa [History of Modern Reform Movement in Korean Confucianism]*. Seoul: Dosô Chulpan Sammun.

Yun, Sa-soon (1998). *Han'gukûi Sônglihakkwa Shilhak [Neo-Confucianism and the Practical Learning in Korea]*. Seoul: Samin.

———— (1997). *Yun Sa-soon Gyosuûi Han'guk Yuhak Sasangron [A Thesis on Korean Confucianism by Professor Yun Sa-soon]*. Seoul: Yemun Sowon.

———— (1980). *Toegye Chôlhakûi Yôn'gu [A Study on the Philosophy of Toegye]*. Seoul: Koryo Daehakkyo Chulpanbu.

Yun, Suk-san (1996). *Huchônûl Yôlmyô [Opening New Heaven]*. Seoul: Donghaksa.

————, ed. with commentary (1996). *Donggyông Daejôn*. Seoul: Donghaksa.

———— (1989). "Donghake Natanan Dokyojôk Yoso [Taoist Elements in Donghak]" in *Dogyo Sasangûi Han'gukjôk Jôn'gae [Contextualization of Taoist Philosophy in Korea]*, ed. by Han'guk Dogyo Sasang Yônguhoe. Seoul: Asea Munhaksa.

Yun, Sung-bum (1964). *Gidokgyowa Han'guk Sasang [Christianity And Korean Thought]*. Seoul: The Christian Literature Society of Korea.

## Journals and Periodicals

*Asian Journal of Theology* (formerly *East Asia Journal of Theology*). Singapore.

*Buddhist–Christian Studies*. Honolulu, Hawaii.

*Ching Feng*. Hong Kong.

*CTC Bulletin*. Bulletin of the Commission on Theological Concerns, Christian Conference of Asia. Toa Payoh, Singapore: CTC-CCA.

*The Ecumenist 24:4 (May-June, 1986)*. New York: Paulist Press.

*Gidokgyo Sasang* [*Christian Thought*]. Monthly. Seoul: Daehan Gidokgyo Sohoe.

*Journal of Chinese Philosophy*. Quarterly. Honolulu, Hawaii: Dialogue Publishing Company.

*Miju Hyôndae Bulgyo* [*Modern Buddhism*]. Monthly. Flushing, NY: Miju Hyundae Bulgyo.

*Philosophy East and West*. Quarterly. Honolulu, Hawaii: University of Hawaii Press.

*Shin In Gan* [*New Humanity*]. Seoul: Chôndogyo Chongbu Publishers.

*Shinhak Sasang* [*The Theological Thought*]. The Quarterly of the Korea Theological Study Institute. Chon'an, Chungnam: Korea Theological Study Institute.

*Spring Wind–Buddhist Cultural Forum*. A quaterly publication of Zen Buddhist Temple. Toronto, Ontario.

# World Wide Web Resources

*http://minjungtheology.org/openeng.htm:* Institute of Minjung Theology.

*http://www.religionstheology.org/main.htm:* Institute for the Study of Theology of Religion.

*http://members.iworld.net/hederein/haein-sa/temple.html:* Haein Temple, which houses the Korean Tripitaka and is an important centre for the study of Avatamsaka (Hwaôm) philosophy.

*http://www.buddhapia.com/:* A useful site for the general introduction to Korean Buddhism in both English and Korean.

*http://www.chondogyo.or.kr:* Headquater of Chondogyo.

*http://my.netian.com/~bookac:* A Korean Confucian Homepage, which includes the emerging Confucian group called, "Minjung Confucians United [Minjung Yugyo Yônhap]."

*http://shamanism.view.co.kr:* For a General Introduction to Korean Shamanism.

*http://plaza.snu.ac.kr/~kahr-bs:* Korean Association for the History of Religion.

# Index

Ahn, Byung-mu  2, 77, 80, 87 94, 98, 99
Ahn, Kye-hyon  104
Analects: see Lun yü
Aristotle  21, 29, 32, 43, 80
Augustine  32–34, 80
Baeklyôn'gyo (White Lotus) sect  110
Balasuriya, Tissa  118
bon-gak  107, 108, 112
Bôpshin  107, 108
Buddha  98, 102, 103, 104, 105, 107–113, 127
bul-gak  107, 108, 112
*Bulssi Japbyôn*  38
Buswell, Robert E.  114
Cha, Ju-hwan  11
Chai, Ch'u (and Winberg Chai)  28, 30
Ch'an: see Sôn  8, 15, 113, 114
Chan, Wing-tsit  28, 34, 37
Chang, Kil-san  110
Chang, Tsai  28, 39
Ch'eng Brothers  33
  Ch'eng Hao  28
  Ch'eng I  27, 28, 35
Ch'eng–Chu School  35–37
Ch'ien Mu/Qian Mu  36
Chiki  4, 49, 52–56, 58, 63–64
Ching, Julia  34, 35
Choe, Chi-won  13
Choe, Dong-hee  51, 67
Choe, Gil-song  12
Choe, Je-U/Suun.  3, 4, 7, 13, 48, 49–67, 75, 78, 82, 96, 98
Choe, Nam-sun  12
Choe, Shi-hyung  55, 59, 67, 68
Chondogyo
Chong, Do-jon  37–38
Chong, Yak-yong  43, 44
Chônju

Chou, Tun-i/Zhou Dunyi  21, 26–32, 44, 50, 57
Chu Hsi/Zhu Xi  26, 28, 30, 32–41, 43, 44, 57, 58
Chuang Tzu/Zhuangzi  14, 16–23, 43
Chun, Chul-hwan  85
Chun, Tae-il  82, 83–84
Chung, Dae-hwan  37
Chung, Hyun Kyung  95, 119, 128
Chung Yung/Zhongyong  41
Confucius  27, 36, 41, 73
Creel, Herrlee G.  17, 22–25
Dae Jong Gyo  15
Dan'gun  11, 12, 15, 18,
de Bary, William Theodore  26, 35
Dharmakaya  107, 108
Dôk: see te/de  20
Donghak  9, 15, 47, 48, 49–71, 73, 74, 78, 96-98, 109, 134, 138–141, 145, 147
  Farmers Revolt  45, 78, 98
Donggyông Daejôn  26, 52, 53, 59
Eight *kua*  28, 30, 31
Fiorenza, Elizabeth Schussler  122–123
Five Elements  29, 31, 32
Four Beginnings  40, 41–43, 59
Four Books  41
Fung/Fêng Yu-lan
Go-un  13
gong li  40
Graham, A.C.  27
guishin  54
Guisso, Richard W. I  75
Gumgang Sammaegyông  114
gunja/kunja  65
Haewol  48, 55, 59, 67, 68
Han  10, 14–16, 25, 51, 57, 63, 75
han  75–77, 118
hanpuri  76–77
Han, Jong-man  13

# Index

Hanalnim 4, 49, 51, 52, 57, 58, 66, 67
Hananim 51, 52
Hanûnim 51
Hegel, G.W.F. 55–56
  Hegelian 63
hexagrams 31
haplyu 94
hobal 42, 43
Hong, Jang-hwa 49, 51, 52, 56, 57, 65, 67
hsien (仙: an immortal): see sôn 10, 12, 16-18, 22-24
hsin/xin 34–38, 40, 41, 59, 98
hsin hsueh/xinxue 35
hsing 29, 31
hsing/xing 28, 37, 38, 40
hu chôn gae byôk 63
Hua-yen or Hwaôm 8, 9, 36, 37, 40, 103
*huo jan chih ch'i* 27
Hwadam 39, 42, 57
Hwan-gôm 12
Hwang, Sun-myong 110
Hwaôm 9, 36, 103, 106
Hwaômgyông 9
Hwa-rang do 14
hyônjang 7, 95–97
i/yi 26
I Ching/Yijing 28–31, 33
ildo 43
Il Yôn 10
jen/ren 26, 27, 35, 36, 38, 41
In nae chôn 98
in ûi ye ji 59, 60
jayôn 15, 16
jen-hsin 35, 36, 41
Jesus (Christ) 79, 81, 88–94, 98, 99, 121, 122, 125, 129, 131
jukiron 42
jung saeng 88, 98
Jûng San Gyo 15, 110
juriron 40, 42
Kang, Kon-kee 105
ki (pron. "gi," 氣): ether, etherial force, breath, matter-energy; ch'i/ qi in Chinese 26, 27, 37–43, 49, 53–60, 64
Kim, Bu-sik (金富軾, 1075–1151) 13

Kim, Chi-ha 44, 54, 87, 88, 147
Kim, Jae-young 104, 105
Kim, Ki-hyon 42
Kim, Kyung-jae 50, 56
Kim, Yong-Bock 129, 146
Kim, Yu-shin 14
Knitter, Paul 130–133, 143
Ko Eun 110
Ko Hung/Ge Hong 22
kua 28, 30, 31
Kwon, Kun (權近, 1352–1409) 38, 57
Lao tzu/Laozi (Noja, 老子): The alleged—now refuted—author of Tao Te Ching 13–21, 28–30, 33, 39
Lau, D.C. 19
Lee, Don-hwa 48, 53, 62
Lee, Hang-nyong 62–63
Lee, Jung-Young 33, 75
Lee, Ki-baek 105
Lee, Kyoung-jik 48
Lee, Nung-hwa 11, 14
Lee, Suk-ho 11
Lee, Ul-ho 15
Lee, Young-ja 105
Legge, James 28, 29
li (ye, 禮): ritual, propriety 59, 60
li (理): principle, noumena 26, 27, 30–43, 58
li-ki (ch'i) 26, 27, 32–43, 58
Li Kuang-ti 31
*Lieh Tzu* 14, 17, 22
Lu Hsing-shan 30, 31, 35
Lun Yü 41
lyông 49, 64
Maitreya 101, 104, 109–112
Marx, Karl 6, 120, 121, 126, 132, 141
  Marxism 69, 70
Mencius 27, 33, 36, 40–42, 59
Maspero, Henri 21
minjung/Minjung 1, 2, 4, 6-9, 25, 44, 46, 60, 65, 67, 70, 73–100, 101, 102, 109, 110, 113, 114, 115, 133, 141, 145, 147
  -consciousness 60
  Buddhism 4, 101–115
  Perspective 1, 87–88, 128

# Index

Theology 1, 2, 4, 6, 7, 8, 60, 70, 73-100, 101, 117, 118, 122, 125, 126, 128, 129, 141, 145
Mugûk 26, 57, 58; see Wu Chi
Daedo 26
mudang 77
muwi 13, 14, 20, 73; see wu wei
nae yu shin lyông 64
Nahn, Andrew C. 103
Neo-Confucianism 25-29, 52, 57, 58, 133
   Buddhist influence 34–37
   in China 29–37
   in Korea 37–44
   and Korean society 44–46
Non'ô (論語): see Lun yü
Oh, Ji-young 68
Overmyer, Daniel L. 109, 111
Paek, Se-myong 53
Panikkar, Raimon 118, 132
Park, Chung-hee 84
Pieris, Aloysius 91, 118, 126, 127, 129
Plato/-nic/-nist 32, 34, 43, 49
Principle: see li (理)
Pung lyu do 10, 12–14, 15
Pyun, Sun Hwan 12
Queen Mother of the West 12, 22
Rainy, Lee 27
Reuther, Rosemary Radford 122
Rhi, Ki-yong 106, 107, 108, 115
Sakyamuni 104, 105, 110
sam shin 10, 11, 12, 16
Samgang Oryun 45
Samguk Sagi 13
Samguk Yusa 10
san shin (山神) 11
san shin (産神) 11, 12
Sangje 51
Schreiter, Robert 6, 7, 80, 81, 96, 97
Seven Emotions 41–43
Shamanism 24–25, 10–16, 17, 18, 24, 25, 52, 64, 74, 75–77
shi-gak 107, 108, 112
Shichônju 4, 49, 52, 53–55, 63, 64, 66
Shih/shi 36, 37
Shih Chi 21
Shim 37, 38, 98

shin 15, 49, 54, 64
Shin, Bok-ryong 67, 69
Shin, Ock Hee 108–109
shin sôn 10–12, 16, 24, 65
sôn (仙) 10–12, 16, 17, 18, 22, 23, 24
Sôn/Ch'an/Zen (禪) 15, 101, 102, 106, 112–114
Sohn, Byung-hee (Uiam) 61, 98
sôn pung do gol 16
sông 37, 38, 40
Sông Lyông/Shin 49, 64
Sponberg, Alan 109, 110, 111, 114
Ssu-ma, Ch'ien 21
su shim jông ki 59, 60
Suh, Kwang-sun David 75, 128
Suh, Kyong-Dok 38–39
Suh, Kyung-su 114
Suh, Nam-dong 83, 86–88, 94–99, 118, 126
Suun: See Choe, Je-U
Supreme Ultimate: see Taegûk/Ta'i Chi
syncretism 78–82, 125, 133
Taegûk/T'ai Chi 26, 27, 28, 29–31, 34, 39, 57, 58
T'ai Chi T'u Shuo 29
Tao/Dao 9, 15, 17, 18–21, 26, 27, 31, 35, 36, 39, 40, 43, 47, 138
Taoism 4, 10, 11, 12, 13, 14, 15, 16–24, 26, 27, 38, 51, 52, 57, 58, 61, 64, 65
Tao Te Ching 19, 87
tao t'ung/do tong (Kor.) 57
te 20
t'ien (chôn) 34, 38, 51
Tillich, Paul 55, 56, 62, 76, 77, 79
Toegye (Yi Hwang) 26, 34, 40–42, 43, 57
trigrams: see kua (koe)
tzu jan (jayôn) 15, 16
Walker, Alice 123
Wang, Yang-ming 35
Watson, Burton 18, 22, 23
Weems, Benjamin B. 48
Welch, Holmes 17
Whitehead, Alfred North 55, 56
Williams, Delores S. 122, 123
Won Bul Gyo 15
Wonhyo 15, 39, 101–109, 112, 114, 115
wu: shaman 24

Wu Chi/Wuji (Mugûk) 26, 29, 30, 57, 58
wu wei (muwi) 13, 14, 20–21, 26, 73
yang (yin-yang) 5, 29, 30, 32, 39, 54, 59, 63
yang-sheng 22, 23
yin (yin-yang) 5, 29, 30, 31, 32, 39, 59, 54, 63
yông se mu gung 16
Yongdam Yusa 16, 46, 48, 52
Yu, Chai-shin 11, 75
Yulgok (Yi I) 26, 42–43, 57, 58
Yun, Sa-soon 38
Yun, Sung-bum 51
Zen (Ch'an): See Sôn. 8, 15, 101, 102, 106, 112, 113, 114

# Asian Thought and Culture

This series is designed to cover three inter-related projects:

- *Asian Classics Translation*, including those modern Asian works that have been generally accepted as "classics"
- *Asian and Comparative Philosophy and Religion*, including excellent and publishable Ph.D. dissertations, scholarly monographs, or collected essays
- *Asian Thought and Culture in a Broader Perspective*, covering exciting and publishable works in Asian culture, history, political and social thought, education, literature, music, fine arts, performing arts, martial arts, medicine, etc.

For additional information about this series or for the submission of manuscripts, please contact:

> Peter Lang Publishing, Inc.
> Acquisitions Department
> 275 Seventh Avenue, 28th floor
> New York, New York 10001

To order other books in this series, please contact our Customer Service Department at:

> 800-770-LANG (within the U.S.)
> (212) 647-7706 (outside the U.S.)
> (212) 647-7707 FAX

Or browse online by series at:

> www.peterlang.com